SHEILA KIRWAN
LINDA P. GARLAND

TEACH ME YOUR WAYS

Teach me your ways, O Lord;
make them known to me.
Teach me to live according to your truth,
for you are my God, who saves me.
I always trust in you.

Psalm 25:4-5

The Light of the World Series 3

Gill and Macmillan

Published in Ireland by
Gill and Macmillan Ltd
Goldenbridge
Dublin 8
with associated companies throughout the world

© Linda P. Garland and Sheila Kirwan, 1991
© Artwork, Gill and Macmillan Ltd, 1991
0 7171 1728 6

Print origination by
Seton Music Graphics Ltd, Bantry, Co. Cork
Design and illustrations by
Design Image, Dublin

Nihil obstat
Oliver V. Brennan B.D., M.A.
Imprimatur
✠ Cahal Cardinal Daly, Archbishop of Armagh

All rights reserved. No part of this publication may be copied,
reproduced or transmitted in any form or by any means without
permission of the publishers.
Photocopying any part of this book is illegal.

In the same series
A New Commandment
Believe the Good News
Teach Me Your Ways

CONTENTS

UNIT I	BELIEFS AND VALUES		
	Chapter 1	My Beliefs	1
	Chapter 2	My Values	8
	Chapter 3	Choosing Values	16
	Chapter 4	Called by God	22

UNIT II	CHRISTIAN BELIEFS AND VALUES		
	Chapter 5	Human Rights	32
	Chapter 6	Justice	40
	Chapter 7	Justice in the World	56
	Chapter 8	Valuing My Own Life	73
	Chapter 9	The Lives of Others	81
	Chapter 10	The Life of the Human Community	86
	Chapter 11	The Environment	93
	Chapter 12	Relationships	106
	Chapter 13	Family	117
	Chapter 14	God	123
	Chapter 15	Idolatry	129

UNIT III	SCRIPTURE—THE OLD TESTAMENT		
	Chapter 16	The Bible	134
	Chapter 17	The Call to Faith	140
	Chapter 18	The Promised Land	147
	Chapter 19	Prophets	160
	Chapter 20	Psalms and Festivals	168

UNIT IV	SCRIPTURE—THE NEW TESTAMENT		
	Chapter 21	Jesus	176
	Chapter 22	The Kingdom of God	182
	Chapter 23	The Beatitudes	188

Chapter 24	Jesus' Resurrection	194
Chapter 25	The Last Things	200

UNIT V THE SACRAMENTS

Chapter 26	Christian Initiation	206
Chapter 27	The Eucharist	214
Chapter 28	Reconciliation	218
Chapter 29	Marriage	223
Chapter 30	Holy Orders	231

UNIT VI THE CHRISTIAN COMMUNITY—THE CHURCH

Chapter 31	The History of the Christian Community	236
Chapter 32	The Mission of the Christian Community	254
Chapter 33	Ecumenism	259
Chapter 34	Dialogue with World Religions	264

UNIT VII THE LITURGICAL YEAR

Chapter 35	The Liturgical Year	277
Chapter 36	Advent	283
Chapter 37	Christmas	293
Chapter 38	Lent	299
Chapter 39	Easter	302

UNIT VIII WORSHIP AND PRAYER

Chapter 40	Worship	305
Chapter 41	Prayer	309
Chapter 42	Pilgrimage	317

ACKNOWLEDGMENTS

The authors wish to thank the following for their helpful assistance during the preparation of this book: Anne Kenna; Fr Bill Reilly; Fr Oliver Brennan; Very Reverend Rabbi Ephraim Mirvis, Chief Rabbi of Ireland; Imam Yahya Mohammed Al-Hussein, Islamic Foundation of Ireland; John O'Neill, the Samyé Trust; John O'Connell and Gearoid O Riain, Dublin Travellers Education and Development Group; School Catechists who reviewed drafts of the text; staff of Gill and Macmillan, Publishers.

COPYRIGHT ACKNOWLEDGMENTS

Unless otherwise stated, Scripture quotations are from the *Good News Bible*, published by the Bible Societies and Collins.
Old Testament © American Bible Society 1976.
New Testament (Good News for Modern Man) © American Bible Society 1964, 1971, 1976.
Reproduced by permission.

For permission to reproduce copyright material grateful acknowledgment is made to the following:
Cassell PLC for an adapted extract from *The Story of Taizé* by J.L. Gonzalez-Bolado;
St Mary's Press, Christian Brothers Publications, for 'A Resurrection Newspaper', adapted from *Sharing III: A Manual for Teachers* by Thomas Zanzig;
Prentice Hall for 'The Wonder Workers' from *Values Clarification: a handbook of practical strategies for teachers and students* by Simon, Howe and Kirschenbaum;
Chicago Liturgy Training Publications for 'Rite of Christian Initiation' by Fr Aidan Kavanagh published in *Liturgy* magazine;
Winston Press for 'Used Cars: A Simulation' and 'College Admissions', adapted from *Moral Education: a handbook for teachers* by Robert T. Hall;
Gujarat Sahitya Prakesh for 'Whistler's Bridge' from *The Prayer of the Frog* by Anthony de Mello and Diaz del Rio S.J.;

Darling-Kindesly from the diagrams 'The Environment under Attack', 'Living on the Land' and 'Living in the City' from *Blueprint for a Green Planet* by John Seymour and Herbert Girardet;

McCrimon Publishers for 'Lord Have Mercy' from *The Israeli Mass*;

FEL Publications for 'We are One in the Spirit';

Collins PLC for 'The Little Box' from *Living the Faith Together* by Wim Saris;

Abingdon Press for 'Preparing to Pray' from *Haircuts and Holiness* by Louis Cassells;

Zondervan Publishing for 'Letter to Amos' from *Far Out Ideas for Youth Groups* by Wayne Rice and Mike Yaconelli;

Ave Maria Press for 'The Rite of Christian Marriage' and 'The Rite of Ordination of a Priest', adapted from *The Sacraments and You* by Michael Pennock;

RTE and the author for 'That Christmas' by Dan Treston published in *Sunday Miscellany 2*, edited by Ronnie Walsh;

Navan Travellers Committee for an adapted outline of UN Declaration of Human Rights, the piece 'A Young Traveller's Story' by Jimmy McCarthy and the Charter of Travellers' Rights prepared by the Irish Centre for the Study of Human Rights in University College Galway, all of which appear in *Pride and Prejudice: the case of the Travellers* by Michael McDonagh;

Dublin Travellers Education and Development Group for six points on Travellers adapted from 'Working with Irish Travellers' by John O'Connell;

Peter Li Publishers Inc. for 'Substance Abuse Quiz' taken from *Today's Catholic Teacher*;

Frederick A. Praeger for 'The Coming of the Pink Cheeks' from *Kabongo* by Richard St Barbé Baker, adapted from *Through African Eyes: Cultures in Change*;

Bantam Doubleday Dell for an extract from *Night* by Elie Wiesel.

The cartoon on page 131 by Girard of Canada appears in *Thin Black Lines* published by Development Education Centre, Sally Oak College, Birmingham.

The publishers have made every effort to trace copyright holders but if they have inadvertently overlooked any, they will be pleased to make the necessary arrangements at the first opportunity.

BELIEFS AND VALUES

MY BELIEFS

CHAPTER 1

A belief is something I consider to be true. My beliefs make a difference in my life. They affect the way I think, feel, speak and behave. In each of the following situations, people mention one of their beliefs.

'Professor, what can you tell us about pulsars?'
 'Well, on the basis of our research so far, we believe that pulsars are stars which are located far outside our galaxy. They emit radiation at regular intervals, and this is what we have picked up on our instruments. We believe that they are a natural part of the universe, and cannot be taken as signs of extra-terrestrial life.'

'Dr Muttson, I believe that these footprints will lead us to the murderer!'

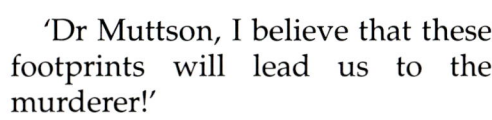

'After this, I'm going straight. I'll never put you through this again, I promise.'
'I know, I believe you, Harold.'

'Some of them think that I'll be no good at this job.'
'Well, I believe in you. I know you can do it.'

'When you think of the size of the universe, people don't seem to be a very important part of it.'
'Well, I believe that people are very important. I believe that each of us is created for a special purpose.'

QUESTIONS

In each of these situations, people mention one of their beliefs.
1. Briefly explain each of the five beliefs.
2. What reasons do you think the people have for each belief?
3. What effect do you think these beliefs could have on the actions or attitudes of the people who have them?
4. What are the similarities between the beliefs? What are the differences?

EXERCISES

1. Write down some important beliefs which you have.
2. Share your answers with the rest of the class.

Beliefs

Beliefs can be looked at under these three headings:
1. Belief in people
2. Belief in ideas
3. Scientific beliefs

> Most beliefs are based on some kind of *evidence*. This evidence can be any piece of information which shows that a belief is true. Evidence gives people reasons for believing that something is true. Different beliefs are based on different kinds of evidence.

Scientific beliefs are based on evidence which can be physically measured and demonstrated—for example, the freezing point of water under normal conditions is believed to be 0°C. This can be measured and demonstrated by using a thermometer. Some of our scientific beliefs are based directly on our own experience. For example, we believe that when we throw a ball up in the air in an open space, it will fall down, because this is what has always happened in our experience. Some of our scientific beliefs are based on what other people have told us about their experiences. For example, we believe that everything in the universe is made up of atoms, not because we have seen them ourselves, but because other people have conducted experiments which show that everything is made up of atoms.

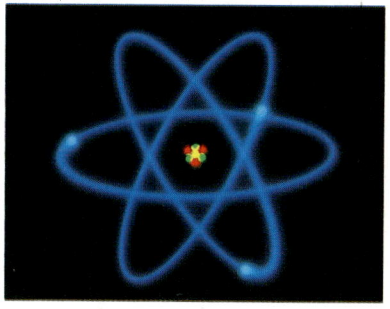

A lithium atom

Our *belief in certain ideas* is based on a different kind of evidence. This kind of belief is based on our personal experiences, our thoughts and feelings about our experiences, and the thoughts and feelings of other people about their experiences. For example, we may believe in democracy as a good form of government. Our experience of living in a democracy may have given us a sense of freedom, a feeling of being able to influence the way things are done in our country. When we think about this experience, we may decide that we would not like to live under any other form of government. When we listen to or read about other people's ideas about democracy, we may want to improve the way democracy works in our country. For example, we may come to believe that a true democracy should try to help the less well-off to get a fair share of the country's wealth.

Our *belief in a person* is based on our experience of knowing that person, our relationship with the person and the experience which other people have had with the person. For example, we may believe and trust in a friend to give us good advice in a difficult situation. This can be based on:
— our experience of listening to his/her advice in the past, with good results;
— our experience of his/her care and concern for us;
— knowing that he/she really wants to help.

Our belief in the person can be strengthened by knowing that other people also trust and believe in him/her and listen to his/her advice.

> Most of us have many different beliefs. These beliefs are based on different kinds of evidence. Some evidence comes from our own personal experience and some comes from what other people have told us. Some beliefs are more important than others. The more important our beliefs are to us, the greater is the influence which they have on the way we live.

EXERCISES

1. Examine the beliefs you listed in Exercise 1, page 2. Try to decide which of the three categories each of your beliefs falls into — scientific belief, belief in an idea, or belief in a person. Are there any beliefs which do not seem to fit into any category? Or which seem to fit into more than one category? Ask the rest of the class and your teacher to help you with these.
2. Examine one or two of your most important beliefs in each category. What reasons or evidence do you have for holding each belief? In each case, explain whether the evidence is based on your own personal experience, or on what you have learned from other people's experiences.
3. Explain how each of your most important beliefs influences the way you live your life. For example, do they affect what you think, feel, say or do?

Christian Beliefs

These are the most important Christian beliefs:
— God loves us.
— God created us so that we could love God and love each other.
— We rejected God's plan for us by sinning and refusing to love.
— God continued to love us and sent Jesus to live among us, to show us how much God loves us and to show us how to love God and each other.
— Jesus defeated the power of sin, evil and death by dying and rising from the dead.
— He gave us the freedom to become children of God, able to love God and love each other.
— The Church is the community of Jesus' followers.
— The risen Jesus continues to love and guide the Church community through the pope and the bishops, the priests, teachers and others who minister in the community.
— The Holy Spirit lives in each Christian and makes it possible for us to follow Jesus in our lives and to love one another.
— Death is not the end, but the beginning of a new stage in life with God.

EXERCISES

1. To which of the three categories does each of these Christian beliefs belong?
2. What reasons or evidence do Christians have for each of these beliefs? Make a note of whether each piece of evidence is based on a person's personal experience, or the experiences of a number of people, or both.
3. Give examples to show how some of these beliefs influence the way people live. For example, do people speak or behave in certain ways because of their Christian beliefs?
4. Examine the beliefs you listed in Exercise 1 on page 2.
   (a) Are any of the beliefs Christian?
   (b) Are any of them non-Christian?
   (c) What beliefs (if any) would you like to add to your list?

Reflection: 'One of the twelve disciples, Thomas (called the Twin), was not with them when Jesus came. So the other disciples told him, "We have seen the Lord!"

Thomas said to them, "Unless I see the scars of the nails in his hands and put my finger on those scars and my hand in his side I will not believe."

A week later the disciples were together again indoors, and Thomas was with them. The doors were locked, but Jesus came and stood among them and said, "Peace be with you." Then he said to Thomas, "Put your finger here, and look at my hands, then stretch out your hand and put it in my side. Stop your doubting, and believe!"

Thomas answered him, "My Lord and my God!"

Jesus said to him, "Do you believe because you see me? How happy are those who believe without seeing me!"' John 20: 24–29

Action: Ask a parent/guardian or another adult you respect to tell you about their beliefs, and their reasons for believing.

Psalm: Protect me, O God; I trust in you for safety.
I say to the Lord, 'You are my Lord;
all the good things I have come from you.'

You, Lord, are all I have,
and you give me all I need;
my future is in your hands.
How wonderful are your gifts to me;
how good they are!

I praise the Lord because he guides me,
and in the night my conscience warns me.
I am always aware of the Lord's presence;
he is near, and nothing can shake me.

And I am so thankful and glad,
and I feel completely secure,
because you protect me from the power of death,
and the one you love you will not
abandon to the world of the dead.

You will show me the path that leads to life;
your presence fills me with joy
and brings me pleasure forever.
Psalm 16: 1–2, 5–11

Some more information

The Apostles' Creed
I believe in God, the Father Almighty,
Creator of heaven and earth;
And in Jesus Christ, His only Son, Our Lord,
Who was conceived by the Holy Spirit,
Born of the Virgin Mary,
Suffered under Pontius Pilate,
Was crucified, died and was buried.
He descended into hell;
The third day he rose again from the dead;
He ascended into heaven,
Where he is seated at the right hand of God,
    the Father Almighty;
From thence he shall come to judge
The living and the dead.
I believe in the Holy Spirit,
    the holy Catholic Church;
    the communion of saints,
    the forgiveness of sins,
    the resurrection of the body,
    and life everlasting.
            Amen.

MY VALUES

CHAPTER 2
▼

A *value* is something I think is very important or worthwhile. My real values make a difference in my life. They affect the way I think, feel, speak and behave. In the following exercise, each of the Wonder Workers has something important or worthwhile to offer you. Your choice should tell you something about your values.

The Wonder Workers

A group of fourteen experts is willing to give their services free to the members of this class. Their extraordinary skills are guaranteed to be 100% successful. If you had to choose the four most useful experts, which four would you choose?

1 *Dr Dorian Grey* — A noted plastic surgeon, he can make you look exactly as you want to look by means of a new painless technique. (He also uses hormones to alter body structures and size!) Your ideal physical appearance can be a reality.

2 *Baron Von Barrons* — A college placement and job placement expert. The college or job of your choice, in the location of your choice, will be yours!

3 *Dr Yin Yang* — A health expert, she will provide you with perfect health and protection from physical injury throughout your life.

4 *Dr Knot Not Ginott* — An expert in dealing with parents, she guarantees that you will never have any problems with your parents again. They will accept your values and your behaviour. You will be free from control and badgering.

5 *Dr Hinnah Self* — Guarantees that you will have self-knowledge, self-liking, self-respect and self-confidence. True self-assurance will be yours.

6 *Rocky Fellah* — Wealth will be yours, with guaranteed schemes for earning millions within weeks.

7 *Dwight D. DeGawl* — This world-famed leadership expert will train you quickly. You will be listened to, looked up to and respected by those around you.

8 *Dr Claire Voyant* — All of your questions about the future will be answered, continually, through the training of this soothsayer.

9 *Stu Denpower* — An expert on authority, he will make sure that you are never again bothered by authorities. His services will make you immune from all control which you consider unfair by the school, the police and the government.

10 *Dr Susie Smart* — She will develop your common sense and your intelligence to a level in excess of 150 I.Q. It will remain at this level through your entire lifetime.

11 *'Pop' Larity* — He guarantees that you will have the friends you want now and in the future. You will find it easy to approach those you like and they will find you easily approachable.

12 *Maisie Methuselah* — Guarantees you long life (to the age of 200) with your aging process slowed down proportionately. For example, at the age of 60 you will look and feel like 20.

13 *Dr Otto Carengy* — You will be well-liked by all and will never be lonely. A life filled with love will be yours.

14 *Prof. Val U. Clear* — With her help, you will always know what you want, and you will be completely clear on all the muddy issues of these confused days.

GROUP WORK

1. Get into groups of three or four.
2. Each person tells the group which four experts they chose, and why.
3. As a group, try to agree on the four best experts.
4. Report your findings to the whole class.

EXERCISES

1. Examine the four Wonder Workers you chose earlier. What important or worthwhile thing did you want from each of them? These are your *values*.
2. What values did your group decide on?
3. What are the similarities between your chosen values and those of the class? Are there any differences?
4. What other values do you have? How do they affect your life?

Values in Action

> It is not always easy to live up to our values. Sometimes we think or speak or act against our values. This can happen because of laziness, or fear or selfishness.

Imagine the following situation. One evening, a group of sixteen-year-olds is out enjoying themselves. Suddenly, a row blows up. A few people in the group start to pick on a boy who is a bit of an outsider, no one's special friend. The incident starts with teasing and jeering, but things quickly get out of control. Most of the group, both the boys and girls, just stand around doing nothing. One of them is Stephen who is quite popular with everyone. Stephen really values courage. He wants to be someone who is never afraid to say what he thinks. Now, however, he just stands there and watches as three of his friends beat up the outsider. Stephen knows he should say something, *do* something, but he does not have the courage. He is not even afraid that the others will turn on him — he is not afraid of a fight. But he is afraid that his friends will laugh and jeer at him, that he might become an outsider himself. So he does nothing — and feels disgusted with himself.

Stephen valued courage, but he found it difficult to be courageous. Many of us also have values, but find it difficult to put them into action. St Paul described this problem in the following words:

'I do not understand what I do; for I don't do what I would like to do, but instead I do what I hate. For even though the desire to do good is in me, I am not able to do it. I don't do the good I want to do; instead I do the evil I do not want to do.'
Romans 7: 15, 18–19

EXERCISES

1. Examine the values which you listed at the beginning of the chapter. Do you always speak and behave as if these values were important to you? Explain, giving examples.
2. Examine each of the following examples. In each case explain:
   (a) What values are important to the main character;
   (b) What do you think the character will do;
   (c) What do you think the character *should* do.

A. Mary and Anna have been friendly for years. Anna's parents were away for a few days, and she did not bother to go to school. Now she wants Mary to forge a 'sick-note' and sign the name of Anna's mother. Mary does not want to write the letter, but she does not want to upset Anna.

B. Justin thinks it is very important to say his prayers every night before going to sleep. However it is usually late when he goes to bed, so sometimes he decides not to pray at all.

C. Colman and Siobhán have been going out together for a few weeks. They like each other very much. Some of Colman's friends talk about their girlfriends in a very sexist way, and they expect Colman to do the same. If he does not, they jeer at him and tell him that he is a wimp. Colman finds it very hard to put up with all the teasing but he is very fond of Siobhán, and respects her.

D. Rita is a reasonably good student, but she has done very little work for the last year. When she is meant to be studying, she watches television, or listens to music. She has an important examination this year, and has promised herself to study hard and do well. However, she is finding it very difficult to keep her promise because she wants to follow all her favourite TV series and she gets bored just concentrating on her homework.

Christian Values

> All Christian values are based on the two great commandments: love of God and love of my neighbour. When the people asked Jesus what was the most important commandment, Jesus answered:
>
> 'Love the Lord your God with all your heart, with all your soul, and with all your mind.' This is the greatest and the most important commandment. The second most important commandment is like it: 'Love your neighbour as you love yourself.' (Matthew 22: 37–39)

Being a Christian means trying to love God and other people in every situation and in all circumstances. The Ten Commandments, the teachings and example of Jesus, and the teachings of the Church challenge us to be truly loving in our thoughts, attitudes, words and actions. Christian love is very practical. It means treating everyone with respect, being fair and honest towards others and protecting them from harm. Christian love means being as concerned about the needs of other people as we are about our own needs. It means being ready to serve others and to make sacrifices for them.

Love means being ready to serve others and make sacrifices for them.

Every Christian value helps us to put love into practice in our lives. For example, stewardship is an important Christian value because when we care for creation, we are showing our love for God who is Lord of Creation. We are also showing our love for other people by protecting and caring for the world in which we all live. Another important Christian value is having an informed conscience. This is important because it enables us to know the difference between a truly loving, caring action and an unloving one.

There are many other Christian values, including mercy, compassion, prayer, chastity, freedom, service and forgiveness. All of these values are important to Christians because they help us to love God and other people.

Love means being concerned about the needs of others.

Exercises

1. How could each of the following Christian values help you to love other people?
   (a) kindness
   (b) self-control
   (c) patience
   (d) courage
   (e) sacrifice
   (f) honesty

Love means treating people with respect.

2. Examine the values which you listed at the beginning of the chapter. Are these values Christian values? That is, do they help you to love God and other people? Explain.
3. Are any of the values unChristian? That is, could they encourage you to be selfish and unloving? Explain.
4. Make a list of the Ten Commandments.
   (a) What value is mentioned in each commandment?
   (b) How does each commandment help us to love God and each other?

QUESTIONNAIRE

Write down whether you agree or disagree with each of the following statements.
1. Look after yourself, because no one else will.
2. Students should respect their teachers.
3. Get revenge on people who have harmed you so that they will not do it again.
4. Children should follow the same religion as their parents.
5. Education is a waste of time.
6. It is better to agree with people so that there will not be a row.
7. Everyone should make up their own mind about the right thing to do.
8. Vandalism is wrong.
9. Everyone should be treated equally.
10. It is wrong to have more money than you need.
11. You have to be rich to be happy.
12. People should give good example to children.

GROUP WORK

1. Get into groups of four or five.
2. Share your opinions about the statements in the Questionnaire. Which statements does everyone agree on? Why?
3. As a group, try to decide what value is referred to in each statement.
4. Make a list of the Christian values which are referred to.
5. Report your conclusions to the whole class.

Reflection: 'Once a man came to Jesus. "Teacher," he asked, "what good thing must I do to receive eternal life?" . . . "Keep the commandments if you want to enter life," answered Jesus. "What commandments?" he asked. Jesus answered, "Do not commit murder; do not commit adultery; do not steal; do not accuse anyone falsely; respect your father and mother; and love your neighbour as you love yourself."

"I have obeyed all these commandments," the young man replied. "What else do I need to do?" Jesus said to him, "If you want to be perfect, go and sell all you have and give the money to the poor, and you will have riches in heaven; then come and follow me." When the young man heard this, he went away sad, because he was very rich.' Matthew 19: 16–22

Action: Choose one of your most important values. Decide on *one* way in which you will put this value into action during the coming week.

Psalm: Happy are those whose lives are faultless,
    who live according to the law of the Lord.
    Happy are those who follow his commands,
    who obey him with all their heart.
    They never do wrong; they walk
    in the Lord's ways.

    Lord, you have given us your laws
    and told us to obey them faithfully.
    How I hope that I shall be faithful
    in keeping your instructions!

    If I pay attention to all your commands,
    then I will not be put to shame.
    As I learn your righteous judgments,
    I will praise you with a pure heart.
    I will obey your laws;
    never abandon me!

    Be good to me, your servant,
    so that I may live and obey your teachings.
    Open my eyes, so that I may see
    the wonderful truths in your law.

            Psalm 119: 1–8, 17–18

CHOOSING VALUES

CHAPTER 3
▼

We learn all our beliefs and values from others. Children usually have the same beliefs and values as their parents, families and friends. As we grow older, we learn about various beliefs and values from other people, books, films, advertisements and other forms of the media. Each of them may give us different messages about people, relationships, God, the world, goodness and evil. Over a period of years we decide on the beliefs and values which are true for us. The following project will give you an opportunity to examine some of the values which are shown in advertisements.

What's on offer?
These products are advertised frequently on television and radio, in newspapers and magazines and in many public places.

Bread	Children's toys
Alcohol	Computers
Chocolate	Make-up
Cars	Clothes
Washing powder/liquid	Holidays
Video/Hi-fi equipment	

Preparation
1. Get into groups of three or four.
2. Each group should choose a different product from the list.
3. Gather as many advertisements for your product as you can. Mount newspaper, magazine or mail order advertisements on poster paper or in a scrapbook. Describe, through written work or drawing, television and radio advertisements and other advertisements which you cannot present directly.

GROUP WORK

1. Let each member of the group present the advertisements he/she has found.
2. As a group, choose three or four advertisements to examine in more detail.
3. Examine each of your chosen advertisements as follows, making brief notes as you go along:
   (a) What information does the advertisement give you about the product?
   (b) Does the advertisement say directly that the product will affect you or your life in some way?
   (c) Does the advertisement give the *impression* that the product will affect you or your life in any way?
   (d) In your opinion, what is the main message of this advertisement?
   (e) What method(s) did the advertisers use to get across their message about the product? (For example, explaining what the product is like, showing people using the product, using music and pictures to give a particular impression of the product etc.)
   (f) Why do you think they chose a particular method?

(g) What value or values does the advertisement show? (For example, what does it say (or imply) is important to people, will make people happy, is necessary to people etc.?)
4. Let each group present its findings to the rest of the class under the following headings:
(a) The advertisements we chose, and why
(b) The message of each advertisement
(c) The values in each advertisement.
5. When every group has reported, make a list of the values presented in the advertisements. As a class try to decide:
(a) Which of the values might Christians agree with?
(b) Are any of the values directly opposed to Christian values? (For example, do the values in any advertisement say or imply that something is good, when Christians believe that the same thing is wrong?)

Try to use cleaning products which are not harmful to the environment.

Learning Beliefs and Values

People who love us teach us their values because they want us to be happy and good. For example, parents teach their children that fighting is wrong because they want their children to grow up in a peaceful world, willing to work for peace.

Other people present values to us for different reasons. For example, advertisers show us certain values so that we will buy their products. Advertisers use very specialised techniques to make us believe what they are saying and sometimes we can be influenced by them without even realising it.

For example, advertisers know that most people want their homes to be clean and healthy. So if they want people to buy a new cleaning liquid for the bathroom, they 'teach' them about the vital importance of 100% absolutely perfectly super cleanliness. They might use an advertisement showing person A who only gets her bathroom *clean*, and person B who gets his bathroom 100% absolutely perfectly *super* clean! When people watch this kind of advertisement often enough, they begin to believe that 'ordinary' cleanliness is not enough, and that they must buy some special super cream or liquid to make sure their bathroom is clean. By getting people to believe in the new value, the advertisers are making it more likely that people will buy the new product. Many people do not realise that their new value has come from the advertisement, and not from their own common sense. As a result, many tons of unnecessary cleaning mixtures are poured into our sinks and toilets. This can cause serious pollution in our seas and rivers.

We can absorb many different values from television advertisements.

One of the reasons why advertisers are so successful is because they 'target' their audience. This means that they create specific advertisements to appeal to particular sections of the population. When you take a look at an advertisement you can usually tell if it is directed at teenagers, mothers, children, retired people, car-drivers or any other group.

> When we become aware of and examine the values which are presented to us through advertising and the other media, then we can make an informed decision about whether or not to accept them.

EXERCISES

1. Examine the values you listed in Chapter 2. Where did you learn each of these values?
2. Who or what has had the greatest influence on the values you have?
3. Give some examples of values which you have learned from people who care about you. In each case explain why they want you to have this value.
4. What kinds of advertisements are directed towards teenagers? Make a list of the values in these advertisements.
5. Do you agree with the values presented to teenagers in advertisements? Explain why or why not for each value.

Choosing Values

Making decisions about values is very important. Christians often use the following process when making important decisions.
1. We pray to God for guidance.
2. We think about the choices we have.
3. We try to work out the consequences of each of the choices for ourselves and others.
4. We ask other people to guide us.
5. We use our conscience to make the right choice, informed by the Scriptures and Church teaching.

As Christians, we have the support and help of the Church community, the teaching authority of the Church, the Word of God in Scripture, the example and teaching of Jesus and the guidance of the Holy Spirit to help us to choose our values wisely.

Each of us can also influence others, either encouraging them to choose Christian values or making it difficult for them to do so.

What values are shown in these posters for Concern?

GROUP WORK

1. Get into groups of four or five.
2. Make up a play, story, poem or cartoon sequence about a teenager who has to decide between a Christian and an unChristian value — for example: peace or violence; love or hatred; forgiveness or revenge; obedience or disobedience; generosity or selfishness.
3. Include any elements of the Christian process of decision-making which you think are useful.
4. Make your play, story etc. as realistic as possible. Remember to show the consequences of the decisions.
5. Present your work to the rest of the class.

Values in Conflict

When we are faced with two contradictory values, we usually know what we *should* do, even if we do not do it. Sometimes we are in a situation in which two good values are in conflict, and we have to decide which is the more important value of the two. Examine each of the following situations and decide:
(a) What values are in conflict with each other?
(b) Which value is the more important one in this situation?

A. You are on your way to school and you see a young child knocked down by a hit-and-run driver. If you wait to help the child, you will be late for school, and you have a very important examination first thing.

B. A friend of yours has spent all their money on the latest hairstyle. Your friend thinks it looks great. You think it looks really terrible, and that everyone will laugh at your friend when they see the hairstyle.

C. Your best friend's boyfriend/girlfriend has let you know that they would rather go out with you than with your friend. You have always liked this person and find them very attractive.

D. You have to do a lot of work at home because your mother is an invalid and your father works long hours. Your examinations are coming up and your teachers have told you that you must do extra study every day if you want to get good results.

Discussion: Advertising should be banned.

Reflection: 'No one can be a slave of two masters; he will hate one and love the other; he will be loyal to one and despise the other. You cannot serve both God and money.' Matthew 6:24

Action: Closely examine one of your favourite TV programmes or an article in one of your favourite magazines. What values are presented? Do you agree or disagree with them?

Psalm: Teach me, Lord, the meaning of your laws,
and I will obey them at all times.
Explain your law to me, and I will obey it;
I will keep it with all my heart.

Keep me obedient to your commandments,
because in them I find happiness.
Give me the desire to obey your laws
rather than to get rich.
Keep me from paying attention to what is worthless;
be good to me, as you have promised.

Keep your promise to me, your servant —
the promise you make to those who obey you.
Save me from the insults I fear;
how wonderful are your judgments!
I want to obey your commands;
give me new life, for you are righteous.

Psalm 119: 33–40

CALLED BY GOD

CHAPTER 4
▼

What do the cartoon, the parish newsletter article and the story have in common?

'We converted the attic last year, but we're thinking of building an extension soon.'

PARISH NEWS

APRIL 29th 1992

Welcome, Emily!

We are delighted to welcome Emily into the Church community. She was baptised last week during the Easter Vigil. Emily has been living in the parish for some years, and decided that she wanted to become a member of the Church community. Emily's conversion is a reminder to us all of the great gift we have received in Baptism.

NEW CURATE IN THE PARISH

Lorem ipsum dolor sit amet, consecteteur adipscing elit sed diam ninniumy euismod tempor incidunt ut labore ut labore et dolore magna aliquam erat volupat.

eu fugiat nilla pariatur. At vero eos et accusam it iusto odio balndit praesent luptatum delenit aigue dios dolor et molestias wxceptur sint dunic non provident

DATES FOR FIRST HOLY COMMUNIONS

Lorem ipsum dolor sit amet, consecteteur adipscing elit sed

Change of Heart

It was lunch-time. The newsagent's was crowded with students from the two nearby schools and with the workers from the building site across the road. Mrs Stephens and her two assistants were completely occupied behind the counter, taking money and giving change, and putting the purchases in paper bags. They were too busy to notice what was going on at the back of the shop.

Seán and Frank stuffed a few more copies of 'League Football' magazine into their schoolbags. The rest of the gang crowded round, pretending to look at the posters above the magazine rack. 'Hey, what about a box of chocs?' whispered Vincent. 'You must be joking,' said Seán in a loud voice. 'Shut up,' whispered Frank. 'They'll hear you.'

Everyone gazed at the boxes of chocolates displayed on a high shelf over their heads. 'Tom, you're the tallest,' said Vincent. 'You would be able to reach them easily.' 'And I'd be *seen* very easily,' answered Tom. 'Go on, I dare you,' said Vincent. 'I'd do it myself, but I'd have to stand on something.' After a few more minutes of urging, Tom reached up and took the nearest box of chocolates. He moved slowly, so as not to attract any attention. Neither Mrs Stephens nor anyone else took any notice of the boys. No one shouted 'Stop, thief!', not even when the boys walked out of the shop laughing and joking, the box of chocolates safely hidden away with the magazines, sweets and pens in their schoolbags. They headed off to the bicycle shed to divide the 'loot' among them.

Everyone else was laughing and joking and telling Tom what a fine fellow he was, but Seán was silent. He took his share, but it gave him no pleasure. He thought of all the other stolen goods he had hidden away at home. They all called it 'loot', but over the last few weeks Seán had been unable to stop thinking about it as 'stolen property'. This excitement of robbing the shop and inventing new hiding places had worn off. Seán could remember the exact moment when he had begun to be sick of it all. His mother had seen him reading his new (stolen) Sports Annual, and had pretended to fall down in shock.

'I don't believe it, Seán. At last you're willing to spend your own money to buy books, instead of making your father or me get them for you. Next thing we know you'll be helping out with the grocery bill.' His mother had laughed, but Seán knew that she felt proud of him because she thought he was growing up, becoming mature, using his money wisely. He wondered what she would say if she knew what he was really like. In that moment he saw himself as a fraud and a thief, and he hated what he saw.

That night he lay in bed, wide awake and miserable. He knew he didn't want to go 'looting' with the gang any more, but he couldn't see how to get out of it. He didn't want to be called 'Chicken', or lose all his friends. He had been so proud to be accepted by the gang — no one would dare to be friends with him if the gang were against him. He knew there would be trouble if he got out; for one thing they would be afraid he might tell someone about the looting. They would make his life a misery, trying to make him afraid to talk to anyone. So he had said nothing and continued going along with the gang, becoming more and more desperate to escape.

The day after they had stolen the chocolates, Miss Cosgrave, the Maths teacher, made an announcement in class. She intended setting up a Computer Club in the school and wanted to know how many students would be interested in joining. 'We can get the use of the computers at lunch-time and after school,' she said. 'There are a few competitions we could enter, when we're good enough,' she added. Seán had his hand up even before Miss Cosgrave had finished her announcement. This was the chance he had been waiting for, the perfect excuse. He knew very little about computers, but he was willing to learn.

Over the next few days, Seán was really happy. The other members of the gang were surprised by his sudden interest in computers but they were not suspicious about his reasons. After a while they even stopped showing him their 'loot', and trying to make him envious. The only problem was that being a member of the club was quite hard work. Everyone else knew far more about computers than Seán did, so while they were having great fun, he was struggling with the basics. But he refused to give up. He liked feeling good about himself and being in control of his own life. He promised himself that, no matter what happened, he would never steal from anyone again.

Conversion

Conversion means a complete change, a transformation.

> Conversion means ending one way of being, of living, of doing, and beginning a new way, having a new purpose. Conversion can happen suddenly, or over a period of time.

EXERCISES

1. Give some examples of different kinds of conversion. Explain why you think they are examples of conversion.
2. Examine the examples of conversion given at the beginning of the chapter.
   (a) What are the similarities between them?
   (b) What are the differences?
   (c) Which of these conversions do you think shows the greatest transformation? Why?

Christian Conversion

We often use the term 'conversion' to describe the change that takes place when someone decides to become a Christian. We can also use the word conversion to describe the way in which people who are already Christians try to become better, more loving people, more Christ-like in their daily lives. This kind of conversion is not a sudden change, but a gradual change.

> Christian conversion means turning towards God and away from sin.

Christian conversion means more than just changing my mind about something; for example, deciding that I do not want to steal any more. Christian conversion means a change in the whole person which leads to a new way of life. It involves not only a change in the person, but also in their relationships with others and their relationship with God.

The first step in Christian conversion is to decide that I really want to follow God's plan for my life, I want to turn away from sin and love God and other people. Every day after that I will have many opportunities to put that decision into practice. There will be many occasions when I will see a loving action I could do, a kind word I could say, someone I could forgive. Each time I do or say something loving, I am becoming a more loving person, I am becoming the 'Me' God wants me to be. On other occasions I will be tempted to sin; I might feel like being mean or cruel, I might want to hurt someone for hurting me. Each time I say no to the temptation to sin, I am turning my heart and mind to God and rejecting sin and evil.

Christian conversion is an on-going process which is only possible for people who are willing to admit that they are sinners, that they hurt others and themselves, and who want to change with the help of God.

EXERCISES

1. In the story of the Prodigal Son (Luke 15:11–3), the younger son had a conversion and came home to his father. Write the story of the next few weeks or months in the life of the younger son, showing the opportunities he had and the difficulties he faced when he was living out his conversion.
2. Imagine there is a new law forbidding people to be Christian in your country. Anyone suspected of being a Christian is brought to trial and, if they are found guilty, they are sent to prison. Someone gives your name to the police and you are put on trial. Would there be enough evidence in your life *as you live it now* to prove that you are a Christian? Remember, only up-to-date evidence is acceptable, that is, evidence from the last month or so. Write an account of your trial as it might be reported in the newspaper.

Personal Development

Throughout their lives, people grow, change and develop. We develop physically, mentally, spiritually, emotionally and socially. In the earlier stages of human development, people grow and change by instinct. In the later stages, people have more freedom and greater opportunities to use that freedom. Adolescents have many opportunities to decide what beliefs and values they will have, and the kind of people they will become.

Because I am unique and special, I must be the best ME I can possibly be. The kind of person I am is extremely important. What I do, say, think, believe and value matters. The Nazi soldier who said 'It's not my fault. I'm not important. I was only following orders' was wrong. His values and actions were vitally important. They made a difference to the kind of person he became, and to the people with whom he came in contact.

When we realise how important it is to have and keep good beliefs and values, then we become capable of standing on our principles and saying 'Yes' to good and 'No' to evil, and we are prepared to take the consequences — death if necessary. The fifteen-year-old who shoplifts because everyone else is doing it, and the shop will never miss it, so it doesn't matter, has missed the point that he/she *does* matter, that his/her life story should be as upright and honest as he/she can make it, no matter what anyone else does or thinks or says.

Prisoners in a Nazi concentration camp.

Christian conversion helps each person to become the best person he or she can be. This is part of God's loving plan for our lives.

Exercises

1. (a) Write a description of the way of life you hope to have in ten years' time.
(b) Write a description of the kind of person you would like to be in ten years' time.
(c) What are you doing at present to ensure that you achieve (a)? What are you doing to ensure that you become (b)?
(d) Are you doing anything which will make it difficult for you to achieve (a) and (b)?

Discussion: Do teenagers need conversion?

St Paul's Conversion

Saul was a devout Jew who believed firmly in God and in God's law. He came from Tarsus in Asia Minor and was a tent-maker by trade. When he first heard of the followers of Jesus, he believed that they were heretics and sinners, trying to destroy all that he believed in. He thought that they should be punished and was willing to hunt them down himself. When Stephen, one of the first Christians, was murdered because of his belief in Jesus, Saul thoroughly approved. From that point on Saul made it his business to destroy the Church, the community of believers. He went from house to house, dragging out the followers of Jesus, both men and women, and threw them into jail.

Saul went to the high priest and asked for letters of introduction to the synagogues in Damascus, so that if he should find there any followers of the Way of the Lord, he would be able to arrest them, both men and women, and bring them back to Jerusalem.

As Saul was coming near the city of Damascus, suddenly a light from the sky flashed round him. He fell to the ground and heard a voice saying to him, 'Saul, Saul! Why do you persecute me?' 'Who are you, Lord?' he asked. 'I am Jesus, whom you persecute,' the voice said. 'But get up and go into the city, where you will be told what you must do.'

The men who were travelling with Saul had stopped, not saying a word; they heard the voice but could not see anyone. Saul got up from the ground and opened his eyes, but could not see a thing. So they took him by the hand and led him into Damascus. For three days he was not able to see, and during that time he did not eat or drink anything.

There was a Christian in Damascus named Ananias. He had a vision in which the Lord said to him, 'Ananias!' 'Here I am, Lord,' he answered. The Lord said to him, 'Get ready and go to Straight Street, and at the house of Judas ask for a man from Tarsus named Saul. He is praying, and in a vision he has seen a man named Ananias come in and place his hands on him so that he might see again.'

Ananias answered, 'Lord, many people have told me about this man and about all the terrible things he has done to your people in Jerusalem. And he has come to Damascus with authority from the chief priests to arrest all who worship you.'

The Lord said to him, 'Go, because I have chosen him to serve me, to make my name known to Gentiles and kings and to the people of Israel. And I myself will show him all that he must suffer for my sake.'

So Ananias went, entered the house where Saul was, and placed his hands on him. 'Brother Saul,' he said, 'the Lord has sent me — Jesus himself, who appeared to you on the road as you were coming here. He sent me so that you might see again and be filled with the Holy Spirit.' At once something like fish scales fell from Saul's eyes, and he was able to see again. He stood up and was baptised; and after he had eaten, his strength came back.

Saul stayed for a few days with the believers in Damascus. He went straight to the synagogues and began to preach that Jesus was the Son of God.

All who heard him were amazed and asked, 'Isn't he the one who in Jerusalem was killing those who worship that man Jesus? And didn't he come here for the very purpose of arresting those people and taking them back to the chief priests?'

But Saul's preaching became even more powerful, and his proofs that Jesus was the Messiah were so convincing that the Jews who lived in Damascus could not answer him.

After many days had gone by, the Jews met together and made plans to kill Saul, but he was told of their plan. Day and night they watched the city gates in order to kill him. But one night Saul's followers took him and let him down through an opening in the wall, lowering him in a basket.

Saul went to Jerusalem and tried to join the disciples. But they would not believe that he was a disciple, and they were all afraid of him. Then Barnabas came to his help and took him to the apostles. He explained to them how Saul had seen the Lord on the road and that the Lord had spoken to him. He also told them how boldly Saul had preached in the name of Jesus in Damascus. And so Saul stayed with them and went all over Jerusalem, preaching boldly in the name of the Lord. He also talked and disputed with the Greek-speaking Jews, but they tried to kill him. When the believers found out about this, they took Saul to Caesarea and sent him away to Tarsus.

Saul, who was also called Paul, became a great missionary and converted many people to Christianity. You can find an account of his travels in the Acts of the Apostles, written by Luke. (See Acts 8:1–3, 9:1–31)

QUESTIONS

1. What is your reaction to this story?
2. What kind of person was Saul?
3. Why did he persecute Christians?
4. What changed his mind about Christians?
5. What do you think Saul's 'blindness' is a sign of?
6. What do you think the other Christians felt about Saul's 'conversion':
   (a) immediately afterwards?
   (b) a few years later?
7. How did Saul change or develop as a person after his conversion?
8. What does this story tell you about Jesus?
9. The Scripture writers teach us about God and about faith. What message or meaning do you think Luke, the author of Acts, wanted to get across in this story about St Paul?
10. Do you think this story has a message for young people today? Explain.

Reflection: 'After John had been put in prison, Jesus went to Galilee and preached the Good News from God. "The right time has come," he said, "and the Kingdom of God is near! Turn away from your sins and believe the Good News!"' Mark 1: 14–15

Action: Choose *one* quality you would like to have. Decide on *one* step you will take to achieve that quality in yourself.

Psalm: To you, O Lord, I offer my prayer;
in you, my God, I trust.
Save me from the shame of defeat;
don't let my enemies gloat over me!
Defeat does not come to those who trust in you,
but to those who are quick to rebel against you.

Teach me your ways, O Lord;
make them known to me.
Teach me to live according to your truth,
for you are my God, who saves me.
I always trust in you.

Remember, O Lord, your kindness and constant love
which you have shown from long ago.
Forgive the sins and errors of my youth.
In your constant love and goodness,
remember me, Lord!

Because the Lord is righteous and good,
he teaches sinners the path they should follow.
He leads the humble in the right way
and teaches them his will.
With faithfulness and love he leads
all who keep his covenant and obey his commands.

Psalm 25: 1–10

CHRISTIAN BELIEFS AND VALUES

HUMAN RIGHTS

CHAPTER 5

Every Christian is called upon to love God and other people. The first step towards loving others is to respect and protect their *basic rights*. A right is something that people are *entitled* to — something which should not be taken away from them.

How do you think *you* should be treated? At home? At school? Use the following activity to decide what *rights* you share with everyone else at your school. Remember — a right is something to which *everyone* is entitled, not just you or your special friends.

1. Working in pairs, make a list of the rights to which every person in your school is entitled. Each right should apply to all students, teachers, domestic staff etc.
2. Make sure to include the basic necessities of life, like food, clothing etc., as well as those rights which apply specifically to school situations.

Group Work

1. Get into groups of four or five.
2. As a group, try to agree on the ten most important rights.
3. Report your list of rights to the whole class. (Keep a record of the rights on the blackboard or flip-chart.)
4. As a class, try to agree on the ten most important rights.

Human Rights

Every human being is a special act of God's creation. Each person is created in God's own image and is called to love God and others. Because of this, every person has certain basic human rights, things they are entitled to just because they are human beings created by God. The most basic human right is the right to life. Many other rights are based on this, including the right to food, shelter and work. All people, regardless of their age, sex, race, religion, intelligence or any other characteristic, are entitled to basic human rights. Rights are not simply nice things that lucky people have; they are necessary for living the dignified and meaningful life that God wants for every human being. Christians are called to respect and protect the rights of all people.

Exercises

1. Do other people always respect your rights as a student? Explain your answer.
2. Do you always respect the rights of other students; teachers; other members of the staff?
3. How do people feel when their rights are not respected? How do they feel when their rights are respected?
4. Give examples to show how your class could show greater respect for each other's rights, both inside and outside the classroom.

Assignment

Examine the summary of the United Nations Charter of Human Rights on page 39. Using some of the ideas in this charter, adapt your 'School Charter' so that it is a full description of the human rights of everyone in the school.

A meeting of the United Nations.

Rights are Limited

Each person's rights are limited by the rights of everyone else. It has been said that 'my right to swing my fist ends where my neighbour's nose begins'. My right to freedom of action is limited by another person's right to personal security.

Sometimes the rights of one person or group seem to be in conflict with the rights of others. For example, if a ship is sinking and there are not enough lifeboats to rescue all the passengers, then some of them will drown. This is an extreme example in which everyone has an equal right to life, but only some of them can actually live. This kind of problem is very difficult to solve unless some people are willing to give up their rights voluntarily for the sake of the others. Any solution must take into account the fact that everyone in the situation has important rights, rather than taking the easy way out and pretending that some people's rights do not matter.

In many situations where rights appear to be in conflict, the solution may be for people to accept limited rights so that the rights of others will be respected. For example, everyone has the right to own and use private property for their own benefit. Parents have the right to use their money to provide what their children need. However, parents do not have the right to spend more than their fair share of the world's resources on their children. If some other children do not have enough to eat, then it would be right for the parents to give some money to help starving children, rather than buying their own children a new music system.

Our rights are limited by the needs of others.

EXERCISES

1. Give some examples to show how and why a person's rights are limited in the following situations:
    (a) In a classroom
    (b) On the roads
    (c) When there is a water shortage
    (d) When a group of friends goes out for the evening.
2. How could each of the following 'conflicts' of rights be resolved?
    (a) Two members of a family want to watch different television programmes at the same time.
    (b) A company wants to make some employees redundant, so that the company will make more profit.
    (c) Fifty students want to study an important subject in a school, but there are only thirty places available on the course.

Poverty

When people are deprived of their basic human rights, they end up in poverty. This poverty can take many different forms, depending on which rights are being neglected. Lack of proper food or shelter brings the kind of poverty most people know about. It means that people do not have enough of the world's goods to be healthy, and to be able to look after themselves and their families.

Lack of education can also bring poverty, as the following account shows.

A shanty-town in Sao Paulo, Brazil.

> Eileen is eighteen years old. She works as a driver for a small company. According to Eileen herself: 'I was never very good at school. When I was in primary school, I never seemed to be able to hear what the teacher was saying. I had an operation on my ears when I was ten, so I could then hear properly, but I could never quite catch up. I was good at art and games, but I hated reading and writing. Later on, the teachers told me I should get special help, since I was actually very bright, but my family couldn't afford a private teacher. The school tried to help me, but it didn't work out. I was glad to leave in the end. I have no qualifications. When I applied for this job, I had to get my dad to fill in the application form for me. I've got no chance of promotion. I feel I'm at a dead end. I'd love to do art and design, but you can't do anything without qualifications, can you?'

Eileen has enough money to live on, but she suffers from another form of poverty. She does not have a basic education. If there was a free adult literacy course at a local school, she could learn to read and write. She could then go on to do her adult education and get some qualifications. However, in some parts of the world, even primary education is expensive and poor people cannot afford it. In this kind of situation, people may never get the kind of education they need.

Lack of respect and dignity can bring another kind of poverty. We can have a poor opinion of ourselves and our abilities if we have been degraded, humiliated or treated with suspicion on a regular basis. When we lose our self-respect, we sometimes feel unable to achieve anything worthwhile.

While people who are rich in some ways can be poor in other ways, the different kinds of poverty often go together to produce what has been called a 'poverty trap'. This means that people like Eileen, who have very little money or resources, often have very little education. So they are not able to improve

Many young people are caught in a poverty trap.

their standard of living by getting a better job. If I have no job at all and no hope of getting one, I may start to feel hopeless and worthless. I may stop applying for jobs because I feel sure that I will never get one. Other people who are lucky enough to have jobs may call me a 'sponger' or a 'waster', which makes me feel worse. I will only be able to escape from the poverty trap when my community begins to show me some respect as a person and gives me a chance to get a job.

> When people do not get their basic human rights they become poor in some way. There are many different kinds of poverty. Everyone in the community has the responsibility to help one another to escape from poverty.

EXERCISES

A Kurdish refugee and her child.

1. (a) Give examples to show the different reasons why people can be poor.
   (b) In each case, try to identify the basic human right or rights which the person might be denied.
2. Comment on the following statement, explaining whether you agree or disagree and why.
   'We should take care of the problems in our own country, and try to get rid of poverty here. It's up to other countries to do the same for their own people. It's not our problem if people are starving thousands of miles away.'

Faith, Hope and Love

Some people feel that trying to make sure that everyone's rights are respected is a hopeless task. Individuals say, 'What can I do? I'm not an important person, no one will listen to me. Surely what I do will not make much difference.' The governments of countries say, 'The task is huge. There will always be people trying to exploit and use other people and deny them their rights. What good is it to pass laws? People will only get around the laws.' When we listen to the news, or read about the appalling conditions in which people live, or see people living in dreadful conditions on the side of the roads, we can feel helpless too.

However, for the Christian, life is never hopeless or helpless. Firstly, the Christian life is a life of faith, faith in God and in God's love and concern for us which was shown in a special way in the life, death and resurrection of Jesus. We believe that God is with us in every situation, no matter how awful it might be, helping us to use all our gifts to improve the situation.

Secondly, Christians have great hope in God's loving plan for the world. This hope means that Christians never give up, no matter how 'hopeless' things seem. It is because of this hope that a poor Christian gives a few pence — all they can afford — to help others, knowing that every contribution, no matter how small, is important in God's eyes.

Thirdly, Christians know that love is more powerful than any other force in the universe. Christians know, from the life of Jesus and from their own experience, that love can transform people, relationships and situations. A loving word, action or prayer is always possible in any situation, so no situation is hopeless.

Christians believe that when we are helping someone we are helping Christ himself.

Because of faith, hope and love, Christians believe that God's will *will* be done, that the rights of every person will be respected, and that as Christians we can work with God's help preparing for that time.

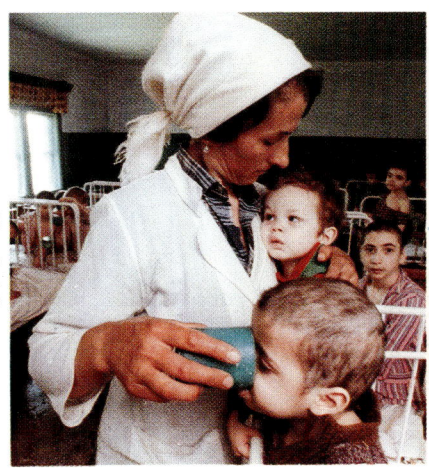

A nurse caring for neglected Romanian children.

Exercises

1. Read Matthew 19: 23–29. In this passage, what words of encouragement does Jesus have for people who are in 'impossible' situations?
2. Give some examples, from your own experience if possible, to show how love can transform people, relationships and situations. For example, you could show how a loving action by one person made a difference to someone's life.
3. How would you answer a person who said, 'There's no need for people to do anything. We must simply wait for God to put everything right.'

Discussion: It's up to the government to do something about poor people — students cannot do anything to help.

Reflection: 'The group of believers was one in mind and heart. No one said that any of his belongings was his own, but they all shared with one another everything they had. With great power the apostles gave witness to the resurrection of the Lord Jesus, and God poured rich blessings on them all. There was no one in the group who was in need. Those who owned fields or houses would sell them, bring the money received from the sale, and hand it over to the apostles; and the money was distributed to each one according to his need.' Acts 4: 32–34

Action: Join, or set up, a group working to help people achieve their basic human rights.

Psalm: Lord, I look up to you,
  up to heaven where you rule.
  As a servant depends on his master,
  as a maid depends on her mistress,
  so we will keep looking to you, O Lord
    our God,
  until you have mercy on us.

  Be merciful to us, Lord, be merciful;
  we have been treated with so much contempt.
  We have been mocked too long by the rich
  and scorned by proud oppressors.

Psalm 123

SOME MORE INFORMATION

A Summary of the United Nations Universal Declaration of Human Rights

1. All human beings are born free and equal, with the same rights and dignity. They have the gifts of reason and conscience, and should treat each other like brothers and sisters.
2. Everyone is entitled to all the rights mentioned in this Declaration, regardless of their race, colour, sex, religion or any other characteristic.
3. Everyone has the right to life and freedom, and the right not to be injured in any way.
4. No one shall be a slave.
5. No one shall be tortured, or given a cruel inhuman or degrading punishment.
6. Everyone is entitled to be protected by the law.
7. No one shall be arrested or detained for no good reason, and everyone is entitled to a fair and public trial when accused of a crime.
8. Everyone shall be presumed innocent until proven guilty.
9. Everyone has the right to freedom of movement.
10. Adult men and women have the right to marry and have a family.
11. The family is the basic group in society, and is entitled to protection by society and by the state.
12. Everyone has the right to own property.
13. No one has the right to take another's property illegally.
14. Everyone has the right to freedom of thought, conscience and religion, and to express his/her opinions openly.
15. Everyone has the right to take part in or elect the government of his/her country.
16. Everyone has the right to social security.
17. Everyone has the right to work, to just conditions at work, and to protection against unemployment.
18. Everyone has the right to form or join trade unions.
19. Everyone has the right to rest and leisure.
20. Everyone has the right to an adequate standard of living.
21. Mothers and children are entitled to special care and help.
22. Everyone is entitled to free elementary education.
23. Parents have the right to choose the kind of education that shall be given to their children.
24. Everyone's rights and freedoms shall be limited only for the purpose of ensuring other people's right and freedoms.

JUSTICE

CHAPTER 6

Every day we have to make decisions about how we will treat people and how we will relate to them. Discover how *you* might relate to other people as a salesperson or a customer in the following game.

'Second-Hand Cars for Sale'
Situation: A second-hand car business with a number of cars for sale.

Players: Four customers, two salespeople, two mechanics and one business manager.

Preparation
1. The customers are asked to leave the room while the salespeople, mechanics and the business manager set up the business.
2. A card is made out for each of the six cars for sale, listing its make, year of manufacture, number of miles travelled etc.
3. The salespeople read out the description of each car and the class decides what price it will be. The cars and their prices are listed on the chalkboard or flipchart.
4. The customers come back into the room and the game begins.

Directions to the Salespeople
1. The salespeople keep the cards. They may show them to the mechanics or the business manager, but not to the customers.
2. If the customers have any questions which the salespeople are not sure about, the salespeople can consult with the mechanics to decide what to tell the customers.
3. The salespeople must answer all the customers' questions truthfully.
4. When a customer decides to buy a car, the salesperson should bring him/her to the business manager to complete the deal and sign the necessary papers.

Direction to the mechanics
The mechanics are stationed to the side, ready to be consulted by the salespeople.

Direction to the business manager
The business manager closes any sales made with the customers and deals with any complaints they may have.

Directions to the customers
1. The customers 'view' the cars on sale and eventually choose one each to buy.
2. They can spend as much money as they want, but should try to make sensible purchases.
3. The customers can ask any questions they want about the cars and will be given truthful answers.

Directions to the rest of the class
Watch the action carefully to find out:
      (a) Who is the best salesperson and
      (b) Who is the smartest customer.

The game is over when all of the car sales have been completed. At this stage, the customer is given the card describing the car he or she has bought.

Have a show of hands to decide which salesperson was the best; which customer was the smartest.

QUESTIONS

1. In your opinion, was anyone treated unfairly in the game? Explain.
2. Did anyone speak or behave dishonestly in the game? Explain.
3. Do you think the game is true to life — does this kind of activity take place in real life? Explain.

Justice means being fair.

Justice

Justice means being fair and honest in my relationships with other people. It means giving people what is due to them, or what they are entitled to. Justice is the first step in establishing good relationships between individuals and between groups of people. Justice allows people to co-operate with one another and live in peace together. All Christians are called by God to think, speak and act justly, at home, at school, at work, and in all other circumstances. Justice shows in a practical way that we are willing to love our neighbour.

EXERCISES

1. In the game at the beginning of the chapter, did the salespeople, mechanics and business manager treat the customers justly? Explain your answer.
2. Do you think that it was right to treat the customers in this way? Why/Why not?
3. How do you think the customers with the faulty cars felt when they discovered what was wrong with their cars? What do you think they might do?
4. Have you ever been treated unjustly? How did you *feel*? What did you do?
5. Write a brief definition of injustice and of how it affects people.

GROUP WORK

1. Get into groups of five or six.
2. Let each group take one of the following and make up a short play about it:
   (a) Injustice in a family
   (b) Injustice between 'friends'
   (c) Injustice towards young, part-time workers
   (d) Injustice in shops, cinemas, discos etc.
3. Present your plays in turn to the rest of the class. After each performance, briefly note:
   (a) Who is being treated unjustly and why;
   (b) What are the consequences of this injustice for the victim and for the other people in the situation;
   (c) What would have to happen so that justice could be done in this situation.

Prejudice and Discrimination

Prejudice is a common form of injustice. It means to pre-judge someone or something. *It means having a negative attitude or opinion before finding out the facts in a situation.*

People can be prejudiced against individuals or groups. For example, people could believe that someone in their neighbourhood was a 'good-for-nothing' and a thief, without ever knowing him, or having any proof, because 'everyone else' says he is a 'good-for-nothing' and a thief. We can be prejudiced against people who are different from us in some way — people of a different colour, race, social class, religion or culture.

When prejudice, which is an attitude of mind, causes people to speak unjustly about or act unjustly towards others, we call this discrimination. Discrimination can take place between individuals or groups of people. A student who refuses to sit beside another student because she is poor; a club which does not allow girls to play football because it is a 'boy's game'; an employer who will not give someone a job because they have the 'wrong' address — they are all practising discrimination.

Under the Apartheid system in South Africa, black people were discriminated against by law.

Prejudice and discrimination are unjust because they are unfair and dishonest. They result in some people being treated as if they were of less worth than other people, as if they were not entitled to respect and dignity as human beings. As Christians, we are called upon to examine our own attitudes and actions, to become aware of our prejudices and to try to overcome them with God's help. We should be able to bring justice to people who are discriminated against for any reason.

EXERCISES

1. Find some evidence to show how the following people can suffer discrimination:
    (a) poor people
    (b) children
    (c) women/girls
    (d) black people
    (e) people of a minority religion in a country.
    You may find some information in the news or in documentary programmes, in the newspapers or magazines. Organisations such as those listed at the end of the chapter will also be able to provide information.

2. Have you ever been discriminated against? If so, briefly explain what happened.
3. Do you think you are prejudiced against any person or group of people? How would you know if you were prejudiced?

Racism

Racism is a particular form of prejudice which believes that all human beings can be divided into certain 'races', each with specific physical, intellectual and cultural characteristics. Usually, people who are racists see one race (their own) as superior to or better than all the others. The 'inferior' races can be treated with various degrees of discrimination — they may be refused jobs, housing in certain areas, or access to education; they may be segregated or kept separate from the 'superior' race by law; they may suffer actual persecution, violence and death. Black people, Asians, Jews and many other groups have suffered and continue to suffer from racism.

Exercises

1. Explain why racism is unChristian.
2. Is there any form of racism in your local community or in your country? Explain.

Ethnic Groups

An ethnic group is a group of people who share a common history, culture and sense of identity. The people of an ethnic group see themselves as different from other people or groups. They believe themselves to be a separate and distinct group. Usually other people also recognise an ethnic group as separate and distinct. Everyone in the world is a member of an ethnic group. However we do not usually think about it until we are in the company of people from a different group. The Aborigines in Australia, white Australians, Irish-Americans, French-Canadians and the Inuit (or Eskimo) people of the Arctic are all examples of ethnic groups.

As people, we tend to fear or be suspicious of anyone or any group who is different from us. Looking down on people who are different from us, or exploiting them, can make us feel superior. For these and other reasons, ethnic groups have been

Australian Aboriginees.

the victims of prejudice and discrimination all over the world. They can be treated unjustly because of racism; for example, people might say, 'Aborigines are not as intelligent as white people'. They can be treated unjustly because they are poor; for example people might say, 'The Irish are filthy; they never work; any money they get goes on drink'. One of the most unjust ways to treat an ethnic group is to deny that they have a right to their identity as an ethnic group, and to say that they should 'be like everyone else'.

Travellers

Travellers are an ethnic group in Ireland. Like the Bedouin of Arabia, the Romanies of Britain and the Gypsies of Continental Europe, Travellers have a nomadic tradition. Travellers are a distinct community, with the following characteristics:

Inuit family outside their buried outpost camp

1. *They have a long shared history*, which, even though largely unresearched, can be traced back for centuries, probably to before the 12th century. (Travellers are not settled people who left or were evicted from their land as a result of the famine, for example.)

2. *They have a shared set of customs, traditions, values and a common lifestyle. These are related to nomadism.* They share a form of nomadism which covers a range of situations from those who travel throughout the year, to those who travel in one period of the year, to those who remain in one place for many years and then move on. The difference between a nomad and a settled person is not just the fact of travelling from place to place. A nomad sees all forms of living accommodation as temporary, even if he or she has stayed there for many years. A settled person, however, will see a tent as temporary, but a house as permanent. Nomadism enables Travellers to carry on traditional activities, such as buying and selling metal. It also enables them to meet other Travellers regularly for social occasions, and to avoid conflict where necessary.

Travellers' traditional horse-drawn caravan.

The extended family is very important to Travellers. They like to live with cousins, aunts, uncles, grannies, as well as parents, brothers and sisters. When a young couple marry, they do not want to go away and live by themselves. Instead, they remain with the larger family group from which they get support and companionship. Weddings and funerals are important times of celebration when large groups of Travellers get together. Travellers do not have to

Many Travellers today live in modern caravans.

Many Travellers deal in car parts and scrap metal.

send out invitations. When there is a wedding, all Travellers know they are welcome. They will travel great distances to join in the celebrations.

3. *They share a common ancestry.* They have a small number of ancestors, and different families are associated with different parts of the country. For example, the Connors are linked with Wexford, while the Wards are associated with Galway. A person is born a Traveller. People cannot decide to 'become' Travellers.

4. *Travellers have their own language* called the Cant, Gammon or Shelta. Travellers can also be recognised by their accents, and by the way they use language. Travellers have a strong oral tradition. This means that they do not have a tradition of writing in their own language; neither do they have a written account of their history and traditions. Instead, the language, stories and customs are passed on orally, by word of mouth, from generation to generation.

5. *The Travellers' oral tradition is rich in folklore.* This has much in common with the folklore of other countries. Travellers also have a distinctive style of singing. Modern life and the influences of the mass media, such as television, are making it more difficult for the folklore tradition to continue. This is especially true among young Travellers.

6. *Travellers are a small minority group* who have a common experience of oppression and discrimination down through the years.

Some Travellers like to live in houses.

Questions

1. What is your reaction to this account of the customs and lifestyle of Travellers? Does anything surprise you in this account? Explain.
2. Are there any advantages in getting to know and understand people of a different culture?
3. Mention some of the difficulties that can arise when people of different cultures live in the same community.
4. To which ethnic group do you belong? How would you describe *your* culture?

A Young Traveller's Story

Like other nomads whose way of life is based on moving from place to place, Irish Travellers are often treated with prejudice and discrimination by the settled population.

Jimmy McCarthy, a young Traveller, describes his own experiences of prejudice and discrimination.

'It started to happen to me in Galway. I went to a dance. There was a friend with me and as we were going in the door we were stopped by a big man who said: "You're not coming in." I got a shock and said: "What do you mean, I'm not coming in?" He said: "No Travellers are coming in."

I turned and walked away. I felt really bad, so I went home. I sat there thinking about it, and I just couldn't get over it. I was saying, "Why are we different from others? Why are Travellers treated like dirt?"

It's very embarrassing when you are turned away like that. A Traveller is treated like dirt because hardly any buffer* will speak to Travellers. You'd get more guards talking to Travellers than you would buffer people. I didn't even know I was a Traveller when I was small because when I was in the school in Tralee, I was an altar boy. I went to Mass every day. I was very religious. It was only years later I left school and lived on the site at Ashline in Ennis that I knew I was a Traveller, when I learnt the way of the Travellers. I didn't know that we were different from townspeople but I soon found out. The first thing I found out was that townspeople didn't like Travellers because Travellers were supposed to be breaking into their houses and robbing them and people were afraid of Travellers. The Travellers wouldn't be served in pubs because they were supposed to be troublemakers. They didn't like Travellers coming around to their houses begging. They didn't like seeing their young ones going round with Travellers.

Now things aren't too bad because I don't go much to discos or dances. Last week we were at Lahinch at a disco. We went back very early. When the disco was starting, Tom, John and I were getting ready to pay. When Tom took out his money the woman said, "Hold on for a minute."

She went out to talk to one of the head men. I knew what it was about. I felt embarrassed just thinking about it. Then the man came over and said, "O.K. lads, I won't have any trouble out of you, will I?" We said "No." He said, "We will have someone watching you." That is the only time it has happened to me in a long time and I hope it doesn't happen to me again, with the help of God.'

* *Settled person*

QUESTIONS

1. What is your reaction to Jimmy's account?
2. Do you think Jimmy was treated justly? Explain.
3. How do you think Travellers should be treated at discos; in pubs; when they call to the houses of settled people?
4. Do you think you are prejudiced against Travellers? Have you ever discriminated against a Traveller in your words or actions? Explain your answers.

Discrimination against Travellers

Travellers make up approximately 0.5% of the population of Ireland, but the laws are made by the settled majority. Many of these laws do not take the needs of Travellers into account, and some actively discriminate against them. For example, the law allows County Councils and other official bodies to use huge boulders to block off areas which Travellers used as halting sites. Travellers' basic rights to water, waste disposal, employment, health care and other social services, accommodation, education, energy supply (electricity etc.) are often either neglected or denied. The state provides houses for people who need them. But it does not provide enough halting sites for Travellers who need them. Cooking, washing and toilet facilities are provided automatically in Council or Corporation houses. However, four families on a halting site may have to share one tap and one toilet among all of them. In many places, no effort is made to provide education for Travellers who move so frequently. Instead of getting respect and recognition as people, Travellers are often forced to live like settled people in order to receive their basic rights.

As well as legal discrimination, Travellers often experience prejudice and discrimination from the people they meet in the settled community. Some settled people will not allow their children to play with Traveller children. Many hotels, shops and other public premises refuse to let Travellers in, or treat them with suspicion if they are admitted.

Many people think that all Travellers are drunkards, criminals, thieves, liars and spongers. This is not true. Travellers, like most settled people, are law-abiding and honest. In 1983, the Report of the Travelling People Review Body stated that Travellers were no more likely than the settled population to become involved in crime or to get drunk. However it is very hard to get rid of the prejudice because it has been part of our society's way of thinking for so long.

Many sites used by Travellers lack proper facilities.

Site blocked off with boulders.

Great efforts are being made by many groups, involving both Travellers and settled people, to make sure that Travellers get their basic human rights, including the right to continue to be Travellers. (You will find a list of these groups at the end of the chapter.) Efforts are also being made to educate the settled population about the Travellers and their way of life, to encourage trust and co-operation between Travellers and the settled community, and to defeat prejudice through knowledge and understanding.

Young Travellers.

CHARTER OF TRAVELLERS' RIGHTS

This charter was prepared by the Irish Centre for the Study of Human Rights in University College Galway. The charter states the rights which Travellers share with all others, including the right to be themselves and follow their own culture and traditions.

Article 1 — Travellers as a Minority

Travellers, as individuals and as a group, have a right to:
- the realisation of their own identity and to follow their traditional way of life;
- their separate identity and the protection of the state;
- be consulted on and involved in decisions affecting themselves.

Article 2 — The right to move and the right to stop

- Travellers have the right to free movement, and the state is obliged to act against threats to their health, their dignity etc.
- Until proper sites are provided, local authorities or others shall not dump materials or erect barriers on sites currently used.

Article 3 — Accommodation

- Travellers have the right to decide whether or not they wish to continue their nomadic way of life.
- The state has the ultimate responsibility to provide accommodation for Travellers whether travelling or settled.
- Travellers should not be forced to accept sub-standard or inappropriate accommodation.
- Sites for Travellers should not present risks or hazards and should take into account family groupings, trades and occupations.

- For Travellers wishing to continue travelling, serviced sites should be provided close to all facilities.
- The state should protect customary sites from interference and compensation should be paid for past interference.

Article 4 — Economic Needs
Travellers have the right to:
- a standard of living adequate for health and well-being (food, clothing, accommodation, medical care etc.);
- work and fair conditions;
- protection against discrimination in work;
- support to pursue traditional ways of life;
- social security services and entitlements.

Article 5 — Health
Travellers have a right to:
- life;
- physical, social and environmental conditions which support improvement in the quality of their lives;
- action by the state to remove causes of ill health;
- water supplies, sanitation, refuse collection;
- medical and hospital services;
- advisory and educational facilities for the promotion of health.

Article 6 — The Family
The Traveller's family has the right to:
- appropriate social, legal and economic protection;
- protection against discrimination;
- legal protection against measures which force them to move on;
- social protection for mothers, especially during pregnancy;
- special treatment for handicapped members;
- opportunities for the physical, mental, moral, spiritual and social development, especially of children.

Article 7 — Education
- Travellers have a right to equality of education at all levels which recognises their history, culture and identity. All education should challenge prejudice and discrimination against Travellers.

Article 8 — The Law
- Travellers have the right to equal protection before the law.

Article 9 — Political Rights
Travellers shall have the right and the opportunity to:
- participate in public life;
- have access to the public service;
- special provision for the exercise of these rights necessitated by mobility or illiteracy.

Article 10 — Free Expression
Travellers shall have, with others, the right to:
- freedom of opinion and expression;
- legal protection from attacks upon their honour, reputation and private and family life;
- reply in equal measure to inaccurate or offensive statements made about them;
- action by the state against those who incite hatred or discrimination.

Article 11 — Privacy
Travellers, in common with all others, have the right to:
- respect for their person;
- legal protection against interference with their private or family life;
- respect for their property.

Article 12 — Discrimination
- Travellers are entitled to the full exercise of their rights and should not suffer any distinction, exclusion or restriction based on the fact that they are Travellers.

GROUP WORK

1. Get into groups of three or four.
2. Read the Charter of Travellers' Rights carefully.
3. As a group, make a note of your answers to the following:
   (a) What is your immediate reaction to the charter?
   (b) Pick out the articles which could apply to you, just as much as to Travellers.
   (c) Which articles apply only to Travellers? Do you believe Travellers are entitled to what they have claimed in these articles? Give your reasons.
   (d) Can you see any way in which the rights mentioned in the charter might lead to conflict between Travellers and the settled population? Explain.

The Work of Justice (Irish Bishops' Pastoral)

Justice means, firstly, giving every [person] what is due to him [or her] . . .

Justice involves returning to another something that is rightly his [or hers] . . . It is about honesty, and truthfulness and straight dealing in work, business, in public service, in political life.

(Taken from Paragraphs 43 and 45)

QUESTIONS

1. Give an example to show that justice means giving people something that belongs to them already.
2. Give examples to show how teenagers are called upon to be just, honest and truthful in the following areas of their lives:
   (a) schoolwork and study
   (b) use of spending money
   (c) asking for money at home
   (d) doing household chores
   (e) relationships with brothers and sisters
   (f) relationships with parents
   (g) keeping promises.
3. Re-write the quotation from the Irish Bishops' Pastoral so that it speaks directly to young people about justice in their lives.

The Work of Justice (Irish Bishops' Pastoral)

This is an appropriate place to make a special reference to our treatment of the Travelling People. Many of them are not poor; yet they are still the most discriminated against minority in this country. We judge them by different standards from those we apply to other groups. If a few of the Travelling People misbehave, we sometimes say this is 'typical' of them all. We do not say this about other sections of society, some of whose members also misbehave. We blame the Travellers as a whole for the unruliness of a few. We are inconsistent in regard to them, we expect them to be good neighbours, yet many refuse to have them as neighbours.

Let a carefully prepared plan to settle a travelling family, however well chosen and however well behaved, be mooted in certain neighbourhoods, and residents will raise an indignant outcry. Surely our values in many such matters are still far from Christian. Property values sometimes seem to be more important to us than Christian values. There are territories in our own hearts and minds which have still to be converted to Christ.

Questions

1. According to this Pastoral, in what ways are Travellers treated differently from other people in our society?
2. Why do the bishops say that the treatment of the Travellers shows that our values are not Christian? What Christian values should be shown in the treatment of Travellers?
3. What do you think the bishops mean by the last sentence in the quotation? Do you agree with them? Why/Why not?

Project

Do a class project on 'Justice in our Community'. Working as individuals, pairs or groups of three to four, choose different topics related to the main theme: for example justice in relation to Travellers, people of Asian and African descent, women, children, poor people, people with a physical disability, single parents, the homeless, work, school, the home etc. Remember to include:

(a) a description of any injustice involved in your topic;

(b) a description of what must be done or what must be stopped so that there can be justice in the situation;

(c) what action is already being taken by individuals or groups to bring about justice in the situation.

(The addresses at the end of the chapter might be useful in helping you to research your project.)

Reflection: 'Remove the chains of oppression and the yoke of injustice, and let the oppressed go free. Share your food with the hungry, and open your homes to the homeless poor. Give clothes to those who have nothing to wear, and do not refuse to help your own relatives.'   Isaiah 58: 6–7

Action: Keep yourself informed of issues relating to justice, using some of the following methods.
— Watch current affairs programmes or documentaries on TV.
— Read local newspapers and listen to community radio.
— If there are any groups working for justice in your area, find out what they are doing and why.

Psalm: Lord, you are a God who punishes;
reveal your anger!
You are the judge of all people;
rise and give the proud what they deserve!
How much longer will the wicked be glad?
How much longer, Lord?
How much longer will criminals be proud
and boast about their crimes?

They crush your people, Lord;
they oppress those who belong to you.
They kill widows and orphans,
and murder the strangers who live in our land.
They say, 'The Lord does not see us;
the God of Israel does not notice.'

My people, how can you be such stupid fools?
When will you ever learn?
God made our ears — can't he hear?
He made our eyes — can't he see?
He is in charge of the nations — won't he punish them?
He is the teacher of all people — hasn't he any knowledge?
The Lord knows what they think;
he knows how senseless their reasoning is.

Lord, how happy is the person you instruct,
the one to whom you teach your law!
You give him rest from days of trouble
until a pit is dug to trap the wicked.
The Lord will not abandon his people;
he will not desert those who belong to him.
Justice will again be found in the courts,
and all righteous people will support it.

Who stood up for me against the wicked?
Who took my side against the evildoers?
If the Lord had not helped me,
I would have gone quickly to the land of silence.
I said, 'I am falling';
but your constant love, O Lord, held me up.
Whenever I am anxious and worried,
you comfort me and make me glad.

You have nothing to do with corrupt judges,
who make injustice legal,
who plot against good people
and sentence the innocent to death.
But the Lord defends me;
my God protects me.
He will punish them for their wickedness
and destroy them for their sins;
the Lord our God will destroy them.

Psalm 94

Useful Addresses

Dublin Travellers Education
   and Development Group,
Pavee Point,
North Great Charles St.
Dublin 1.
Tel. (01) 732802

The Irish Commission for
   Justice & Peace,
169 Booterstown Ave,
Blackrock,
Co. Dublin.
Tel (01) 2885021

Combat Poverty Agency,
8 Charlemont Street,
Dublin 2.
Tel. (01) 783355

Focus Point,
15 Eustace Street,
Dublin 1.
Tel. (01) 776421/718086

Jesuit Centre for Faith and
   Justice
26 Upper Sherrard St.
Dublin 1.
Tel. (01) 740814

Society of St Vincent de Paul
   (SVP),
18 Nicholas Street,
Dublin 8.
Tel. (01) 757043

Irish Anti-Apartheid
   Movement (IAAM),
20 Beechpark Rd,
Foxrock,
Dublin 18.
Tel. (01) 2885021

Irish Traveller Movement
C/o Holy Faith Convent
Barry Rd, Finglas
Dublin 11.
Tel. (01) 341145

JUSTICE IN THE WORLD

CHAPTER 7

There are many situations in which one group of people has to make a decision which will affect the life of another person or group of people. In the following role-play, one group of people must try to make a just decision which will affect the lives of at least two people.

College admissions

City College is a community college for third-level students. It is a very popular college because most of its graduates get very good jobs. For this reason, there are usually more applicants than there are places. This year 100 places are available. Ninety-nine of these places are soon filled by early applicants. Then, two late applications arrive from the following students.

1. **Justin, aged 18.** He got excellent results in his final examinations — two As and three Bs. Justin comes from a well-off family. He has always had a room of his own in which to study. His parents paid for private tutors to help him with his study, particularly in his weaker subjects. Justin feels that all his hard work will have been worth it if he gets a place at City College.

2. **Jennifer, aged 18.** She got one B, two Cs and two passes in her final examinations. She comes from a poor family. Her mother died when she was twelve. Jennifer did not have much time for study because she had to mind the younger children and do a lot of work around the house. This is the only chance she has of going to college, getting a good job and being able to help support her younger brothers and sisters.

Both Justin and Jennifer are equally intelligent and hard-working. The College Admissions Board cannot decide which candidate should have the last place. Some of them feel that Justin should get the place because he got such good exam results. Others feel that Jennifer has had more problems than Justin and that she needs to get the college place in spite of her results.

The Board invites the family and friends of both candidates to come to a meeting and speak on their behalf. The members of the Board feel that listening to both points of view will help them to come to a decision.

Role Play: the Meeting.
1. Divide the class into three groups:
   Group One — Justin's family and friends
   Group Two — Jennifer's family and friends
   Group Three — the College Admissions Board
2. Each group meets and plans what it will say or do at the meeting.
   (a) Group One will decide the arguments they will put forward to persuade the Admissions Board to give Justin the place.
   (b) Group Two will decide the arguments they will put forward to persuade the Admissions Board to give Jennifer the place.
   (c) Group Three will decide *how* to conduct the meeting, who will be allowed to speak and for how long, whether they will allow any debate or discussion etc.
3. When every group is ready, the Admissions Board Chairperson calls the meeting to order, and the role-play begins.
4. After the meeting, the Board has to decide whether to give the last place to Justin or Jennifer. The Chairperson reports this decision to the whole class.

QUESTIONS

1. What happened during the meeting? What did you think or feel as it was going on?
2. Do you agree with the decision made by the Admissions Board? Why/Why not?
3. Was the Admissions Board's decision a just decision? Explain your answer.
4. Are there any other situations in which one group of people has to make a decision affecting the life of another person or group of people:
   (a) in your local community
   (b) in your country
   (c) in the world?
   Explain your answers, giving examples.

Different Forms of Justice

Justice is not a simple issue. It is often easy to see that something is unjust, but it is not always easy to see exactly how justice can be done. There are usually a number of choices of action in any situation, and we have to decide which is the best or more just action to take. In the case of the College Admissions Board, there are at least three actions which could be taken, each of which is just in its own way.

1. Both students should be given an equal chance to go to the college. Put their names into a hat and choose one at random. This action is just because *Justice means equality*.
2. Jennifer's needs are greater than Justin's needs, so Jennifer should get the place. This action is just because *Justice means giving people what they need*.
3. Justin got the best results, so he deserves to get the place. This action is just because *Justice means giving people what they deserve*.

> There are many other situations, involving both individuals and groups of people, in which these three types of justice could apply. In each situation, Christians are called to use the form of justice which is the most loving. As individuals and as communities we have the Word of God in Scripture, the example of Jesus, and the teaching of the Church to guide our consciences in making the right choices.

EXERCISES

Examine the following situations. In each case decide:
- as an individual and then
- as a class, which form of justice — equality, need or merit (what people have earned or deserved) — should apply in each situation.

1. A number of artists have entered portfolios of their paintings for the 'Artist of the Year' competition. Some of them are young people just out of art school; others have been painting for years. Some have achieved fame, success and wealth; others barely earn enough to keep themselves. Some of the artists have great talent, others are mediocre and a few have no real talent at all. What would be the just way to choose the 'Artist of the Year'?

2. Two countries, one rich and one poor, both manufacture shoes which are sold in both countries. The rich country runs an advertising campaign to encourage people to buy only those shoes which are made in their own rich country. They advise their citizens to boycott the shoes from the poor country in order to safeguard employment and increase profits in the rich country. The poor country is depending on good sales in the rich country to increase its profits and safeguard employment. How should the people of the rich country make their decision about which shoes to buy?

3. Chris and Joan both work for the local town council. Joan works 35 hours a week in an office and earns £150 a week. She is a parent with two small children to support. She is well educated and good at her job. Chris is a roadsweeper. He earns £120 for a 40 hour week. The work is tiring, and often dirty and unpleasant. He is a middle-aged man who lives alone. He is well educated and does his work well. Both Chris and Joan have applied for a £20 raise. The council can only afford to spend £30 on wage increases. What would be the just way to divide up the money?

4. A family is planning to go away for a short summer holiday. The father wants to go to a holiday resort beside a golf course because he loves golf and finds it relaxing. He works very hard all year round to support his family, and this is the one holiday he will take this year. The two teenagers want to go to a resort with more night-life, discos and the chance of meeting other young people. They have always gone on holiday wherever their parents decided, but this time they think they should get what they want. The mother wants to go to a health resort, with a fitness and healthy eating programme, with dieticians, nurses, physiotherapists and a doctor on call. She has recently been told that she has very high blood pressure, and must change her lifestyle if she is not to become seriously ill. She believes that a health resort programme will give both her and the rest of the family a chance to start a healthy lifestyle. The family cannot afford separate holidays, so how should they decide where to go on holiday?

Justice between countries

Throughout history, the people of different countries have made decisions that have affected the lives of people in other countries.

Chief Kabongo of the Kikuyu tribe of Kenya describes what happened to his people when the Europeans took control of Kikuyu land. (Chief Kabongo lived from the 1870s to the 1950s.)

The Coming of the Pink Cheeks

It was in these days that a Pink Cheek man came one day to our Council. He came from far, where many of these people lived in houses made of stone and where they held their own Council.

He sat in our midst and he told us of the King of the Pink Cheeks, who was a great king and lived in a land over the seas.

'This great king is now your King,' he said. 'And this land is all his land, though he has said you may live on it as you are his people and he is as your father and you are as his sons.'

This was strange news. For this land was ours. Our ancestors had bought this land with cattle in the presence of the Elders and had taken the oath and it belonged to us. We had no King, we elected our Councils and they made our laws. A strange King could not be our King and our land was our own. We had no battle, no one had fought us to take away our land as, in the past, had sometimes been. This land we had from our fathers and our fathers' fathers, who had bought it. How then could it belong to this King?

With patience, our leading Elder tried to tell this to the Pink Cheek and he listened. But at the end he said, 'This we know. But in spite of this, what I have told you is a fact. You have now a King — a good and great King who loves his people, and you are among his people. In the town called Nairobi is a council or government that acts for the king. And his laws are your laws.'

For many moons this thing was much talked of by us. Then, when no more Pink Cheeks came and things went on as they had always been, we spoke no more.

Sometimes we heard of strange happenings, or even saw them ourselves, but for the most part life was still as it had always been. The Iron Snake, which I had never seen, had come and had carried men on it, not of our people. Then a big path was made through the country half a day from our land. It was wide enough for three elephants to walk abreast. And stones were laid on it and beaten flat, so that grain could have been threshed there.

As the years passed and more and more strange things happened, it seemed to me that this path or road was a symbol of all changes. It was along this road now that news came from other parts; and along it came the new box-on-wheels that made men travel many days' journey in one day and that brought things for the market that the women wanted to have, clothes or beads to wear and pots for cooking. Along this road the young men went when they left to work with the Pink Cheeks and along it too they went when that day came that they travelled to fight in the war over the sea that the Pink Cheeks made against each other.

Along the road, too, went the trees that men cut down when they made more and more farms. Without trees to give shade the ground was hot and dry and food grew not well.

By the time that my father, Kimani, died and his spirit joined those of our ancestors, our own land was poor too. For even though many of our family had gone away to work for the Pink Cheeks, our numbers had increased and there was now no room for the land to rest and it was tired. The food it grew was poor and there was not enough grown on it for all to eat. Those of our family who worked for the Pink Cheeks sent us food and coins that we could buy food with, or else we could not live.

As there was now so little land and we were so many, the boys as they became men would go away, some to work on farms for the Pink Cheeks, some to a new kind of school-farm for men, where they learned the new customs and also some curious ways; for these grown men were made to play games like little boys, running after balls which they threw. This they did instead of good work.

Munene, one of my younger brothers, had been one of these. He had been away a long time, and when he came back he wore clothes like a Pink Cheek and he came with one of them, in a box-on-wheels, which is called a motor-car, along the new road.

The Pink Cheek called a Council together and when all, both Elders and the young men, were assembled and sat round, he spoke. He spoke of Munene; he told us of his learning and of his knowledge of the customs of the Pink Cheeks and of his cleverness at organising.

'Because of this,' he said, 'and because he is a wise man, the Government, the Council of Muthungu that meets in Nairobi, have honoured him and, in honouring him, are honouring you all.'

He paused and looked around at us. Beside him Munene stood smiling.

'He has been appointed Chief of this district and he will be your mouth and our mouth. He will tell us the things that you want to say and he will tell you the things that we want to say to you. He has learned our language and our laws and he will help you to understand and keep them.'

We Elders looked at each other. Was this the end of everything that we had known and worked for? What magic had this son of my father made that he who was not yet an Elder should be made leader over us all who were so much older and wiser in the ways of our people? It was as if a thunderbolt had fallen among us. The Pink Cheek went on:

'Your new Chief will collect the tax on huts, and choose the places for the new schools that you will build everywhere, so that your children may be taught to read and write. He will raise the money for that from you all. I have spoken.'

When the Pink Cheek had gone there was much talk. We asked Munene to tell us how this had come about and why he was set above the Elders in this way.

'It is because they do not understand our laws and Councils,' he told us. 'Because I speak their language and because when I went away in their wars I had many medals.'

The medals we knew about, for we had seen them. Many had them.

We spoke then of the tax on huts. It was heavy, for some men had many huts. Those men who had gone to work on the farms of the Pink Cheeks sent us money, but this we needed to buy food. More men, therefore, must go.

Munene gave us some good advice. He told us that men were wanted in Nairobi to build the new houses made of stone, both for the Pink Cheeks to live in and where they sat to make business and trading. Our men could go there and earn coins and then they could come back when they had plenty.

This was good, for in this way we would pay our tax and no man would be taken by the Pink Cheeks for not paying. So our young men went away down the new road. We were left to grow what food we could, and all was as usual.

It was while these men were still away to make money for our hut tax that ten of our people came back from the farms where they worked. They were not needed, they said, there was no work for them there. With many others, they had been sent back without money and without food, because there were bad people who troubled the land.

This was the beginning. Along the new road had come big boxes-on-wheels that they called lorries in which they had carted logs from the forest. Now these came filled with people. Many had no homes, for their land had gone to the Pink Cheeks. Some had no homes because their land had gone to be mined for gold. We could not let them starve, so we took them on our land.

It was the end of the dry season and there was little food left in the storehouses. Our *mbari* (community) had now grown big, and all these newcomers on our land must eat too. Altogether there were 1,200 people on the 200 acres of land our ancestors had bought. There was not enough room to grow all the food.

In the dry season many goats and cattle had died for want of water. The harvest had been thin and there was little left, and there was no money to buy food; the last had gone for our hut tax. I heard the crying of children and I saw the women weaken in their work. The old men would sit near their huts, too feeble to walk.

Wangari, whose once-strong breasts hung like empty bags and whose eyes were deep in her head, came to me where I sat by my hut.

'Kabongo, son of Kimani,' she said, sitting close, 'we women are tired; there is no food and the children are hungry; the young men have no stomachs and the old men are withering as dry leaves. You yourself are weak or before this you would have taken counsel with the Elders. Speak now, for our people wait to hear your word.'

I was roused. What she said was true. This was no time to sit and wait. We must hold Council.

The Council met again under the Mugomo tree. There were few, for the new laws of the Pink Cheeks had forbidden big meetings. I looked round at my friends and was sad. Their faces were anxious and their skin was loose on their bones. Even Muonji, who always used to joke, had no smile. For each one had been hungry for many days, and each one told the same story. Everywhere there was a shortage of food, for there was no land and all the time people were being sent back from distant parts. There was uneasiness and some of our tribesmen were troubling our people too much because they wanted to drive the Pink Cheeks from our country. This the Elders told in Council and were uneasy, for we wanted no war with the Pink Cheeks; we only wanted land to grow food.

'We must ask the Council of the Pink Cheeks to lend us some of the land we had lent them,' said one who came from a place where there was land held by the government for future farms and not yet in use.

All agreed that this would be good and for Munene, who as Chief was our spokesman, we made a message to give to the Governor. What we told to Munene he made marks with and, when we had finished, he spoke it to us again and it was good.

Munene took our message and he took also a gift of honey and eggs and went away down the long road and left us to wait.

We waited many days, with hope. It was a whole moon before Munene came back. He came to us slowly and sadly, and we knew from his way that the news was bad.

'They will not give the land,' he said. 'They say they have no more land for us.'

So I am sitting before my hut and I wait. For soon the time will come for me to creep away into the forest to die. Day by day my people grow thinner and weaker and the children are hungry; and who am I, an old man, to eat the food that would come to them?

As I sit I ponder often. . . .

Has the Pink Cheek brought good to my people? Are the new ways he has shown us better than our own ways?

Something has taken away the meaning of our lives; it has taken the full days, the good work in the sunshine, the dancing and the song; it has taken away laughter and the joy of living; the kinship and the love within a family; above all, it has taken from us the wise way of our living in which our lives from birth to death were dedicated to Ngai, supreme [God] of all, and which, with our system of age groups and our Councils, insured for all our people a life of responsibility and goodness. Something has taken away our belief in our Ngai and in the goodness of men. And there is not enough land on which to feed.

These good things of the days when we were happy and strong have been taken, and now we have many laws and many clothes and men dispute among themselves and have no love. There is discontent and argument and violence and hate, and a vying with each other for power, and men seem to care more for disputes about ideas than for the fullness of life where all work and live for all.

The young men are learning new ways, the children make marks which they call writing, but they forget their own language and customs, they know not the laws of their people, and they do not pray to Ngai. They ride fast in motorcars, they work fire-sticks that kill, they make music from a box. But they have no land and no food and they have lost laughter.

Adapted from *Through African Eyes*

QUESTIONS

1. What is your reaction to this story?
2. Why have the 'Pink Cheeks' taken over the country?
3. What are the differences between the Kikuyu way of life and the Pink Cheeks' way of life, according to this story?
4. Make a list of:
   (a) the good effects and
   (b) the bad effects that the coming of the Pink Cheeks has had on the people.
5. Are there any examples of injustice in the story? Explain.
6. Give examples to show how each of the three forms of justice — based on equality, on need and on what people have earned or deserve — are needed in order to bring about justice in this situation.

EXERCISES

1. In many colonies, including Kenya, the problems caused by European colonisation did not end when these countries achieved their independence, because of the damage that had been done to the way of life of the people. Give some examples from the story, to show the kind of problems the Kikuyu might have even after the Europeans had gone.
2. Look up some text-books or encyclopaedias to see what they say about colonialism. Write a brief report on your findings, stating whether colonialism is presented as a good or a bad thing; whether the point of view of both colonists and the people who were taken over is given; whether the injustices of colonialism are mentioned.

International Relationships Today

Today, most of the former colonies are independent countries which rule themselves. However, the 'rules' of international relationships still tend to treat the poorer, developing countries as if they were colonies, since the rich countries make those rules to suit themselves. The richer countries are rich mainly because they have exploited the colonies in the past, and continue to exploit the poorer countries today.

For example, the rich countries decide together, as a group, what price they will pay for raw materials like coffee, tea, copper and fruit from the developing countries. The poorer countries have to sell their produce, even if the prices are very bad, because they desperately need any money they can get.

One of the reasons developing countries need to earn foreign money is to pay back their growing debt to the rich countries. In the early 1970s, Western banks had a lot of money which they needed to lend so that they could make a profit. They encouraged the governments of poor countries such as Brazil and Mexico to borrow money to develop their industries, transport and communications, health services and education. They also lent them money to improve their 'defence' systems with bigger and 'better' weapons. At this stage, the interest rate was low. In the years since then, the interest rates have soared. This means that the amount owed by the poor countries has got bigger and bigger. The main way in which poor countries can make enough money to repay some of their debt is by exporting their goods to the rich countries. During the economic recession, the rich countries have paid less money for these goods. Most poor countries have found it more and more difficult to increase their exports and pay off their ever-increasing debt. The total debt of Sudan in North Africa is four and a half times what it makes from exports. This means, if nothing is done to tackle the problem, Sudan and many other poor countries will *never* be free of debt. Instead, they will get poorer and poorer, and less and less able to help themselves.

The International Monetary Fund (the IMF) is supposed to help countries which get into financial difficulty like this. But the IMF does not take into account the real needs of the people in the developing countries. Its only interest is in making sure that the poor country pays back its debt to the rich countries. In order to receive a loan from the IMF to help them out of their difficulties, the poorer countries must cut their public spending, which means spending much less money on hospitals, education and other services.

Women picking tea in Sri Lanka.

Many developing countries rely on selling their produce to developed countries.

Some of the aid given to developing countries by the wealthy countries consists of arms and ammunition.

These cuts affect the poorest people the worst. The standard of living of the world's poorest people has dropped dramatically in the last thirty years. In Brazil, a thousand children die of starvation every day, while the country exports food to pay Brazil's debt. Millions of poor people get lower wages, less health care and less education because of the cuts imposed by the IMF and other organisations. In order to pay their debts, many countries such as Sudan grow cash crops like cotton for export instead of growing food for their hungry populations.

Worst of all, no money is available for further development, so that the poorer countries are caught in a trap. While they have such huge debts, they cannot develop their own country; while their country is underdeveloped, they can never pay off their debts.

Children die while food is exported to rich countries.

There are a number of ways in which the problem of international debt can be tackled.

1. The richer countries can pay fair prices for the goods from the poorer countries instead of exploiting them. This would enable the poorer countries to build up their own economies.

2. The richer countries could lower the interest rate on international debts. At present, the richer countries, in particular the United States, decide what the interest rate will be to suit themselves only.

3. Some or all of the debt could be cancelled. Many poorer countries have already paid back more than double the amount of money which they had borrowed originally.

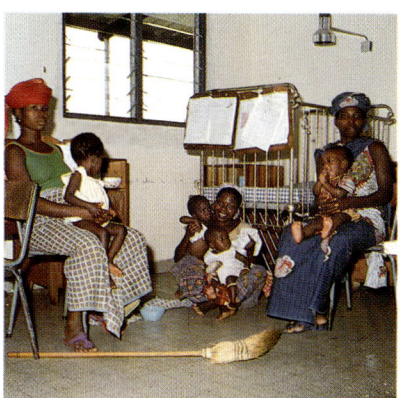

Health care suffers because of cut-backs in public spending.

Solving the international debt problem would help not only the developing countries, but also the developed countries. If the economies of the poorer countries collapse, the developed countries would also suffer, because they would lose markets in which to sell their goods.

> The well-being of every country in the world depends on good international relationships. Only when co-operation, mutual respect and justice become the 'rules' of the interaction between countries will the people of the world be able to look forward with hope to the future.

Coffee is grown as a cash crop.

EXERCISES

1. In what ways are the richer countries being unjust to the poorer countries?
2. Give examples to show how each of the three different forms of justice are needed by the developing countries — to be given an equal chance; to be given what they need; to be given what they have earned or deserved.
3. How could the rich countries be building up trouble for themselves by being unjust to the poor countries?

ASSIGNMENT

Listen to or watch the news once a day on one radio or TV station for a week. Make a note of any country which is mentioned. What kind of news are you given about it? Is it a developed or a developing country? Are you told anything about the relationship between your own country and the country mentioned? At the end of the week, write a brief report for the class, mentioning the frequency with which different countries are part of the news, and the reasons why. Distinguish between the kind of news given about developing and developed countries. Are there any important countries (or continents) which are not mentioned? Give your opinion as to why they are not mentioned. Compare your report with the rest of the class. What do your reports tell you of your country's attitude to other countries? Is this a just attitude?

Social Problems (Apostolic Letter of Pope Paul VI)

There is a need to establish a greater justice in the sharing of goods, both within national communities and on the international level. In international exchanges there is a need to go beyond relationships based on force, in order to arrive at agreements with the good of all in mind.

. . . The most important duty in the realm of justice is to allow each country to promote its own development, within the framework of a co-operation free from any spirit of domination, whether economic or political.

(Adapted from Paragraph 43)

EXERCISES

1. What does Pope Paul say must be done to achieve justice in the world?
2. Give some examples to show how the relationships between countries are based on force. Do you think this is unjust? Explain your answer.
3. Why do the poorer countries need the co-operation of the richer countries in order to develop fully?
4. Why do the richer countries need the developing countries in order to develop fully themselves?

The Work of Justice (Irish Bishops' Pastoral)

The Church's social teaching has been misrepresented as being concerned with the defence of private property. The Church never taught an absolute or unqualified right to private property. *She has always qualified the right of ownership in two ways. She has insisted firstly that all ownership comes from God, who designed the good things of creation for the benefit of all humanity. Ownership is therefore really a stewardship of property given by God to owners for the benefit of all. Ownership carries with it obligations towards others and towards society and especially towards the poor. The Church has insisted secondly that ownership should be widely distributed throughout society, so that all [people] may have their just share of the things God has given for the benefit of all. There is no such thing in justice and no such thing in Catholic teaching as an absolute right to do what I like with my property, or my land. The proper description of Catholic teaching about property or wealth is 'private ownership with social function'.*

(Paragraph 65)

QUESTIONS

1. According to this paragraph, what are the reasons why Christians cannot do exactly what they like with their own money or possessions?
2. What is your reaction to the points made in this paragraph?
3. If everyone took this teaching to heart, how would the following situations be affected:
   (a) the relationship between the rich and the poor in your local community;
   (b) the relationship between the rich and the poor countries of the world.

Project

Choose one developing country or region in the world. Research the geography, history, culture and way of life of the people. Research the present social and economic conditions in the country or region. Find out about the relationship between this country and your own. (The resources and addresses listed at the end of the chapter should help you with your research.)

When you have gathered the information, present it in project form to your class (or to the whole school), together with your comments on any injustices which you have found, the reasons for them, and your suggestions as to how justice could be achieved.

Discussion: Rich countries should give more financial aid to poor countries.

Reflection: 'My heart praises the Lord;
>my soul is glad because of God my Saviour,
>for he has remembered me, his lowly servant!
>From now on all people will call me happy,
>because of the great things the Mighty God has done for me.
>His name is Holy;
>from one generation to another he shows mercy
>to those who honour him.
>He has stretched out his mighty arm and scattered
>the proud with all their plans.
>He has brought down mighty kings from their thrones,
>and lifted up the lowly.
>He has filled the hungry with good things,
>and sent the rich away with empty hands.
>He has kept the promise he made to our ancestors,
>and has come to the help of his servant Israel,
>he has remembered to show mercy to Abraham and
>to all his descendants forever!'

Luke 1:46–55

Action: You could ask to have your name put on the mailing list of one of the agencies mentioned at the end of the chapter so that you could keep informed about justice in the world.

Psalm: Teach the king to judge with your righteousness, O God;
   share with him your own justice,
   so that he will rule over your people with justice
   and govern the oppressed with righteousness.

   May the land enjoy prosperity;
   may it experience righteousness.
   May the king judge the poor fairly;
   may he help the needy
   and defeat their oppressors.

   May your people worship you as long
   as the sun shines,
   as long as the moon gives light, for ages to come.

   May the king be like rain on the fields,
   like showers falling on the land.
   May righteousness flourish in his lifetime,
   and may prosperity last as long as
   the moon gives light.

   He rescues the poor who call to him,
   and those who are needy and neglected.
   He has pity on the weak and poor;
   he saves the lives of those in need.
   He rescues them from oppression and violence;
   their lives are precious to him.

   Praise the Lord, the God of Israel!
   He alone does these wonderful things.
   Praise his glorious name forever!
   May his glory fill the whole world.
   Amen! Amen!
                    Psalm 72: 1–7, 12–14, 18–19

Useful Addresses
Action from Ireland (AFrI),
P.O. Box 1522,
Dublin 1. Tel. (01) 786755/555453

Amnesty International,
Seán MacBride House,
8 Shaw St,
Dublin 2. Tel. (01) 776361

Comhlámh,
61 Lower Camden St.,
Dublin 2. Tel. (01) 783490

Concern,
1 Upper Camden St.,
Dublin 2. Tel. (01) 751463/681237

GOAL,
P.O. Box 19,
Dun Laoghaire,
Co. Dublin. Tel. (01) 2809779

GORTA,
12 Herbert St,
Dublin 2. Tel. (01) 615522

National Council for Unicef,
4 St Andrew St,
Dublin 2. Tel. (01) 770843

Oxfam Ireland,
202 Lr. Rathmines Rd,
Dublin 6. Tel. (01) 972195/966792

Trocaire,
169 Booterstown Ave.,
Blackrock,
Co. Dublin. Tel. (01) 2885385

Traideireann,
P.O. Box 20,
Athlone,
Co. Westmeath. Tel. (0902) 92064

VALUING MY OWN LIFE

CHAPTER 8

In the following play, a number of people take risks with their own lives and the lives of others.

Characters: Barry, Dan, Marian, Frank, Susie, Car Driver, Ambulance Driver, Doctor

THE MOTORBIKE

Scene One. Barry is showing his new motorbike to Dan.

Barry: What do you think of it?

Dan: It's terrific! I wish my folks would let me have one.

Barry: My Dad was keen on bikes when he was young, so I think he sees me following his footsteps.

Dan: Or his skid marks!

Barry: They wanted me to get something smaller to start with, but then this came up in the paper, and Dad said it was too good an opportunity to miss. 500 cc's — I couldn't believe my luck.

Dan: It's powerful, all right. You'll have no trouble with the girls now, Barry.

Barry: Since when did I ever have trouble with girls? Anyway, Marian is thrilled. She's got all the gear and everything, helmet, boots, the lot. She's going to get her own bike next year, when she's old enough.

Dan: Some people have all the luck.

Barry: Are you going to the party in Redmond's tonight?

Dan: No, I don't really know any of that crowd.

Barry: Marion and I are going — everyone says they give great parties.

Dan: Well, have a good time.

Barry: I intend to.

Scene Two. Barry and Marian are at the party.

Marian: I hardly know anyone here — they're all years older than us.

Barry:	What does that matter? You get fed up talking to kids all the time.
Frank:	Hello you two. I'm Frank, and this is Susie.
Susie:	Hi.
Frank:	What are you drinking?
Marian:	Well, I don't know really . . .
Barry:	I've got my own wheels, now, you know. Can't risk drinking and driving.
Frank:	Well, I think I drive better with a load of drink.
Susie:	He does better wheelies, too.

(*Everyone laughs*).

Frank:	Come on, you have to have a drink at a party, everyone else does, and they're all driving. You don't have to get drunk or anything.
Barry:	All right. Just one, then. What about you, Marian?
Marian:	Why not, if it's just the one.

Scene Three. At the party, two hours later. A lot of people have gone on to another party. Barry and Marian are having a singing session with five or six other people.

Barry:	(*thinks to himself*) Better be careful. Don't want to smash up the bike on the way home.
Marian:	(*thinking anxiously*) I've had two drinks. I'm not sure how many Barry's had. I hope the party breaks up soon.
Frank:	Let me get you another drink, Mary.
Marian:	No thanks. And my name is Marian.
Frank:	Don't worry about it. I'm not. (*He laughs*) What about you, Barry, are you being sober and sensible too?
Barry:	Well . . . one more won't make much difference.
Frank:	Good for you. That's what I like to hear.
Marian:	Barry, I think you've had enough.
Frank:	I suppose you'll have to do what you're told, Barry.
Barry:	Just give me the drink, Frank, and take no notice of her.

Scene Four. The party is over. Marian and Barry are standing beside the motorbike.

Barry:	We'll have to leave the bike and walk home. I can't drive when I've had so much to drink. It wouldn't be safe.

Marian: You must be joking! I'm not going to walk all that way at this time of night.
Barry: But it's not really safe to . . .
Marian: Look, if you won't take me home, I'll go and find someone who will.
Barry: All right, all right. I'll do it. Let's go.

Scene Five. A car and motorbike have crashed. The ambulance and fire brigade are at the scene.

Car Driver: He came round the corner straight at me. I couldn't help hitting him. I couldn't help it, he had no chance, no chance at all.
Ambulance Driver: Now just relax, you've had a bad shock. Put this blanket around your shoulders.
Barry: *(he is lying on the ground, moaning)* Marian . . . where's Marian?
Car Driver: How is the girl? Will she be all right?
Ambulance Driver: We're doing everything we can.
Doctor: I'm afraid it's no use.
Car Driver: You mean . . . she's dead?
Doctor: I'm afraid so.
Car Driver: Oh no. The poor girl. What about him?
Doctor: He was very lucky. He'll be all right.
Car Driver: Very lucky? I wonder if he'll think he's lucky when he realises what's happened.

QUESTIONS

1. What are your thoughts and feelings about this drama?
2. List all the important decisions Barry made on the night of the party. In each case explain:
   (a) What were his reasons for making that decision?
   (b) What were the consequences of that decision?
3. List all the important decisions Marian made the night of the party. In each case explain:
   (a) Why did she make that decision?
   (b) What were the consequences of that decision?
4. What kind of person is Barry? Marian? Frank? What values do each of them seem to have?

5. Were there any examples of conflicting values in this drama? Explain.
6. Do any important changes take place during the drama? Explain.
7. What do you think is the most important moment in the drama? Why?
8. In your opinion, what is the most important meaning or message of this drama?

EXERCISE

Write a story, drama or poem with a similar message or meaning.

The Value of Human Life

> Human life is a very important Christian value. The life of a person is precious because it is a gift from God, given to each of us for a purpose. Life must be protected so that each person can live his/her life to the full as God intends.

Human beings, created in the image and likeness of God, are able to love, to create and to understand. In this way, people are the high-point of God's creation.

Each individual person is totally unique. Everyone, no matter what their background, position in life, or abilities has a contribution to make to the world that no one else can make. The factory worker, doctor, artist, person with a disability, the unborn child, each of their lives is of vital and equal importance.

> All Christians are called to protect human life, including their own. This means taking reasonable care of ourselves and others.

Each person is totally unique.

EXERCISES

1. In the drama, did Barry value his own life? Explain.
2. Did Marian value her life? Explain.
3. Why did (a) Barry and (b) Marian risk their lives?
4. Do you value your own life? Explain your answer, giving examples.

Substance Abuse

One of the ways in which people endanger their lives is through substance abuse. Abusing substances like marijuana, heroin, alcohol, tobacco and glue can lead to illness, injury, permanent disability or death. People abuse drugs for many different reasons — personal problems, anxiety and worry, wanting a thrill, or because 'everybody is doing it'. Young people whose parents, families or friends abuse drugs are more likely themselves to do so. The addiction which follows the abuse of drugs can be extremely difficult to beat.

Use the following short quiz to see how much you know about substance abuse. In your copy, write down the number of the statement, and beside it put T (true) or F (false).

1. Marijuana gives you a temporary 'high' feeling and doesn't do any permanent damage.

    ☐ True   ☐ False

2. You don't really have to worry about becoming an alcoholic unless you drink 'hard' liquor, like whiskey.

    ☐ True   ☐ False

3. Crack is not as addictive or as physically damaging as drugs like heroin.

    ☐ True   ☐ False

4. Most 'real' alcoholics are down and out, living on the streets.

    ☐ True   ☐ False

5. Almost all young people agree that alcohol should be considered a drug.

    ☐ True   ☐ False

6. Once you stop using drugs, you'll be all right.

    ☐ True   ☐ False

7. Crack cocaine is such an expensive drug that few young people would be able to try it.

    ☐ True   ☐ False

8. Drug users hurt only themselves.

    ☐ True   ☐ False

9. Alcohol is just as threatening to young people as it is to adults.

   ☐ True   ☐ False

10. Drugs can make some people perform better in sports or in the arts.

    ☐ True   ☐ False

Adapted from 'Today's Catholic Teacher', Nov./Dec. 1990

Compare your answers with the rest of the class. Now check your answers with your teacher. Are you well-informed as a class?

Exercises

In each of the following situations, describe (a) What action you would take and (b) What would be the consequences of that action.

1. You are watching a video with your friends in someone's house. One of them lights up a marijuana cigarette and begins passing it around. The person beside you passes it to you.
2. You are at a party. The group you are with begin to smoke cigarettes. One person offers you a cigarette. You refuse. The person says, 'I suppose your daddy says you are too young to smoke, then?' and everyone laughs.
3. You are doing your homework with a friend in her house. There are no adults at home. She takes out a bottle of whiskey from the cupboard and pours out a drink for herself and you.
4. You are studying for a very important examination, but you find that you cannot study late at night because you keep falling asleep. An acquaintance in school tells you he can get you some pills to keep you awake.
5. You are out with your older brother and his girlfriend, who is driving. She is very drunk and your brother has had three pints of beer. You are too young to have a driver's license.

Human Life is Sacred (Irish Bishops' Pastoral)
The Christian principle of respect for human life at every stage of its existence is firm and clear. God alone is the Lord of

life. [People] are made in His image and likeness. We come from God. We go to God. We belong to God.

Some will argue that not every life is of equal value. But in the eyes of God, every life is of equal and priceless value. We must see every life as having the value which it has for God.

Each human being is called to live with God forever. Each human life is one of whom Christ thought so much that he died for him [or her]. Here is where each human being gets his [or her] value. Some people have answered the question, 'What is that person worth?' by stating the value of his or her assets or the amount of his or her annual earnings. The true answer is 'That person is worth the life's blood of Christ'. There and only there is the true standard for judging the value of life.

(Taken from Paragraphs 4 and 5)

QUESTIONS

1. List the reasons, given in this passage, why the value of human life is so important to Christians.
2. Give examples of how teenagers could show that they really value their own lives — physically, mentally, emotionally, socially and spiritually.

The Work of Justice (Irish Bishops' Pastoral)
The quantity of harm done and unhappiness caused in Ireland by excessive drinking is almost incalculable. The results of abuse of drink, in terms of marriage strain or breakdown, disturbed children, battered wives and battered babies, pressure on health and welfare services, and handicaps to national economic recovery represent a great mass of misfortune. Yet drinking abuses seem to be spreading constantly and to be involving new groups of the population — women, young boys and girls, even sometimes schoolchildren. It is surely time for thorough investigation of causes and planning of remedies.

(Taken from Paragraph 55)

QUESTIONS

1. Why is it difficult to know exactly how much damage is caused by alcohol abuse?

2. Does the abuse of other substances lead to the same kind of harm and unhappiness as alcohol abuse? Explain your answer.
3. What evidence is there in this paragraph to show that substance abuse harms human life?

Reflection: 'You created every part of me;
you put me together in my mother's womb.
I praise you because you are to be feared;
all you do is strange and wonderful.
I know it with all my heart.
When my bones were being formed,
carefully put together in my mother's womb,
when I was growing there in secret,
you knew that I was there —
you saw me before I was born.
The days allotted to me
had all been recorded in your book,
before any of them ever began.'

Psalm 139: 13–16

Action: If you are doing anything at present which shows that you are not valuing your own life, decide on one step you will take to increase the value you place on your own life.

Psalm: I look to the mountains;
where will my help come from?
My help will come from the Lord,
who made heaven and earth.

He will not let you fall;
your protector is always awake.

The protector of Israel
never dozes or sleeps.
The Lord will guard you;
he is by your side to protect you.
The sun will not hurt you during the day,
nor the moon during the night.

The Lord will protect you from all danger;
he will keep you safe.
He will protect you as you come and go,
now and forever.

Psalm 121

THE LIVES OF OTHERS

CHAPTER 9

There are many occasions in our lives when our words and actions can have a great effect on the lives of others.

Carefully examine each of the following situations and answer the questions which follow:

1. You know for certain that two members of your class are terrorising a young first year student, taking money and physically attacking the student. No one else knows what is going on — you found out by accident. Neither the bullies nor the victim know that you know.

2. There has been a week of heavy snow. You have not seen the old man across the street for at least three days, although you see the lights going on and off at different times. He is a very cantankerous person who hates interference from 'nosey neighbours'.

3. Some members of your class are going mountain-climbing for the weekend. Only those with experience are allowed to go, as it is a difficult climb. Your best friend is going, but you know he/she has no climbing experience.

4. One day you see your younger sister going for a cycle with her friends. She is riding your old bicycle which has no brakes.

QUESTIONS

1. What do you think you *would* do in each situation? Why?
2. What do you think you *should* do in each situation? Why?

Group Work

1. Get into groups of four or five.
2. Let each member of the group give their answers to the two questions.
3. As a group, try to agree on what would be the best thing to do in each situation.

Protecting Human Life

> Valuing human life means more than just not harming it, or taking it away. It means protecting and caring for people, so that the quality and dignity of their lives are respected. This particularly applies to the life of the weak, the poor and others whose lives are at greater risk.

Sometimes the society in which we live dismisses some people's lives as if they were of no account.
— Many countries, such as the United Staes and Great Britain, have legalised abortion and sometimes allow newly-born babies to die rather than perform life-saving operations on them.
— The world community allows 40,000 children to die every day from disease and malnutrition.
— Many countries, including Ireland, do not provide the proper facilities for people with mental handicap or other disabilities.
— The world community does not provide work or an adequate share of the world's wealth for most of the people in the world.
— Some people want to legalise euthanasia so that people who are old, sick or do not want to live can be legally killed.
— Some communities leave many old people to live in poverty and loneliness.

> Christians are called upon to protect and improve human life in these and in every other situation in which life is threatened or degraded. As Christians, we must try to show through our attitudes, words and actions that we truly value the lives of other people. This is one of the most basic ways in which we try to love our neighbour.

Exercises

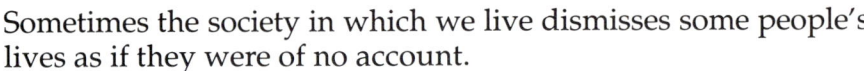

1. Give examples of how you could show that you value the lives of others:
   (a) at home   (b) at school   (c) in your local community

2. Is there any evidence to show that some people's lives are not valued in your local community? Explain.
3. Is there any evidence to show that your local community values the lives of others? Explain.

Human Life is Sacred (Irish Bishops' Pastoral)

The Church says 'Yes', not just to human existence, but to the quality and dignity of human life. The Christian demand is that all human life should be permitted and enabled to develop to the full dignity and quality of living which befit a human person and child of God. Nothing less than that is what is commanded by Christ's command to love our neighbour as we love our own self. The Christian 'Yes' to life includes a call for freedom, for adequate education, for proper living conditions, for more just distribution of wealth and opportunity, for protection of the human environment, and for more responsible use of the resources of nature.

(Taken from Paragraph 31)

QUESTIONS

1. List the ways in which Christians show in a practical way that they value human life, and want to protect it.
2. Give examples of (a) attitudes and (b) actions which threaten the 'quality and dignity' of human life.

Human Life is Sacred (Irish Bishops' Pastoral)

God's commandment, as we have seen, is that no human being may deliberately take away innocent human life. What life could be more innocent than the life of the unborn child? Deliberate abortion is therefore always gravely sinful. The embryo or foetus possesses its fundamental right to life from the moment of conception. From that moment the foetus is already provided with all the genetic elements which will shape its future development as an adult human person.

Each single embryo, even though so small as to be invisible to the naked eye, is unique and unrepeatable. Strictly speaking, so far as in-built potential for future development is concerned, the newly fertilised mother-cell has the same potential as the newly-born baby.

(Taken from Paragraph 9)

QUESTIONS

1. According to the Irish bishops, why is abortion wrong and gravely sinful?
2. Apart from making abortion illegal, what do you think the community should do to protect the life of the unborn child and the mother? (For example, how could we help unmarried mothers or the mothers of large families; what kind of health care should we provide etc.)

Human Life is Sacred (Irish Bishops' Pastoral)

'Euthanasia' is, of course, derived from two Greek words meaning 'pleasant or painless death'. This is one instance, among many in modern society, where a good motive is supposed to make wrong things right. A merciful motive (preventing pain or hardship) is held to make right something which, in itself and in other circumstances, would be admitted to be wrong (putting an innocent person to death).

What must always be remembered is that certain actions are good or evil in themselves already, apart from the motive or intention for which they are done. Deliberately to take one's own life is suicide and is gravely wrong in all circumstances. To co-operate with another in taking his [or her] own life is to share in the guilt of suicide. Deliberately to terminate the innocent life of another is murder, no matter how merciful the motives, no matter how seemingly desirable the result.

(Taken from Paragraphs 50 and 54)

QUESTIONS

1. (a) What is the 'good motive' which makes people think that euthanasia is good?
   (b) Could there be any 'bad motives' for euthanasia?
2. Why is euthanasia wrong, whatever the motive?
3. Can you give other examples of actions which are (a) good or (b) evil in themselves already, apart from the motive or intention for which they are done?
4. Apart from making euthanasia illegal, what do we need to do in a practical way to protect the life of the sick, the old, the terminally ill, the depressed and their families and carers?

Discussion: What can teenagers do to protect the lives of others and improve the quality of other people's lives?

Reflection: 'Cain said to his brother Abel, "Let's go out in the fields." When they were out in the fields, Cain turned on his brother and killed him.

The Lord asked Cain, "Where is your brother Abel?"

He answered, "I don't know. Am I supposed to take care of my brother?"

Then the Lord said, "Why have you done this terrible thing? Your brother's blood is crying out to me from the ground, like a voice calling for revenge. You are placed under a curse and can no longer farm the soil. It has soaked up your brother's blood as if it had opened its mouth to receive it when you killed him. If you try to grow crops, the soil will not produce anything; you will be a homeless wanderer on the earth."' Genesis 4: 8–12

Action: Plan to visit someone who is sick, old or lonely on a regular basis.

Psalm: Lord, your constant love reaches the heavens;
your faithfulness extends to the skies.
Your righteousness is towering like the mountains;
your justice is like the depths of the sea.
People and animals are in your care.

How precious, O God, is your constant love!
We find protection under the shadow of your wings.
We feast on the abundant food you provide;
you let us drink from the river of your goodness.
You are the source of all life,
and because of your light we see the light.

Psalm 36: 5–9

THE LIFE OF THE HUMAN COMMUNITY

CHAPTER 10
▼

Whistler's Bridge

In the early 1850s American painter, James McNeill Whistler, spent a brief — and academically unsuccessful — period at West Point, the US Military Academy. The story goes that when he was assigned to draw a bridge he drew a romantic stone one, complete with grassy banks and two small children fishing from it. 'Get those children off that bridge!' said the instructor. 'This is an engineering exercise.'

Whistler got the kids off the bridge, drew them fishing from the bank of the river and resubmitted the drawing. The angry instructor yelled, 'I told you to remove those children. Get them completely out of the picture!'

But the creative urge was too strong in Whistler. His next version had the children 'completely out of the picture' indeed. They were buried under two small tombstones on the riverbank.

QUESTIONS

1. Why did the instructor want Whistler to get rid of the children from the drawing?
2. Do you think Whistler would have been a good military engineer? Why/Why not?
3. Why do you think Whistler 'buried' the children in the last drawing? Was he just being smart, or was there a deeper reason?
4. What is the message or meaning of this event for you?

Discussion: What can teenagers do to protect the lives of others and improve the quality of other people's lives?

Reflection: 'Cain said to his brother Abel, "Let's go out in the fields." When they were out in the fields, Cain turned on his brother and killed him.
  The Lord asked Cain, "Where is your brother Abel?"
  He answered, "I don't know. Am I supposed to take care of my brother?"
  Then the Lord said, "Why have you done this terrible thing? Your brother's blood is crying out to me from the ground, like a voice calling for revenge. You are placed under a curse and can no longer farm the soil. It has soaked up your brother's blood as if it had opened its mouth to receive it when you killed him. If you try to grow crops, the soil will not produce anything; you will be a homeless wanderer on the earth."' Genesis 4: 8–12

Action: Plan to visit someone who is sick, old or lonely on a regular basis.

Psalm: Lord, your constant love reaches the heavens;
  your faithfulness extends to the skies.
  Your righteousness is towering like the mountains;
  your justice is like the depths of the sea.
  People and animals are in your care.

  How precious, O God, is your constant love!
  We find protection under the shadow of your wings.
  We feast on the abundant food you provide;
  you let us drink from the river of your goodness.
  You are the source of all life,
  and because of your light we see the light.

  Psalm 36: 5–9

THE LIFE OF THE HUMAN COMMUNITY

CHAPTER 10
▼

Whistler's Bridge

In the early 1850s American painter, James McNeill Whistler, spent a brief — and academically unsuccessful — period at West Point, the US Military Academy. The story goes that when he was assigned to draw a bridge he drew a romantic stone one, complete with grassy banks and two small children fishing from it. 'Get those children off that bridge!' said the instructor. 'This is an engineering exercise.'

Whistler got the kids off the bridge, drew them fishing from the bank of the river and resubmitted the drawing. The angry instructor yelled, 'I told you to remove those children. Get them completely out of the picture!'

But the creative urge was too strong in Whistler. His next version had the children 'completely out of the picture' indeed. They were buried under two small tombstones on the riverbank.

QUESTIONS

1. Why did the instructor want Whistler to get rid of the children from the drawing?
2. Do you think Whistler would have been a good military engineer? Why/Why not?
3. Why do you think Whistler 'buried' the children in the last drawing? Was he just being smart, or was there a deeper reason?
4. What is the message or meaning of this event for you?

Leaving people out

Sometimes we ignore people and the needs of people, because other things are more important to us. 'Yes, human life is important', some people say, 'but we need to win this war, and you cannot win wars without killing people'. In the story, Whistler was told to leave the children out of the picture. In the world today, when people are making plans, they frequently leave other people out of the picture. People's needs often take second place to some other consideration. For example, the banks and governments of the richer countries want to get their money back from the developing countries. So they ignore the fact that millions of adults, children and babies must die in order for the money to be paid. In the classroom, if some students want to have fun and not do any work, they can ignore the needs of the other students who want to work and do well in their examinations.

Soldiers are sometimes specially trained to ignore the needs of other people. It is easier for them to kill a 'target' than it is to kill a real person. Soldiers are therefore trained to think about 'the enemy' as a killer, an inhuman being, a 'Hun', a 'Brit' or a 'Provo'. When civilians are killed in a bombing raid, they may be referred to as 'collateral damage' rather than dead people.

A nuclear explosion has a devastating effect on people and their environment.

> When we ignore other people and their needs, we build up hatred, fear and misery in our own local community and in the world community. We make it difficult for people to live together in peace.

EXERCISES

1. Give some examples to show how the needs of the following people can be left out of the picture in different situations:
   (a) students
   (b) teachers
   (c) parents
   (d) unborn babies
   (e) sick people
   (f) workers.

2. In what way are the needs of people left out of the picture in the following situations?
   (a) Soldiers are ordered to 'wipe out' an entire village to make sure that no terrorists escape.
   (b) Soldiers are ordered to 'defoliate' (or remove all the vegetation from) an area, with a poisonous substance, in order to drive out the enemy from cover (nothing will grow in a defoliated area for many years).

The nuclear winter theory predicts that the smoke from fires burning after a nuclear war would block sunlight, causing a rapid drop in temperature that would trigger serious ecological disturbances.

A 'search and destroy' mission during the Vietnam War, 1966.

British soldiers in the Falklands, 1982.

(c) An enemy soldier is tortured to get information about the enemy's movements.
(d) Shooting a civilian to show the government that a person does not approve of what the government does.
(e) Blowing up an aeroplane full of people to draw attention to an injustice in a country.

Defence

Many countries in the world spend huge sums of money on elaborate and complicated 'defence' systems. For example, more than half of the money paid in taxes by the citizens of the United States is used for military and defence purposes. This is supposed to protect the people of the country from attack by other countries. However, many of these defences leave people, even the people of the country itself, completely out of the picture. For example, when so much money is spent on defence, less money is available to provide for health, education and welfare. It can also be dangerous to live near the factories where weapons are made or the military installations where they are kept.

At present, there are enough nuclear weapons in the world to kill every person sixteen times over. These weapons are for 'defence', but no one can be defended from a nuclear war. The scientists tell us that even if some people survived the nuclear blast, the raging fires, the effects of radiation and the contamination of food and water, nuclear war would be the end of civilisation, and possibly the end of the human race. The earth's atmosphere would be full of radioactive dust, which the sun's light and heat could not penetrate. No crops could be grown, so the people who did not die of the cold would probably die of starvation in a 'nuclear winter'.

People use a number of arguments to try to prove that countries need huge military defence systems, including nuclear weapons, in order to protect themselves. For example: 'We have to have these weapons if "they" do, to prevent them attacking us by making them afraid to attack us'. This argument, in favour of a nuclear 'deterrent', is based on the idea that nuclear weapons will not be used to start a war; they will only be used for defence. However, the most important nuclear powers, the USA and the USSR, both have 'first strike' policies. They both plan to detonate a bomb (or bombs) in the enemy's country before the enemy can detonate a bomb in their country. This means being able to guess that the other country is *planning* to attack them, rather than waiting to be attacked and then defending themselves. So while the governments claim to have nuclear weapons as a deterrent, they plan to use them offensively.

Another problem with the 'deterrent' theory is that people tend to use weapons when they have them. It is easier to find reasons for using your most lethal weapons than to find reasons for not using them in a war situation. The fact that countries have nuclear weapons makes it likely that any war which starts with conventional (or non-nuclear) weapons will end up as a nuclear war. One of the main problems with nuclear weapons is that the 'protection' we get from them is as dangerous to our lives and the life of the human community as the dangers we are protecting ourselves from.

Perhaps the most serious argument against the build-up of nuclear and other weapons is their cost in terms of human suffering and death now, even before they are used. It has been estimated that it would cost less to solve the problem of world hunger than the world spends on defence in a week. Every unnecessary pound spent on weapons is a pound taken from the poorest and most oppressed people in the world. This is the real scandal of the nuclear age.

Many people in the world, including those who are members of the Campaign for Nuclear Disarmament (CND), have been working for many years to encourage governments to abandon nuclear weapons. The end of the Cold War between the USA and the USSR and their allies is a hopeful sign. Both sides have agreed to cut down their manufacture of nuclear missiles and to try to build up peaceful relationships in the world community.

> However, as long as there are stockpiles of any kind of weapon in the world — chemical, biological or nuclear — then the lives of people are under serious threat. Christians believe that the only true protection of life comes from co-operation rather than competition. Peace is the result of justice, trust and love, rather than force, suspicion and hate.

Egyptian commandos during the Gulf War, 1991.

Guerrilla warfare in Eritrea, 1990.

EXERCISES

1. Give some examples from films, stories, comics or your own experience to show that people try to 'de-humanise' the enemy, and pretend that his or her life does not count.
2. List the ways in which nuclear weapons are a threat to human life.
3. How many wars are being fought at present in the world? Find out by listening to the news, reading newspapers etc. Try to discover *why* the wars began and how people's lives are being affected by them.

Peace activists protest against nuclear weapons.

ASSIGNMENT

Find out about the atomic (nuclear) bombs which were dropped on Hiroshima and Nagasaki in 1945. Try to discover:
   (a) Why they were used and
   (b) What were the short and long term effects of their use.

Present your findings to the class. Do your findings tell you anything about the possible effects of an all-out nuclear war today?

The call to fullness of life

One of the most important instincts in any person is the instinct for survival. We all know that we need food, clothing, shelter and protection from danger in order to survive. Over the thousands of years of our existence, human beings have adapted to very many different circumstances in order to survive, from the Arctic to the desert.

When Jesus was on earth, he showed that he took people's survival very seriously indeed. He was concerned for the crowd in the wilderness, that they would faint for lack of food, and he worked a miracle so that they would have enough to eat. When people were in pain or unable to work because of a crippling disease, he cured them.

But Jesus wanted more than mere 'survival' for the people. He said, 'I came that you may have life, and have it to the full.' This fullness of life does not simply mean having enough to eat. As he said, 'People do not live by bread alone, but by every word that comes from the mouth of God.' The fullness of life does not simply mean being free of suffering. Jesus tells us that if we want to follow him we must be prepared to suffer: 'If anyone wants to be a follower of mine, let him take up his cross daily and follow me.'

> The fullness of life means knowing God, and living the way God wants us to live. God's plan for us is that we should love one another and co-operate with one another. God asks us to risk trusting one another, instead of being suspicious; to share with each other instead of being selfish; to make decisions based on love, and not fear of one another.
>
> If we make love of others and God the first thing we take into consideration when making a decision, then we will never be able to 'leave' people out of the picture. We will never be able to decide that it is all right to kill innocent people, or to defend ourselves by using weapons which could annihilate the human race.

EXERCISES

1. How could it be risky for (a) a person and (b) a country to make decisions based on love?
2. Can you think of any circumstances in which it would be right for your country to fight a war against another country? Explain your answer.
3. What kind of things can people do to prevent war?
4. Can teenagers do anything to prevent war?

The Challenge of Peace: God's Promise and Our Response (US Bishops' Pastoral letter, 1983)

The arms race is one of the greatest curses on the human race; it is to be condemned as a danger, an act of aggression against the poor, and a folly which does not provide the security it promises.

QUESTIONS

1. The arms race means the stockpiling of weapons by different countries, in an effort always to have more, bigger and better weapons than other countries. In what way is this arms race 'an act of aggression against the poor'?
2. In what way is the arms race a danger to people?
3. In what way is the arms race a folly, or a foolish action?

Christians and the Ecological Crisis (Pope John Paul II's message for 1990 World Day of Peace)

But there is another dangerous menace which threatens us, namely *war*. Unfortunately, modern science already has the capacity to change the environment for hostile purposes. Alterations of this kind over the long term could have unforeseeable and still more serious consequences. Despite the international agreements which prohibit chemical, bacteriological and biological warfare, the fact is that laboratory research continues to develop new offensive weapons capable of altering the balance of nature.

Today, any form of war on a global scale would lead to incalculable ecological damage. But even local or regional wars, however limited, not only destroy human life and social structures, but also damage the land, ruining crops and vegetation as well as poisoning the soil and water. The survivors of war are forced to begin a new life in very difficult environmental conditions, which in turn create situations of extreme social unrest, with further negative consequences for the environment.

(Paragraph 12)

QUESTIONS

1. What types of warfare threaten human beings and their environment today?
2. What does it mean to 'alter the balance of nature'?
3. Give examples to show how the people of a small town could be harmed by:
   (a) a war between two groups in their own country
   (b) a global war.
4. Why would modern warfare tend to lead to further violence, even when the war was over?

Discussion: Could it ever be right and just to have a war?

Reflection: 'Today I am giving you a choice between good and evil, between life and death. If you obey the commands of the Lord your God, which I give you today, if you love Him, obey Him and keep all His laws, then you will prosper and become a nation of many people. The Lord your God will bless you in the land that you are about to occupy. But if you disobey and refuse to listen, and are led away to worship other gods, you will be destroyed — I warn you here and now . . . . I am giving you the choice between life and death, ... Choose life.'
Deuteronomy 30: 15–19

Action: Hold an anti-war day in your school. Use posters, debates, projects and perhaps a guest speaker.
   Useful address: Irish Campaign for Nuclear Disarmament,
   Peace, Neutrality,
   29 Lower Baggot St,
   Dublin 2. Tel. (01) 613987

Prayer For Peace
Let us go up the hill of the Lord,
   to the Temple of Israel's God.
He will teach us what he wants us to do;
we will walk in the paths he has chosen.
For the Lord's teaching comes from Jerusalem;
from Zion he speaks to his people.

He will settle disputes among great nations.
They will hammer their swords into ploughs
   and their spears into pruning-knives.
Nations will never again go to war,
   never prepare for battle again.

Isaiah 2: 3–4

THE ENVIRONMENT

CHAPTER 11

Are YOU environmentally friendly? Find out by using the following questionnaire. Keep an account of your answers in your copy; for example, if your answer to question one is (a) then write 1(a) in your copy. When you have answered all the questions, the scoresheet shows you how to work out your score.

1. If you had to travel a short distance (less than half a mile) would you choose to:
   (a) Walk, run or cycle
   (b) Use public transport (bus, train etc.)
   (c) Get a lift in a car or other other private vehicle using unleaded petrol and/or a catalytic converter
   (d) Get a lift in a car or other private vehicle using leaded petrol.

2. When you wash the dishes, would you prefer to use:
   (a) Hot water and ordinary soap
   (b) A phosphate free and biodegradable liquid
   (c) A small amount of ordinary wash-up liquid
   (d) A large amount of ordinary wash-up liquid.

3. If you had any partly-used copies at the end of the last school year did you:
   (a) Throw them away or just forget about them
   (b) Use them for the same subjects this year
   (c) Use up the blank pages for rough-work, taking notes etc.

4. Do you use recycled paper?
   (a) Never
   (b) Always
   (c) Sometimes.

5. Do you collect paper in your own home/school/neighbourhood for recycling?
   (a) Yes
   (b) No.

6. Do you put glass jars and bottles into the bottle bank?
   (a) Sometimes
   (b) Never
   (c) Always.

7. Do you throw away empty cans?
   (a) Always
   (b) Never
   (c) Sometimes.

8. If you are cold at home do you:
   (a) Put on more clothes
   (b) Increase the heating in the house
   (c) Increase the heating in one room.

9. When you are washing yourself at the sink do you:
   (a) Leave the water running
   (b) Put in the plug and run some water into the sink.

10. Make a note of any of the following statements which are true for you:
    (a) You turn off any lights which are not needed.
    (b) You leave the television on, even when no one is watching it.
    (c) You use aerosols with CFCs in them.
    (d) You throw things in the sea, rivers, lakes.
    (e) You never throw litter on the streets or out in the countryside.
    (f) You have planted or helped to plant a tree.

The score-sheet shows how many points you receive for your answers.

	1	2	3	4	5	6	7	8	9	10
(a)	5	5	0	0	5	3	0	5	0	5
(b)	3	4	5	5	0	0	5	0	5	0
(c)	1	3	5	3		5	3	3		0
(d)	0	0								0
(e)										5
(f)										5

More than 40 points

You seem to be very aware of your environment and you are very friendly towards it! See what you can do to encourage others to be as thoughtful about the environment as you are.

20 to 40 points

You seem to be aware of some issues relating to your environment and you have made some effort to be friendly to it. Perhaps there are some issues raised in this questionnaire which you have never considered before. If so, think about them now and see if you can become even more environment-friendly.

Less than 20 points

Do not be too disheartened by this low score. Many of us are totally unaware of how we can affect our environment and of the ways in which we can become more friendly to it. Choose *one* of the areas in which you did not score well and try to become more environment-friendly by putting *one* of the suggestions into practice.

The Environment

Everything in the world is part of a vast network of relationships called the environment. This environment is not something 'out there', like a stage on which I move about. *I am* the environment, and so are other people, animals, crops, rocks, mud, streets, cities, farms, rivers, seas, air, heat, cold, sunlight, rain, houses, shops, gardens, walls, cars, roads, fish, insects, trees and flowers. Every part of the environment is linked in some way to every other part. Even a remote desert island is linked to Tokyo and Cork by the earth's atmosphere and by the oceans.

Everything in the environment affects and is affected by the rest of the environment to some extent. Plants take in carbon dioxide and give out oxygen. Animals eat plants and other animals, fertilise the ground with their droppings, and in turn provide food for other animals.

Human beings affect the environment more than any other creatures. One reason for this is that we have a greater ability than any other creature to adapt and change things to suit ourselves. The other reason why we have such an impact on the environment is because there are so many of us — 5 thousand million in 1986.

The introduction of farming, the domestication of animals, the development of mining, trade and industry, as well as the building of homes for the billions of people who live on the earth today, have all had serious effects on the environment,

Modern farming has had a huge impact on the environment.

and have even changed the landscape forever in some parts of the world. Whatever human beings are doing to the environment, we are also doing to ourselves, since we are part of that environment. We are affected by sunlight, by the quantity and kind of food we eat and by the air we breathe. When we destroy part of the ozone layer in the atmosphere, which protects us from the sun's harmful rays; or use harmful pesticides on our crops; or pass laws to remove some of the pollution from our air, we are helping or harming ourselves as much as we are helping or harming the rest of the environment.

EXERCISES

1. Look back over the questionnaire at the beginning of the chapter. Based on your answers to it, try to work out the relationship between you and certain other parts of the environment — how you affect and are affected by:
   (a) The air
   (b) Water
   (c) Trees
   (d) The energy supply
   (e) Streets/local countryside
   (f) Other people.
2. Give examples to show how your environmental decisions could have an effect in the long term on:
   (a) You
   (b) Other people
   (c) The world.

Stewardship

Christians believe that God calls all people to be the stewards of the environment of which they are part (Genesis 1:27–28). Being a steward means looking after and protecting all of creation. The call to stewardship applies to every individual as well as to groups of people — families; local communities; the people of a country; and all forms of government, local, national and international.

> The call to stewardship means that every individual and group must take into account how their choices will affect the environment. As stewards we must reject any options which could harm the environment. This does not mean that we should never change or adapt the world around us. However any action we take, or any changes we make, should respect the balance of nature, the system of relationships which makes the world a healthy, harmonious place. As stewards it is our privilege and our responsibility to hand on the care of the world to future generations, and to avoid making their task harder by our action, or failure to act now.

Sometimes stewardship involves making simple and straightforward choices — to waste paper or to use it wisely; to throw litter on the ground or in the bin; whether or not to sign a petition against cruelty to animals. But in many situations, stewardship is very difficult. This may be because people are selfish and do not want to bother about stewardship, or it may be that they genuinely do not know what is the best thing to do in a situation.

For example, many people are not sure about the value and safety of nuclear energy. Some 'experts' say that we need nuclear energy to keep up with the demand for light, heat and other forms of power in our world. They claim that producing energy using a nuclear power station is less harmful to the environment than fossil-fuel (coal, gas) burning stations. They also believe that when the fossil-fuels run out (around 2050), we will need nuclear energy as a substitute.

Cooling towers at the Three Mile Island nuclear plant near Harrisburg, Pennsylvania, USA. Reactor Unit 2 was severely damaged in an accident on 28 March 1979. The clean-up operations have been in progress for over 10 years, and are expected to continue for another 30 years.

Other 'experts' say that nuclear energy has too high a price in terms of risk to the environment. They point out that accidents at nuclear power stations, such as the one at Chernobyl in 1987, have cost many lives already, destroyed vast areas of land and left many people permanently disabled. They say that even without accidents, the nuclear waste generated by nuclear power stations is already causing damage to the sea, the land and the atmosphere, harming the people, animals, fish and plants

Two-blade wind turbine in Scotland.

which come into contact with it. They believe that the solution to the 'energy crisis' lies in (a) reducing our consumption of energy, particularly by eliminating waste and (b) investigating other sources of energy which are not harmful to the environment, such as solar and wind power.

This is one of the many complex issues facing individuals, communities and governments. Some individuals would prefer not to make stewardship decisions in this kind of situation. They prefer to let 'the government' or some other organisation make the decision. Even governments often leave the decision to 'economic experts' or 'natural market forces'. This means that important environmental decisions are made on the basis of 'how can we make more profit?'.

> Christians have the responsibility, both as individuals and as a Church community, to face up to even the most difficult environmental issues. We can never leave it to someone else to decide for us. Our faith and hope in God give us the courage to keep on trying to be good stewards. Our love of God and of each other gives us the commitment and dedication necessary to be self-sacrificing and unselfish, to give up what might benefit us in the short term for the good of the whole environment in the long term.

Exercises

1. Give examples to show how each of the following can act as stewards towards the environment:
   (a) A ten year old child
   (b) A fifteen year old adolescent
   (c) A twenty-five year old single person
   (d) A parent
   (e) A tenants' or residents' association
   (f) A local water authority (in charge of water supply to homes)
   (g) A farmer
   (h) A fisherman/woman
   (i) The Department of Agriculture in a country
   (j) The government of a country
   (k) The United Nations
   (l) The management and staff of a mine
   (m) The owner of a chemical factory.

2. In each of the following situations, explain:
   (a) the possible effects which the action (or inaction) could have on the environment. (For example on animals, birds, fish, plants, trees, people, water, air etc.)
   (b) whether the person in each situation is a good or bad steward. Explain your answer.
   (i) A person builds twenty new houses in a large field at the edge of a town.
   (ii) A person builds twenty high-rise flats in the centre of a city.
   (iii) A farmer regularly gives antibiotics to the animals to prevent them from developing a disease.
   (iv) A farmer uses artificial fertiliser to help the land produce more crops.
   (v) A person insulates their attic, doors and windows to keep in the heat.
   (vi) A person cycles to school.
   (vii) A person buys products which are guaranteed 'environmentally friendly'.
   (viii) A person's house is full of things they do not want and never use.
   (ix) A person buys mahogany furniture.
   (x) A student does a project on 'the environment'.

Stewardship and Justice

Justice means treating every person fairly, having the right relationships between people. *Stewardship is a form of justice.* Through good stewardship of the earth's resources, we provide for ourselves, for everyone else in the world and for future generations of people the following rights:
- the right to live in a clean and healthy world, with unpolluted air
- to have clean water for drinking and cleaning purposes
- to have enough good food
- to be happy and healthy
- to be able to earn a living and raise a family.

Unfortunately, as stewards, people have a poor record of achievement. The destruction, neglect, and selfish use of much of the world's natural resources has upset the balance of nature in many parts of the world. As a result, the environment of which we are part is sick, and many people all over the world are suffering as a result.

Flooding in Bangladesh.

For example, in order to maintain their present way of life, the people in the rich countries of the world contaminate the air with carbon dioxide, methane, sulphur dioxide and other poisonous gases. Many of these gases cause the atmosphere to heat up. As a result, the earth's temperature has risen. This has led to flooding in many parts of the world, like Bangladesh. People have lost their homes, their land, their way of life, their lives, so that other people can live selfishly.

Another example is the destruction of the tropical rainforests. The rainforests of the equatorial region are the home of many groups of people. At least two-fifths of the world's species of plants and animals live there, and many modern medicines are based on plants which only grow in the rainforests. For example, the Yellow Wood tree, which grows on the island of Réunion in the Indian Ocean, contains substances which may help to treat leukaemia. However the Yellow Wood tree may become extinct very soon.

The rainforests act as a kind of filter for the atmosphere of the whole world — taking in harmful carbon dioxide and releasing oxygen into the atmosphere. They ensure adequate water supply to the surrounding regions, soaking up the rainfall quickly and trapping it (so that it is not immediately lost in evaporation); then releasing it slowly into the rivers. The rainforests also regulate global climate conditions; for example, by removing harmful CO_2, they keep down the global temperature.

Because of the rich countries' demand for hard timber like mahogany and teak, vast areas of the forest have been felled. Because of the demand for beefburgers, whole miles of forests have been destroyed to make grazing land for cattle. The countries which have rainforests tend to be poor, developing countries, like Zaire, Brazil and Indonesia. They are under pressure from the governments and banks in the rich countries to produce more timber, more cattle, so that they can pay back their massive debt.

Meanwhile, because these poor governments cannot afford to develop their countries properly, the poorest people cause even more harm to the rainforests in order to survive. They use a 'slash and burn' farming technique. This means that they cut down the forest, burn the stumps of trees, and grow their crops. The land is poor, so after a few years, the people must move on to a new area of forest, and so the cycle continues.

Rainforest being destroyed in Ecuador.

As a result of all these factors, the rainforest is disappearing. One hundred acres are cleared every minute. The people who once lived in the forests are being driven out and killed, and this vital natural resource is being destroyed because of bad stewardship and greed.

Through bad stewardship, the world community is being unjust to millions of people in the world today by destroying their natural surroundings and depriving them of their rights. This bad stewardship may also be making life impossible on the planet for the generations to come.

*E*XERCISES

1. Give examples to show how bad stewardship means being unjust to other people.
2. Examine each of the diagrams on pages 102 and 103.
   (a) What is the relationship between people and their environment in Diagram 1? What is the relationship between people and other people? (Explain your answers, giving examples.)
   (b) What is the relationship between people and their environment in Diagrams 2 and 3? What is the relationship between people and other people? (Explain, giving examples.)
   (c) What are the similarities and the differences between the diagrams?
   (d) Do the diagrams show any examples of (i) justice or (ii) injustice?

Project

Working with at least one other class group in the school, plan to make some contribution towards protecting your environment; or making other people aware of our responsibility as stewards; or finding and sharing more information about our environment and the problems we face as a world. Use the opportunity to build up a good relationship between your class and the other class.

(The addresses and sources listed at the end of the chapter should help you to plan your project.)

The Environment under attack (Diagram 1)

The global environment can be broken down into three main elements - land, water and air. Through our daily activities, we manage to pollute and contaminate all three different elements. If it continues, the damage caused by this may become irreversible.

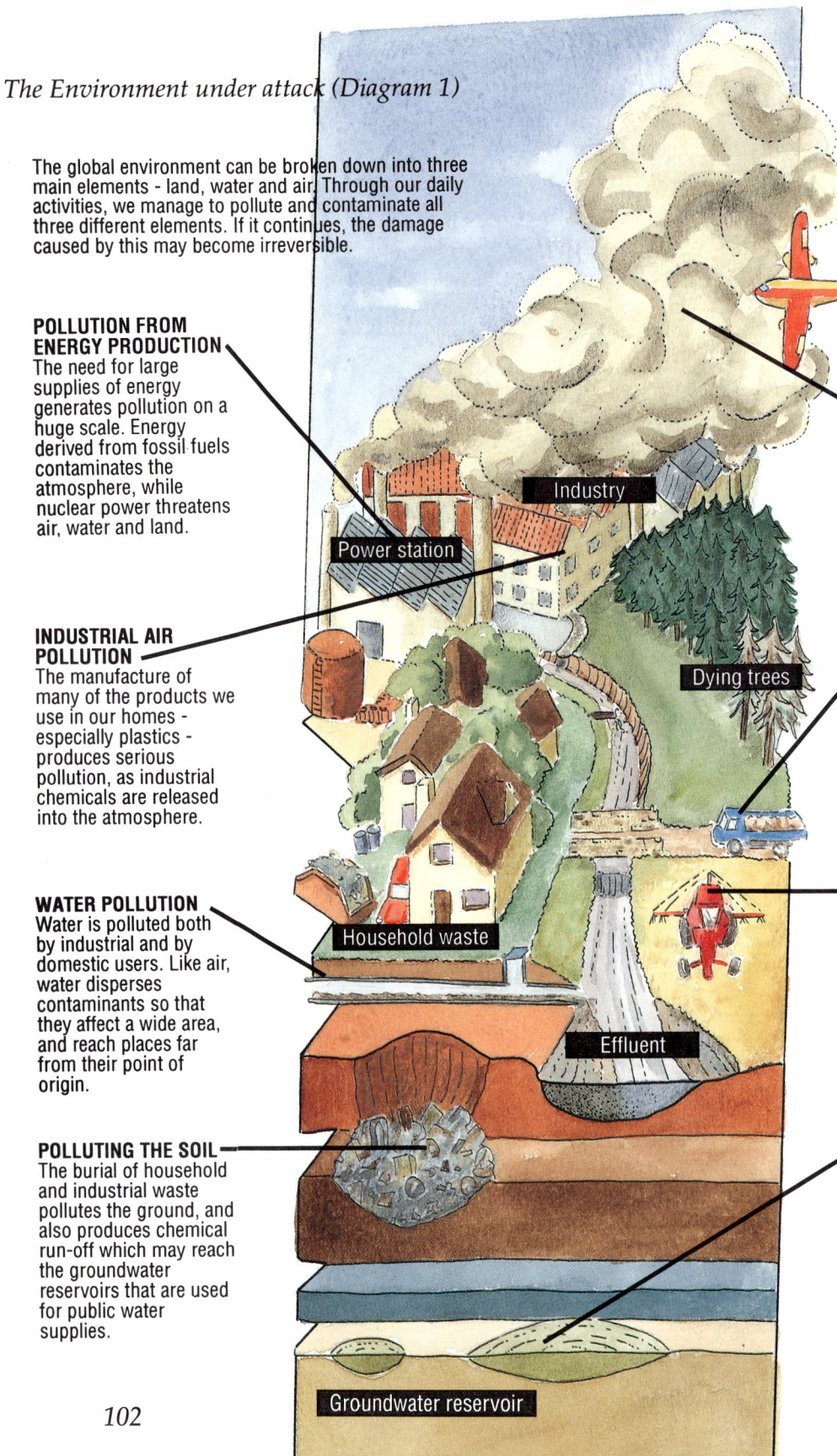

POLLUTION FROM ENERGY PRODUCTION
The need for large supplies of energy generates pollution on a huge scale. Energy derived from fossil fuels contaminates the atmosphere, while nuclear power threatens air, water and land.

INDUSTRIAL AIR POLLUTION
The manufacture of many of the products we use in our homes - especially plastics - produces serious pollution, as industrial chemicals are released into the atmosphere.

WATER POLLUTION
Water is polluted both by industrial and by domestic users. Like air, water disperses contaminants so that they affect a wide area, and reach places far from their point of origin.

POLLUTING THE SOIL
The burial of household and industrial waste pollutes the ground, and also produces chemical run-off which may reach the groundwater reservoirs that are used for public water supplies.

ACID RAIN
This relatively new form of pollution is a by-product of atmospheric contamination. The gases that are released into the air from cars, factories and power stations react with atmospheric moisture to form rain which is potentially lethal to trees.

TRANSPORT POLLUTION
Fossil fuels provide the chief sources of energy for transport. They are a major source of air pollution, one which over the last two decades has grown enormously.

AGRICULTURAL CHEMICALS
The food we eat is prepared from crops grown with the aid of a wide range of agricultural chemicals. These chemicals may end up in our food and in the water supply.

GROUNDWATER CONTAMINATION
Much of the world's fresh water lies in natural reservoirs deep underground. These are slowly becoming contaminated by dissolved chemicals which are washed through the ground.

Living on the land (Diagram 2)

ORGANIC FARMING
By recycling organic waste and following natural methods of pest control, the need for injurious agricultural chemicals would be avoided.

RECYCLING ORGANIC WASTE
All the manure produced by farm animals would be collected and then taken back to the land where it would be used as a valuable natural fertilizer.

SUSTAINABLE TIMBER
The planting and cropping of both hard and soft woods would provide fuel and building materials without depleting the lands all-important forest cover.

DUAL WATER SYSTEM
The dual system for water input and output would cut out unnecessary water treatment and ensure that all waterborne waste was returned to the land instead of being poured into rivers.

COLLECTING AND CONSERVING ENERGY
Domestic solar panels and heat recycling pumps combined with thorough insulation would reduce the need for mass-produced power to a minimum.

GROWING FOOD
Growing food locally would keep down the need for processed food, with its attendant problems of excessive packaging and transportation.

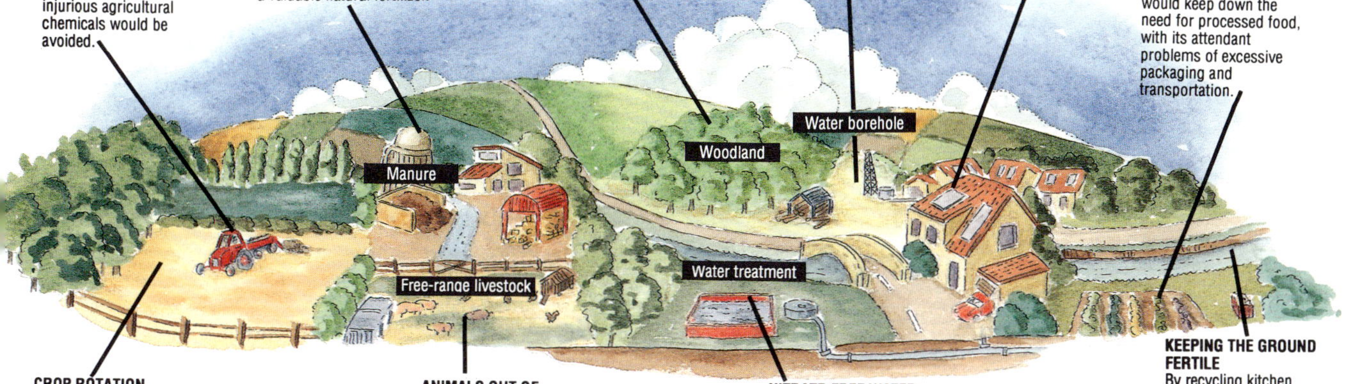

CROP ROTATION
Growing a different crop in each field every year would ensure that the natural fertility of the soil was not depleted and that pests did not have a chance to become a permanent problem.

ANIMALS OUT OF DOORS
Farm animals kept outside would fertilize the soil and use up any organic household waste. They would supply a useful amount of food for a minimum amount of investment.

NITRATE-FREE WATER
No artificial fertilizer on the land would mean less nitrate in river water. Without this nitrate, the water's biological balance would be left undisturbed, and the water would also be safer for human use.

KEEPING THE GROUND FERTILE
By recycling kitchen waste, a compost heap in every garden would improve the fertility and productivity of the soil.

Living in the city (Diagram 3)

RENEWABLE ENERGY
Wind farms and wave generators would collect energy without creating pollution. This could be used either to supplement the energy produced from fossil fuels, or to replace it entirely.

COLLECTING ENERGY
Solar radiation would be collected by solar panels and either used immediately or stored by heating water in underground tanks for use during the winter.

BACK TO THE LAND
Organic waste from the urban sewage system would be transported back to farmland for use as fertilizer.

LOW-POLLUTION INDUSTRY
Careful cleaning of waste gases and the treatment of chemical waste would ensure that industrial processes did not contaminate the environment.

NON-POLLUTING TRANSPORT
Public transport powered by electricity from renewable sources would keep the city air clean and reduce congestion.

NATURE IN THE CITY
Parks and waste ground would be planted with trees. These would play a part in cleaning the urban air and would also provide habitats for wildlife in the city.

THE WATER SUPPLY
Unpolluted river water would require no chlorination and little other treatment before being piped to houses and factories for all uses except drinking.

RECYCLING WASTE
All recyclable materials—glass, metals and paper—would be collected separately and processed in a recycling plant for re-use.

Reflection: 'But once more God will send us his Spirit. The waste land will become fertile, and fields will produce rich crops. Everywhere in the land righteousness and justice will be done. Because everyone will do what is right, there will be peace and security forever.' Isaiah 32: 15–17

Action: Choose *one* action which you can take every day to protect the environment. Put up posters or other reminders at home and at school to remind yourself to perform this action.

Psalm: Praise the Lord from heaven,
>you that live in the heights above.
Praise him, all his angels,
>all his heavenly armies.

Praise him, sun and moon;
>praise him, shining stars.
Praise him, highest heavens,
>and the waters above the sky.

Let them all praise the name of the Lord!
He commanded, and they were created;
by his command they were fixed in their places for ever,
>and they cannot disobey.

Praise the Lord from the earth,
>sea-monsters and all ocean depths;
lightning and hail, snow and clouds,
>strong winds that obey his commands.

Praise him, hills and mountains,
>fruit trees and forests;
all animals, tame and wild,
>reptiles and birds.

Praise him, kings and all peoples,
>princes and all other rulers;
girls and young men,
>old people and children too.

Let them all praise the name of the Lord!
>*Psalm 148: 1–13*

Useful addresses

Earthwatch
Harbour View
Bantry, Co. Cork
027-50968

Enfo
(Environmental Information Centre)
17 St Andrew St
Dublin 2
01-679-3144

Friends of the Earth
26–28 Underwood St
London N1 7JQ

World Wide Fund for Nature
(WWF)
Education Department
Panda House
Catteshall Lane
Godalming, Surrey GU7 1XR

Greenpeace
44 Upper Mount St
Dublin 2
01-605240

Concern:
Trees for Africa Campaign
1 Upper Camden St
Dublin 2
01-681237

Crann
Killegar, Co. Leitrim
049-39820

Irish Wildbird Conservancy
Ruttledge House
8 Longford Place
Monkstown, Co. Dublin
01-280-4322

Irish Wildlife Federation
Conservation Centre
132A East Wall Road
Dublin 3
01-366821

RELATIONSHIPS

CHAPTER 12

Everyone has many different relationships. Some relationships are more important than others. Some make us feel good about ourselves, while others make us uncomfortable or unhappy. The following exercise should help you to discover more about *your* personal relationships and the effects they have on your life.

Relationships Survey
1. Make a list of some of the different people with whom you have a relationship. Try to include as many different kinds of relationships as possible — family, friend, acquaintance etc.
2. Put the list of names in order of priority. That is, put the people who are most important to you first on the list, the next most important second, and so on.
3. Draw a chart similar to the one shown into your copy, and fill it in as best you can.

Person	Time	Activities	Topics	Physical contact

Person: Fill in the name or initials of the person with whom you have the relationship.

Time: Fill in the amount of time you usually spend together in one week — e.g. two hours.

Activities: Fill in the activities that you share with this person — e.g. playing basketball.

Topics: Fill in the kinds of topics you usually talk about together — e.g. music.

Physical contact: Fill in the kind of physical contact you usually have with each other — e.g. handshake.

EXERCISES

1. Note the similarities between your relationships. Which of the relationships tend to be similar?
2. Are there any major differences between your relationships? Is any relationship completely different from all the others?
3. Is there any item in your chart that makes you proud or happy?
4. Is there anything you would like to be able to change about any of these relationships?
5. If you did a survey of your relationships ten years from now, do you think the chart would look the same as your present one? Why/Why not?

Relationships

From birth to death our relationships are a vital part of our lives. Relationships make it possible for us to be conceived, to be born, to grow, develop and mature. Without relationships we would have no language, no culture, no sense of human identity. Other people teach us how to talk (by speaking to us), how to get food (by shopping or hunting), what to do if we are sick, and so on. It is through our relationships that we learn how to live as people.

Children learn from older people.

There are a number of examples of children who were separated from other people at a very young age, and yet who managed to survive in the wild. When they were found years later, these people did not know how to communicate. They were afraid of other people because they did not know that they themselves were human. One girl in South Africa was lost in the bush when she was very young. She survived by living with a pack of wild dogs. When she was found at the age of twelve or thirteen, she could not walk upright. She went on all fours, like the dogs. This girl never learned to walk like a human being because her spine was permanently curved. Some of these lost children, through the love and care of other people, manage to realise that they are human beings, and learn to communicate. Those who are treated without love and compassion never discover their true identity as people.

We usually discover who we are through our relationships with the members of our family, our neighbours and friends, and other people with whom we come in contact. We may learn: 'I am a daughter; I am the youngest; people like me; I live in Cork; I can write my name; I am a fast runner' and so on. Everything we learn about other people through our relationships with them also teaches us something about ourselves. For example: 'Grandad is old — why am I not old? When will I be old? Old people die — will I die?'.

> Every relationship is different because every person is unique. Every relationship teaches us something different about ourselves and other people. Relationships based on love, trust, respect and justice help us to learn the truth about ourselves and others and make it possible for us to be happy. Relationships based on hatred, suspicion, exploitation or injustice can prevent us from becoming the people we are meant to be. The better our relationships are, therefore, the better and happier we will be. No relationship is perfect, although some are better than others. Even people we love will let us down sometimes, and we sometimes let others down.

EXERCISES

1. Examine your list of relationships again. In the case of each relationship explain:
   (a) What have I learned about myself from this relationship?
   (b) What have I learned about other people?
2. In the case of each of your relationships, can you give examples to show:
   (a) that there is love, trust, respect or justice in the relationship?
   (b) that there is hatred, suspicion, exploitation or injustice in the relationship?
   (c) how you could improve the relationship?

Sexual relationships

Every human being is sexual, from the smallest baby to the oldest grandparent. This means that, in a way, all our relationships are sexual, because the people in the relationship are sexual. To say that people are sexual is to say that they have female or male physical characteristics. These include reproductive organs, hormones and the genetic material in every cell of their bodies.

In most human societies, being sexual also involves learning certain ways of behaving, for example, wearing 'male' or 'female' clothes, having a 'female' or 'male' hairstyle, or doing 'male' or

In some countries, women farm the land.

'female' jobs. *Most of these distinctions are not a basic part of being male or female; they are simply customs which have been used for a long time in some societies.* For example, in some societies it is the custom for women to farm the land, ploughing, sowing the seed and harvesting the crop. In these societies the women are seen as fertile, because women give birth, and so it is 'natural' for women to work with the fertile earth. In other societies, it is the custom for men to farm the land, because the men are seen as the providers, who have a duty to bring food to the women. There are other societies in which both men and women farm the land. In these societies, farming is not an activity which depends on a person's sex.

In some countries farming is a male occupation

The relationships between people are greatly influenced by the sexual customs in a society. Some customs encourage relationships based on love and justice, while other customs encourage hatred, exploitation and injustice. In many parts of the world, for example, women are paid less than men for doing the same job. In many countries, a married woman officially belongs to her husband, and she may not own any money or property of her own. These and other customs mean that most of the women in the world are poorer than most of the men. In fact, women form half of the world's population, but they own only a small proportion of the world's wealth.

Sexual customs which respect the rights and needs of both women and men make life better for both sexes. When girls and boys have an equal chance to get a good education, it means that everyone has the opportunity to develop his or her talents fully. When men and women have an equal chance to use their talents and to be well paid for their work, they can be equal partners together in the home and in the community.

*E*XERCISES

1. Give some examples of sexual customs which encourage love and justice.
2. Give some examples of sexual customs which encourage hatred and injustice.
3. Examine your relationships chart again. Could any of your relationships be described as sexual relationships? Explain your answer.

Teenage magazines and books can influence young people's ideas about sexuality.

Sexual attraction

During adolescence, most people become aware of being attracted in a special way to people of the opposite sex. This happens partly because of the sexual changes that take place in adolescence. Our own sexual development makes us more aware of the sexuality of others. The increased level of hormones in our bodies can make us feel sexually excited or aroused, particularly when we are close to or thinking about someone of the opposite sex.

The society in which we live also has an influence on the way adolescents feel about the opposite sex. Films, television programmes, soap operas, teenage books and magazines and many advertisements often presume that even very young adolescents are interested in the opposite sex and always have a boyfriend or girlfriend, especially if they are good looking. This can put adolescents under pressure, and make them feel that there is something wrong with them if they do not want to go out with anyone, or if no one has asked them out.

Sexual attraction is a normal part of human experience. Some people experience it from a young age, while others are adults before it is an important part of their lives. We can feel sexually attracted to someone with whom we have no real relationship, for example a pop star, an actor or actress, or a casual acquaintance. This is particularly common in adolescence when people are discovering more about their sexuality. After a while most of us grow out of our attraction for 'unreal' people like pop stars. We realise that a good relationship involves two people being attracted to each other, getting to know each other, caring for and respecting each other.

QUESTIONS

1. In general, what do you think girls find most attractive about boys?
2. In general, what do you think boys find most attractive about girls?
3. Do you think that films, magazine stories and so on give young people a good idea of what relationships should be like? Explain.
4. Why do you think young people are sometimes attracted to people they have never met?

Sexuality and love

Some relationships begin because two people are sexually attracted to each other. They want to spend time together and to get to know each other better. This can lead to friendship between them, as they begin to be interested in each other as people. They are still sexually attracted, but they are also attracted for other reasons.

Some relationships begin as friendship between two people who enjoy being together. As they get to know each other better, they may discover that they are sexually attracted to each other.

> When sexual attraction leads to, or is part of, a just and loving relationship, it can improve the relationship. It can make us more aware of the other person, and can help us to appreciate how unique and special they are. In the same way, when we know that someone who cares about us and respects us also finds us sexually attractive, we can often feel more confident about ourselves and more aware of the joy of being a sexual person.

Some sexual customs make it more difficult for people to have just and loving relationships with each other. If boys and girls only meet each other at discos and never have much opportunity for talking to each other, then it is difficult for their relationship to develop into a real friendship. If both sexes frequently read magazines and watch films which show people as sex objects, then they may be more inclined to treat the people they know as sex objects as well.

Some relationships begin as friendship between people who enjoy being together.

EXERCISES

1. Examine the following situation and answer the questions at the end.

    Alexander wants to have a relationship with Penelope, his sister's friend. He is sexually attracted to her and thinks she is very good-looking. He thinks that going out with Penelope will be something to be proud of, and to boast about to his friends.

    Penelope wants to have a relationship with Alexander, her friend's brother. She is sexually attracted to him and thinks he is very good-looking. She knows they both like the same kind of music and that they both love sport of all kinds, so she hopes they will get on well together.

(a) What kind of a relationship does Alexander seem to want with Penelope?
(b) What kind of a relationship does Penelope seem to want with Alexander?
(c) What are the similarities and the differences between what Alexander wants and what Penelope wants?
(d) If the two of them have a relationship, do you think it will be based on caring for and respecting each other? Explain your answer.
2. (a) Compare your answers to the previous exercise with the rest of the class.
(b) After listening to each other's points of view, try to come to some agreement about your answers as a class.

Group Work
1. Working on your own, write down whether you agree or disagree with each of the following statements, and explain why.
(a) Every relationship between teenagers of opposite sexes is based on sexual attraction.
(b) If two people are sexually attracted to each other they cannot be 'just good friends'.
(c) It is possible to be sexually attracted to many different people.
(d) Sexual attraction for someone and loving them are the same thing.
2. Get into groups of three or four and compare your answers.
3. Try to come to some agreement, as a group, about each sentence.
4. Report your findings to the whole class.

Exclusive sexual relationships
All loving relationships are life-giving. Loving others and being loved in return makes us feel more fully alive, more enthusiastic and hopeful, and better able to cope with life's problems. For example, a drug addict who is trying to beat an addiction has a much better chance of success if he or she has support from family and friends. Without love, people do not always physically die, but they may feel emotionally, intellectually or spiritually 'dead'. The children who were abandoned in Romanian orphanages during the reign of Nicolai Ceaucescu were almost lifeless when they were discovered. This was because they had no one to love them and to care for them. Everyone needs loving relationships in order to be fully alive as God wants us to be.

Some people are called to form a special loving relationship with another person of the opposite sex. In this relationship which is called marriage, a woman and a man give themselves totally to one another. The physical union of sexual intercourse is a powerful symbol of their total union, in heart and in mind as well as in body. This total self-giving in love greatly enriches the lives of the two people concerned, as they experience the joy of sharing, trusting, companionship and total commitment. Both of them feel special because each was specially chosen by the other. When they make decisions, they try to do what is best for both of them. Their happiness is contagious, as their love for each other makes them more loving towards other people in the community, and so they can brighten the lives of everyone with whom they come in contact. People who are miserable often have no time for other people's problems because they are unhappy themselves. Happy people want other people to be happy as well, so they try to help others if they can.

Children are a powerful symbol of the loving union between two people.

Through their marriage, the woman and man can also bring new life into the world. The children who may be born to the couple are a symbol of the loving union between them. The presence of children in our community reminds us powerfully of the link between love and life.

Because marriage involves total self-giving by one person to another, it is an exclusive relationship which lasts until death. It is exclusive in that I can only form this relationship with one person at a time, if I am to give myself fully in the relationship. It lasts until death, because total giving means having no time limits. It means absolute faithfulness and complete commitment, no matter what happens.

Marriage is an exclusive relationship that lasts until death.

Problems in marriage

Being married is not easy because total self-giving is never easy. Personality differences, selfishness, money difficulties and other problems can make it hard for people to love and trust each other completely. Even two mature people who really love each other often have rows, act selfishly and hurt each other.

People have to work at their marriage relationship so that it can continue to be loving and life-giving. This means making time to talk to each other when problems arise. It means being ready to say they are sorry and to forgive each other. It means being able to make sacrifices for the good of the other person.

Sometimes, a marriage relationship breaks down. This is a very tragic situation in which everyone is hurt — the woman and man, their children, their families and their friends. The

Pre-marriage courses help people to prepare for marriage.

Christian community has a special responsibility to help people whose marriages are in difficulty and to give them support.

> Christians believe that marriage is a vocation, a way of showing God's love to the world, and the ideal basis for family life. This is why we try to protect marriages and to help married people as much as possible by organising pre-marriage courses, marriage counselling and courses to help people improve their marriages.

Exercises

1. Give examples to show how the love between two married people can be life-giving.
2. Give examples to show how other loving relationships can give life to people.
3. Do you agree that being married can be difficult? Why? Why not?

Sexual relationships in adolescence

Most adolescents are not ready for a marriage relationship. They need to have relationships with many different people before they can decide with whom they would like to spend the rest of their lives. They may be physically capable of being parents, but they are unlikely to be ready or able to look after a family of their own.

Although most adolescents realise that they are not ready for marriage, some of them may feel a strong sexual attraction for someone, even wishing to be sexually intimate with that person. However, if I make love to a person physically when I am not giving myself totally to that person forever, then I am cheating myself and the other person as well. Sexual intercourse and the actions which prepare the body for intercourse (such as intimate kissing and caressing) are not just physical acts which give pleasure to people. They are actions which have deep meaning and significance. They should be a sign of total love and commitment between two people. Casual sex, between people who cannot or will not commit themselves to each other for life, takes away the true meaning of sexual intimacy.

> Chastity is an important Christian value. Chastity means respecting myself as a sexual person; it also means respecting the sexuality of others. Being chaste in a relationship means treating someone as a sexual person and not as a sex

object. It means loving the other person rather than using them to get a sexual thrill, or to show off. Chastity helps people to build up just and loving sexual relationships.

Adolescents who are involved in a loving sexual relationship show their love to each other in many different ways. They talk about their feelings and ideas, their hopes and their dreams. They spend time together, helping each other and socialising with the rest of their friends. They hold hands and kiss or hug each other as friends. However, if they truly love each other, they will not put pressure on each other to be more physically intimate. They will respect the strong sexual attraction between them by avoiding situations in which it would be difficult to control their sexual desires.

Respecting our sexuality means being open and honest in our relationships. It means giving our intimate sexual actions their full meaning and significance in an exclusive relationship. One of the best ways to prepare for a happy marriage is to practise being an unselfish, self-controlled and loving person in our relationships during adolescence.

Group Work
1. Working on your own, decide whether you agree or disagree with each of the following statements.
   (a) If a boy and girl really love each other, they should have sexual intercourse with one another.
   (b) Sexual actions such as open-mouth kissing and 'petting' are good ways in which to show you love someone when you are both teenagers.
   (c) If two people love each other, they should be allowed to get married at sixteen.
   (d) If a girl of sixteen gets pregnant, she should marry her boyfriend (of the same age) if they love each other.
2. Get into groups of three or four and compare your answers, giving your reasons.
3. As a group, try to reach an agreement about each statement.
4. Report your findings to the whole class.

Love is For Life (Irish Bishops' Pastoral)
Sex is a means of communication, a language. We all know the importance of communication. We communicate with words; and we communicate with our bodies. Sometimes gestures speak louder than words and say things better than words can say them. There are many ways of expressing love by bodily language and the deepest physical expression of love is sexual

union. Sexual union says, 'I love you', in a very profound way. By sexual union a man and woman say to each other: 'I love you. There is nobody else in all the world I love in the way I love you. I love you just for being you. I want you to become even more wonderful than you are. I want to share my life and my world with you. I want you to share your life and your world with me. I want us to build a new life together, a future together which will be our future.'

QUESTIONS

1. What is your reaction to this statement?
2. Give examples to show how the following people could express their love for each other through bodily language:
   (a) Parent and child
   (b) Teenager and parent
   (c) Friends
   (d) Boyfriend and girlfriend.
3. What are the similarities and the differences between the Christian understanding of sexual union (or sexual intercourse) and the understanding of sexual union in films, TV programmes and magazines aimed at young people?

Reflection: 'I may be able to speak the languages of men and even of angels, but if I have no love, my speech is no more than a noisy gong or a clanging bell. I may have the gift of inspired preaching; I may have all knowledge and understand all secrets; I may have all the faith needed to move mountains — but if I have no love, I am nothing. I may give away everything I have, and even give up my body to be burnt — but if I have no love, this does me no good.' 1 Cor 13: 1–3

Action: Tell a good friend three things you really like or admire about them, and why you are glad to be their friend.

Song of Love
Love is as powerful as death;
passion is as strong as death itself.
It bursts into flame and burns like a raging fire.
Water cannot put it out;
no flood can drown it.
But if anyone tried to buy love with his wealth,
contempt is all he would get.

Song of Songs 8: 6–7

FAMILY

CHAPTER 13
▼

'Its two o'clock, everyone, time to go.' Susan Malone spoke cheerfully, but inside she was feeling depressed. She hated the thought of another row. There was no sign of Teresa, Seán or Aidan. She went to the bottom of the stairs. 'Teresa, Seán, are you ready?' she called. There was still no answer. She ran quickly upstairs. All the doors were shut. She knocked on the boys' door and went in. Seán was lying on his bed wearing earphones. Aidan was sprawled on the floor reading a comic.

'Come on, boys,' said Susan, briskly, 'time to go.' Aidan groaned.

'Aw Mum, I want to read my comic.'

'You can read it in the car. Go on, off you go.'

'What about Seán?' asked Aidan, suspiciously. At ten years of age he was used to having less freedom than his fourteen year old brother, but he still did not like it.

'Seán will be along in a minute,' said his mother, sternly. Slowly, Aidan got up and left the room, still grumbling.

Susan looked at Seán for a moment without saying anything. With his eyes closed he said, 'I'm not going, so don't try to force me.' Susan sighed. 'It's only one afternoon a month. Surely that's not too much to ask?' Seán took off the ear-phones and sat up. He tried to speak calmly and reasonably.

'Mum, I hate it there. Nothing to do except sit around all day watching television, and listening to Granny and Grandad going on and on about nothing.'

'I never heard you complain before about having to watch television,' said Susan.

'But they never watch anything good. It's all religious programmes and soppy films.'

'The point is, they're your grandparents. They like to see you. They've always been very good to you. The least you can do is to give them a few hours of your time.'

Seán said nothing. He just sat on the bed and stared at the floor.

'I suppose you want your father and me to tell lies for you when we get there,' said Susan. 'Maybe "Seán couldn't come,

he was sick", or "Seán had a football match", that sort of thing.'
Seán still said nothing.

'How would you like it if we told the truth? Sean said he didn't want to come and see you because you're old and boring and he hates it here.'

'That's not true,' Seán burst out. 'I never said that.'

'But that's what you meant, isn't it?' Susan said quietly.

'No,' said Seán. 'Well, partly. I hate going on Sundays. I don't mind it during the holidays, going round the farm with Grandad, or walking around on my own. I just want to do my own thing on Sundays. It's the only day that I have really free.'

Susan had one last try.

'Seán, would you not go for my sake? You know how upset . . . everyone will be if you don't go with us.' They both knew she was talking about his father. Seán shrugged.

'Dad can't always have everything his own way,' he said.

Susan went into Teresa's room. Teresa was sitting at her desk, studying. She was sixteen, and doing well at school. She looked up as her mother came in.

'Mum, I can't go with you today. I have a maths test tomorrow, and I have to study for it.'

'You weren't too worried about that when you were out all day yesterday with Debbie,' said Susan.

'Oh, Mum, you know I had to get shoes.'

'Anyway, Sunday isn't a day for studying. It's a day for rest, for family, for visiting your grandparents who love you,' said Susan.

'But what about my test tomorrow?' said Teresa.

'Well, you can get up early in the morning and study.'

'That's no good! I'm always too tired to study in the morning.'

'What about going to bed on time the night before?' asked Susan.

'Oh, Mum, please *please* let me stay home today, will you?'

Susan looked helplessly at her daughter. Why did everything have to be so difficult? She remembered when the children were small, she and Gavin used to bring them out every Sunday. Once a month they always went to see Susan's mother and father — Gavin's parents were dead. The children had always enjoyed the Sunday outings. But recently, they had all changed.

First it was Teresa, who couldn't come with them because she was going to a birthday party, or doing a school play. Then it was Seán, doing extra band practice, or going orienteering with the club. Gradually they had stopped going out together as a family on the other three Sundays, but they had still gone down to the farm on the first Sunday of every month. Now all the children, even Aidan, were making excuses not to go there either. Susan was upset by this, but she didn't think it was worth forcing them to go. However, Gavin always insisted.

'We're your parents,' he would say firmly. 'As long as you live with us you'll do what's right, and we'll have no argument about it.'

But unfortunately there were arguments about it, and Susan was getting fed up with it all.

Gavin came into the room and said, 'Right, we're off. Aidan's already in the car.'

'What about Seán?' asked Susan.

'Seán thinks that he would rather visit his grandparents than have no pocket money for a month,' said Gavin cheerfully.

'I have to study for my maths test,' said Teresa in a small voice.

'Bring the books with you if you like,' said Gavin.

'But . . .' said Teresa.

'No buts,' said Gavin, and went out of the room. Teresa slammed her books, copies and pens into her bag and stalked out of the room after him. Susan followed more slowly. As she went downstairs she began to calculate how many more visiting Sundays there would be before the children left home.

QUESTIONS

1. What is your reaction to this story?
2. What are the characters like in the story? With whom do you have the most sympathy? Why?
3. What values do the different characters have?
4. Do these values cause any conflicts in the story?
5. Does anyone or anything change from the beginning to the end of the story? Explain your answer.
6. In your opinion, what is the most important moment in the story? Why?
7. What do you think is the meaning or message in this story?

Family

Many of us learn about love, relationships, values and life from the members of our immediate family. These are often the people we know best in the world, people we depend on and who depend on us. It is from these people who are closest to us that we usually learn most about ourselves. It is hard to have illusions about yourself when you are a member of a family. It is often said that 'familiarity breeds contempt', and it is certainly

true that we tend to be more selfish and uncaring, rude and unappreciative towards our family than we are towards people we know less well. Family life shows us just how difficult it can be to see things from the other person's point of view; to explain our point of view to them; to forgive someone who has hurt us and not to hold a grudge.

> Conflicts are common in most families. They can occur because of a difference of opinion; because children want to be independent; because parents want to protect their children; because people are jealous, or angry or afraid or self-centred. The way in which we deal with conflict is more important than the cause of the conflict. Sulking, 'not speaking', throwing dishes, shouting and screaming are all natural reactions to a difficult situation, but they are not much help in the long term. Some families cope with conflict by pretending it does not exist — acting as if the row never happened, for example—rather than sorting out the problem.
>
> The best way to try to deal with conflict is to talk about the problem calmly; to try to understand the other person's point of view; to work together to find a solution which is fair to everyone involved.

It is from the people who are closest to us that we learn the most about ourselves.

Resolving conflicts is not easy. Without love it is sometimes impossible. It is worthwhile, however, to take the time and make the effort to improve our relationships at home for two reasons. Firstly, it adds greater joy and happiness to our family life, and encourages us to be just and fair in our dealings with the members of our family. Secondly, it gives us an attitude towards relationships and a way of dealing with people which will help us in all our future relationships. Sometimes we imagine that when we leave home everything will be different — there will be no more conflicts, meanness or laziness, no one bossing us around. The fact is that the very same type of problems and difficulties arise whenever a group of people live in close contact with one another. If we are grouchy and mean at home in the morning, then we will probably be the same when we live in a flat with other people or when we set up our own homes. If we constantly have rows with our brothers and sisters about whose turn it is to clean up, we will probably have similar rows with the people we live with in the future. The self-control and the attitudes of love and justice that we can learn in our homes today can help us to bring peace and harmony to any future relationship.

EXERCISES

1. Do you think that the Malones resolved their conflict well? Explain your answer.
2. Give examples of minor conflicts in everyday family life. What do families normally do about these conflicts? Do you think there is anything else that could be done in each case?
3. Write a brief account of a major conflict which could occur in a family. Swap your account with someone else in the class.

   Each of you should write down how you think the other person's major conflict could be resolved. Share your answers with each other. Any 'impossible' conflict should be shared with the whole class, to see if anyone can come up with a possible approach to solving it. (The list of organisations at the end of the chapter may also give you some ideas.)

Christian Family in the Modern World (Encyclical letter from Pope John Paul II)

All members of the family, each according to his or her own gift, have the grace and responsibility of building, day by day, the communion of persons, making the family 'a school of deeper humanity': this happens where there is care and love for the little ones, the sick, the aged; where there is mutual service every day; when there is a sharing of goods, of joys and of sorrows.

(Taken from Paragraph 21)

QUESTIONS

1. What examples does Pope John Paul II give to show how families can become a 'communion of persons'? Try to explain this in your own words.
2. In what way is a family like a 'school' of 'humanity'? (For example, what can people learn in a family that will make them more human, more loving, more just?)
3. Do you think that parents can learn from their children? Can older children learn from younger ones? Explain your answers.

Reflection: 'So then, we must always aim at those things that bring peace and that help to strengthen one another.'
Romans 14:19

Action: Write down a list of the things that you and the rest of your family agree on. Show the list to the family, and tell them why you like being a member of the family.

Psalm: Happy are those who obey the Lord,
who live by his commands.
Your work will provide for your needs;
you will be happy and prosperous.
Your wife will be like a fruitful vine in your home,
and your sons will be like young olive trees round your table.
A man who obeys the Lord will surely be blessed like this.

May the Lord bless you from Zion!
May you see Jerusalem prosper all the days of your life!
May you live to see your grandchildren!

Psalm 128

Useful organisations
Catholic Marriage Advisory Council (CMAC)
Central Office
All Hallows College
Drumcondra, Dublin 9
(Your local telephone directory will give you the address of the nearest branch.)

Al Anon (an organisation for the relative of alcoholics)
Information Centre
19 Fleet St, Dublin 2
(See local church noticeboards for nearest branch of Al Anon and Alateen, the organisation for teenagers whose lives are affected by alcoholism.)

Cura (an organisation for unmarried mothers)
South Anne St
Dublin 2
(See local church noticeboards for nearest branch.)

GOD

CHAPTER 14

▼

No one has ever seen God. And yet many people have an idea of what God is like.

'What are you drawing, dear?'
'It's a picture of God.'
'But nobody knows what God looks like.'
'They will when I'm finished.'

QUESTIONS

1. Do you agree with the mother that no-one knows what God looks like? Why/Why not?
2. Have you ever seen any 'pictures' of God? Describe them if you have.

EXERCISES

1. Draw any 'picture' of God that comes into your mind, for example when you pray, or when you hear people talking about God.
2. Put everybody's drawing up on the wall. Notice the similarities and the differences between the drawings.

3. Select the picture (not your own) which most appeals to you, and explain why.
4. If you do not understand any of the pictures, ask the people who drew them to explain to you what they meant.

Images of God

When we think about, talk about, or pray to God, we often have an image in our minds of what God is like. Some images of God help us to know and love Him, and to trust in Him no matter what happens.

Some images of God seem to say that God is far away, that God is harsh and cruel, or that God is like Santa Claus who gives presents to you if you ask nicely. These images are not helpful because they do not tell us what God is really like. Any image of God which is not like Jesus' image of God is not a helpful image. Some images of God can harm our relationship with God by making us afraid of God, or encouraging us to ignore God or to blame God for anything that goes wrong in our lives.

Our image of God usually changes as we grow older and get to know God better. Young children sometimes see God as a kind old man living in the sky, who can make the sun shine for a picnic if they ask. However, an older person who knows that there are no old men walking around in space would not find the child's image helpful. This person might have an image of God as a loving Spirit who is near people at all times. This image helps the person to pray to God and to feel close to God.

One of the most common images of God is that God is a father. This is the image that Jesus used frequently when he spoke about God. This image helps us to see that God gives us life, that God loves and cares for us. However, it is equally true to say that God has the characteristics of a mother, giving us life and caring for us. This is shown in Hosea 11: 1–4, for example, when God speaks about the Chosen People, Israel.

> 'When Israel was a child I loved him . . .
> I was the one who taught Israel to walk.
> I took my people up in my arms . . .
> I drew them to me with affection and love.
> I picked them up and held them to my cheek;
> I bent down to them and fed them.'

Christians believe that Jesus is the true image of God, because Jesus is God the Son made human. Jesus himself said 'Whoever has seen me has seen the Father . . . Believe me when I say that I am in the Father and the Father is in me.' (John 14:9–11). It gives Christians great hope and joy when Jesus shows us that God is loving, merciful, compassionate, forgiving, powerful, and willing to suffer with and for all of us. Through Jesus' life, death and resurrection we learn that God loves justice and peace, that God is with us through every joy and sorrow and that no matter what happens, we are never alone.

Exercises

1. Examine the images of God which your class has drawn. Pick out three images which you think are helpful images of God.
2. Do you think any of the images could be unhelpful?
3. Where do you think you get your false images of God?
4. Every person is made in the image and likeness of God. Do you ever see an image of God in other people? In yourself? Explain.

Jesus often used the image of God as a father . . .

Group Work

1. Get into groups of four or five.
2. Look up each of the following Scripture references, and in each case decide:
   (a) What image of God is used in each passage?
   (b) What does this image tell us about God?
   (c) Do you think the image is *literally* true?
   References:
   (i) Genesis 1:26–27 (iv) John 8:12
   (ii) Psalm 23:1–6 (v) Mark 6:34
   (iii) Psalm 99:1–3 (vi) John 2:1–10.
3. As a group, pick out the image of God which you like best out of the six, and explain why.
4. Report your findings to the rest of the class.

. . . but God also has the characteristics of a mother.

The following story from World War II decribes an image of God which the author found in a concentration camp.

'Death in a Concentration Camp'

One day, the electric power station at Buna was blown up. The Gestapo, summoned to the spot, suspected sabotage. They found a trail. It eventually led to the Dutch Oberkapo (supervisor). And there, after a search they found an important stock of arms.

The Oberkapo was arrested immediately. He was tortured for a period of weeks, but in vain. He would not give a single name. He was transferred to Auschwitz. We never heard of him again.

But his little servant had been left behind in the camp in prison. Also put to torture, he too would not speak. Then the SS sentenced him to death, with two other prisoners who had been discovered with arms.

One day when we came back from work, we saw three gallows rearing up in the assembly place, three black crows. Roll call. SS all round us, machine guns trained: the traditional ceremony. Three victims in chains — and one of them, the little servant, the sad-eyed angel.

The SS seemed more preoccupied, more disturbed than usual. To hang a young boy in front of thousands of spectators was no light matter. The head of the camp read the verdict. All eyes were on the child. He was lividly pale, almost calm, biting his lips. The gallows threw its shadow over him.

This time the Lagerkapo (deputy supervisor) refused to act as executioner. Three SS replaced him.

The three victims mounted together onto the chairs.

The three necks were placed at the same moment within the nooses.

'Long live liberty!' cried the two adults.

But the child was silent.

'Where is God? Where is He?' someone behind me asked.

At a sign from the head of the camp, the three chairs tipped over.

Total silence throughout the camp. On the horizon, the sun was setting.

'Bare your heads!' yelled the head of the camp. His voice was raucous. We were weeping.

'Cover your heads!'

Then the march past began. The two adults were no longer alive. Their tongues hung swollen, blue-tinged. But the third rope was still moving; being so light, the child was still alive.

For more than half an hour he stayed there, struggling between life and death, dying in slow agony under our eyes. And we had to look him full in the face. He was still alive when I passed in front of him. His tongue was still red, his eyes not yet glazed.

Behind me, I heard the same man asking:

'Where is God now?'

And I heard a voice within me answer him:

'Where is He? Here He is — He is hanging here on this gallows . . .'

That night the soup tasted of corpses.

Taken from *Night*, by Ellie Wiesel

QUESTIONS

1. What is your reaction to this story?
2. Who are the most important people in it?
3. Does anything or anyone change by the end of the story? Explain your answer.
4. What is the most important moment in the story? Why?
5. What does this story tell you about people? about God?
6. What is the most important message or meaning in this story for you?
7. (a) What image of God did the author see in the concentration camp?
   (b) Do you think this is a helpful image? Why? Why not?

The Trinity

Christians believe in one God. We believe that there are three distinct persons in the one God, completely united in love and purpose and being. We believe in God the Father, the Creator of everything that is.

'Oh Lord, you have always been our home. Before you created the hills, or brought the world into being, you were eternally God, and will be God forever.' (Ps. 90:1–2)

We believe in Christ, God the Son made man, who lived among us, died, and rose from the dead, so that we could become children of God. St Paul, in his letter to the Romans, tells us that 'The Good News was promised long ago by God through the prophets, as written in the Holy Scriptures. It is about God's Son, our Lord Jesus Christ: he was born a descendant of David, he was shown with great power to be the Son of God by being raised from death.' (Romans 1:2–4).

We believe in the Holy Spirit, who fills us with life and love, and makes it possible for us to respond with love to God and other people.

Jesus said 'The Helper, the Holy Spirit, whom the Father will send in my name, will teach you everything and make you remember all that I have told you.' (Jn 14:26)

St Paul wrote 'The Spirit produces love, joy, peace, patience, kindness, goodness, faithfulness, humility and self-control.' (Galatians 5:22–23)

We believe that God is a Trinity of persons, a divine family who wants to reach out in love to the whole human family. Each person in the Trinity shows love for us in different ways. The Father creates us and cares for us and the whole of creation.

Jesus shows us how to love God and each other and saves us from the power of evil. The Spirit lives in each of us, guiding us and giving us the power to love God and each other.

EXERCISES

1. Briefly describe what you know about God the Father; God the Son; God the Holy Spirit.
2. Do you have any questions about the Trinity? Share them with your teacher and with the rest of the class, and see if you can find some answers.

Reflection: 'The grace of the Lord Jesus Christ, the love of God, and the fellowship of the Holy Spirit be with you all.'
2 Corinthians 13:13

Action: Listen carefully to the readings at the next Eucharistic celebration in your community. Notice the images of God which you get from them. Choose *one* of these images, and spend some time thinking about what it tells you about God.

Psalm: God is our shelter and strength,
　　　　always ready to help in times of trouble.
　　　　So we will not be afraid, even if the earth is shaken
　　　　and mountains fall into the ocean depths;
　　　　even if the seas roar and rage,
　　　　and the hills are shaken by the violence.

　　　　Come and see what the Lord has done.
　　　　See what amazing things he has done on earth.
　　　　He stops wars all over the world;
　　　　he breaks bows and destroys spears, and sets shields
　　　　　　on fire.
　　　　'Stop fighting,' he says,
　　　　'and know that I am God,
　　　　supreme among the nations.
　　　　Supreme over the world.'

　　　　The Lord Almighty is with us;
　　　　the God of Jacob is our refuge.

Psalm 46: 1–3, 8–11

IDOLATRY

CHAPTER 15
▼

Which of the following activities are Christian, and which are unChristian?

1. Reading your horoscope every week.
2. Walking around ladders, because it is bad luck to walk under them.
3. Praying every night, asking God to help you make lots of money so that you can be really happy.
4. Water divining — using a forked stick to discover sources of water.
5. Doing astronomy — predicting the movements of the stars, planets and other heavenly bodies.
6. Doing astrology — studying the influence of the stars on human life.
7. Doing nothing except study, for a few months before an important examination, and having no time for any activity not related to work.
8. Performing conjuring tricks, making objects 'appear' and 'disappear'.
9. Staying in bed on Friday 13th, because it is a very unlucky day.
10. Making a Novena of prayer to help someone do well in their examinations.

Idolatry

Worship means giving God the honour, respect, praise, love and thanks that are due to God as the Creator of us all. When we worship God by praying or by celebrating the sacraments, we are showing that we depend on God completely, for everything — life, love, happiness, forgiveness, growth and peace. For a Christian, every good thought, word, action or feeling is in a sense a way of worshipping God, because without God there would be nothing at all.

Idolatry means behaving as if God were not God. It can mean treating someone or something as if it were God, or as if it had God's power. It can mean trying to use God, or make God do what I want by treating God as my servant. *The word 'idolatry' means to worship an idol, to give to someone or something the love, honour and praise that belongs only to God.*

The stories of the Old Testament show us how difficult it was for the Israelites to keep away from idols or false gods, and remain true to their covenant with God. The Canaanites who lived in the Promised Land worshipped a pagan god called Baal, whom they believed made their crops grow and gave them many children. It was very tempting for the Israelites to pray to Baal to see if he would make *their* crops improve. The prophets reminded the people that Baal, and Dagon, the god of the Philistines, and any other idols were only wooden or metal statues, totally unable to help or harm people because they were not real.

> 'They have mouths, but cannot speak, and eyes, but cannot see. They have ears, but cannot hear, and noses, but cannot smell. They have hands, but cannot feel, and feet but cannot walk.' (Psalm 115:5–7)

Most of us would not dream of praying to a tree, or a rock or a wooden idol, but many of us waste our time and make ourselves unhappy by 'worshipping' other idols. For example, many of us worship money, wealth and possessions. This does not mean that we bow down in front of a stack of money and pray to it. Worshipping money means that we think nothing is more important than money. We believe that money will make us happy and the more money we have the happier we will be. For people who worship money, anything that makes them financially rich is a good thing; anything that makes them financially poorer is a bad thing. In business, they believe that cheating people, paying poor wages, selling inferior goods is all right because the profits will be better. They believe that buying cheap goods which were made with slave labour in a developing

country is all right because then they will have more money to spend. They think that giving money to a charity, or to people in need, is stupid, because they want that money themselves. All of these attitudes and actions can show that money is the most important thing in a person's life.

Other people believe in luck — a mysterious force which follows them around causing good or bad things to happen to them. Some people think that 'luck' can be bribed or prevented from doing harm to them if they do certain actions so many times; or if they avoid doing certain actions on special days. Some people even believe that the stars and planets have power over them, and can make things happen to them. Still others believe in magic — special words and objects which can help human beings to control nature, other people, or events.

> Modern idolatry means thinking and acting as if something like money, luck, the stars, magic, success or even another person is the most important and powerful thing in the world. Idolatry means we are ignoring the fact that it is God who brings happiness, who shows us how to live, who is the Lord of the Universe.

The first commandment forbids us to worship anything or anyone except God. The greatest commandment tells us that we must 'love the Lord our God with all our heart, with all our mind, with all our soul and with all our strength'. Idolatry makes us believe that there might be another way to be happy, perhaps an easier way than the way God shows us. 'Magic' promises to be easier than working and sharing together. 'Money' seems to be an easier god than the real God, because it does not demand self-sacrifice or self-denial.

However, modern idols are just as useless as Baal and Dagon ever were. They cannot bring real happiness. Real happiness comes from loving other people and being loved by them. Real happiness means knowing that God loves us and will never abandon us. Every idol will let people down in the end because no idol can make people happy forever. Only love, which comes from God, can last forever.

Exercises

1. Examine again the statements at the beginning of the chapter. Which of them describe idolatry of some kind? Explain your answer.
2. (a) What kinds of things can be most important in the life of a teenager?
   (b) Can this be idolatry? Explain.
3. Give examples to show how teenagers can worship God, apart from praying and celebrating the sacraments.
4. Do you agree that love brings more happiness than an idol like money or power? Why? Why not?

Human Life is Sacred (*Irish Bishops' Pastoral*)

St Paul frequently warns us not to throw away the true freedom which Christ has brought us and revert to old forms of enslavement to passion and to false gods.

Modern [people] would be shocked to be accused of idolatry. But we have to ask whether the worship of false gods really has been abolished in our Western way of life. Perhaps money, alcohol, drugs and sex are being given a place and a status in modern secular society which is not too different from the place occupied by the gods of money, wine and sex in pagan times.

(Taken from paragraph 88)

Questions

1. What forms of idolatry do the bishops mention in this passage? Give examples to show how a teenager could become involved in these forms of idolatry.
2. Try to explain how idolatry is a form of enslavement.
3. Could pleasure become an idol or the most important thing in a person's life? Explain your answer.

Reflection: 'Then the Devil took Jesus to a very high mountain and showed him all the kingdoms of the world in all their greatness. "All this I will give you," the Devil said, "if you kneel down and worship me."

Then Jesus answered, "Go away, Satan! The scripture says, "Worship the Lord your God and serve only him!"

Then the Devil left Jesus; and angels came and helped him.'
Matthew 4:8–11

Action: Write an examination of conscience which would help young people to avoid idolatry in their lives, and encourage them to base their lives on God's love and power.

Psalm: To you alone, O Lord, to you alone,
    and not to us, must glory be given
    because of your constant love and faithfulness.

Why should the nations ask us, 'Where is your God?'
Our God is in heaven;
he does whatever he wishes.
Their gods are made of silver and gold,
    formed by human hands.

They have mouths but cannot speak,
    and eyes, but cannot see.
They have ears, but cannot hear,
    and noses, but cannot smell.

They have hands, but cannot feel,
    and feet, but cannot walk;
    they cannot make a sound.
May all who made them and who trust in them
    become like the idols they have made.

Trust in the Lord, you people of Israel.
He helps you and protects you.
Trust in the Lord, you priests of God.
He helps you and protects you.
Trust in the Lord, all you that worship him.
He helps you and protects you.

                  Psalm 115: 1–11

UNIT III

SCRIPTURE — THE OLD TESTAMENT

THE BIBLE

CHAPTER 16

Match the following Scripture references, Column A, with the correct type of literature, Column B. For example:
1. Philemon 1:1–25 = (f) a letter.

A.	B.
1. Philemon 1:1–25	(a) Poetry
2. Lamentations 1:1–4	(b) Myth*
3. Ruth 1:1–4:22	(c) Legal contract
4. Luke 8:4–8	(d) History
5. 2 Samuel 10:1–19	(e) Sermon
6. Genesis 6:1–8:19	(f) A letter
7. Psalm 67:1–7	(g) Wise sayings
8. Acts 2: 14–36	(h) Prayer
9. Nehemiah 10:28–29	(i) Parable
10. Proverbs 17:1–10	(j) Short story

* A *myth* is an imaginative story which uses symbols to get across its meaning or message.

The Bible

The Bible is not just a book. It is a library of books. The word 'Bible' comes from a Greek phrase 'ta biblia', meaning 'the books'. The Romans took this phrase and made it into a single word 'biblia' meaning 'the book'. It was in this form that it came into the English language and became the 'Bible'.

The people who wrote the different books of the Bible came from many different backgrounds, and had different interests and points of view. There were poets, composers, historians, short story writers, priests, penitents, teachers, farmers, fishermen, exiles, sick people, young, old, joyful and unhappy people. They lived at different times — from 1000 B.C. to 100 A.D. approximately. They lived in many different places — Jerusalem, Babylon and Ephesus, for example.

Stories were often passed on by word of mouth.

They were probably not aware that what they were writing would become part of 'the Bible', although they knew that their work was very important. Many of them wrote down stories and myths, heroic tales, poems and songs that had been passed on from generation to generation by word of mouth, or 'oral tradition'. Others wrote accounts of the history of their people, some of which had also been part of oral tradition, and some of which they had seen in their own lifetime. Some wrote prayers and hymns which were part of the community worship at the Temple in Jerusalem, and others wrote prayers of anguish while they suffered in exile, far from the Temple. (Many Israelites were forced to live in exile in Babylon from 721 BC to 583 BC.)

> The one thing that all of these writers had in common was that they were *inspired* by God to write as they did. All of their writings describe the way in which God acted in their lives, or in the life and history of their people. Because they were inspired, their writings tell us what God wants to tell us about God. That is why we call the Bible God's word.

To say that the writers of the Bible were inspired does not mean that God dictated to them what they were to write, or that they were like robots with no minds of their own. God inspired them by giving them a special insight or understanding of their relationship with God. God gave them the gift of being able to see more clearly what God is like and what God wants people to be like. Each of the writers wrote down what they believed about God to help the people of their own time to get to know God, to understand what God had done for them and to realise how much God loved them.

God speaks to us through the Scripture readings at Mass.

> God speaks to us today through these writings. When we read or listen to the Scriptures, God is communicating with us in a special way, telling us about God and about ourselves. God's word in Scriptures gives us a chance to get to know God personally, and to discover how God acts in our lives.

EXERCISES

1. Look back at the Scripture references given at the beginning of the chapter. In the case of each passage referred to, try to find out:
   (a) What kind of person wrote it;
   (b) What background or situation do you think the writer came from;
   (c) What message do you think the writer was trying to give in this passage;
   (d) Do you think that God is speaking to you in this passage? Explain.
2. What do the following Scripture passages tell us about the Bible?
   (a) 2 Timothy 3:15–17
   (b) Hebrews 1:1–2
   (c) 1 Peter 1:10–12
   (d) John 20:30–31
   (e) Isaiah 1:1
3. Give some examples of Scripture stories or poems or sayings which have a message for you.

Understanding the Bible

Because each of the Biblical writers was writing for the people of their own time, we sometimes find it difficult to understand what they mean. Part of the problem is that the books of the Bible were originally written in Hebrew, Greek or Aramaic, and the writers used ideas, symbols and customs from their own cultures to get across their messages. We are from a different culture, with our own customs and symbols, and so we sometimes do not understand the message because we do not understand the kind of language or symbols the writer is using. For example, blood was a very important symbol for the Biblical writers. In the account of the Covenant between God and the people at Mount Sinai, we read that:

'Moses took half the blood of the animals and put it in bowls; and the other half he threw against the altar. Then he took the Book of the Covenant, in which the Lord's commands were written, and read it aloud to the people. They said, "We will obey the Lord and do everything that he has commanded."

Then Moses took the blood in the bowls and threw it on the people. He said: "This is the blood that seals the covenant which the Lord made with you when He gave all these commands."'

This account might seem very odd to us, because we would not use blood to seal or finalise an agreement. In order to understand what this incident meant to the Israelites, and in order to understand what the message of this incident is for us today, we have to know that in the culture of the time, blood was a sign of life. When Moses threw the blood on the altar (which represented God) and on the people, it was a sign that God and the people now shared one life as partners in the Covenant. When we read this Scripture passage today, one message that God gives us is that God wants to be part of our lives, and wants us to share His life.

The better we understand the culture, language and symbols of the Bible, the more we will be able to understand what God's message is to us. The pope and bishops of the Church have a special vocation to help the rest of the community to understand God's word in Scriptures, and to teach us what it means for Christian life today.

EXERCISES

1. Are there any Scripture passages which you find difficult to understand? Ask your teacher and the other members of the class to help you find out what these passages mean.
2. Read each of the following Scripture passages. In each case explain:
   (a) What message do you think this passage had for the people at the time?
   (b) What message do you think it has for us today?
   (i) Ephesians 4:22–32
   (ii) 1 Peter 4:12–16
   (iii) Luke 5:27–32
   (iv) Exodus 3:7–10
   (v) Genesis 1:1–2:4
   (vi) Leviticus 5:1–13

Reflection: 'The word of God is alive and active, sharper than any double-edged sword. It cuts all the way through, to where soul and spirit meet, to where joints and marrow come together. It judges the desires and thoughts of man's heart.' Hebrews 4:12

Action: Find out about the Dead Sea Scrolls (copies of Scripture writings dating back to pre-Christian times) in your school or public library.

Psalm: Your word, O Lord, will last forever;
It is eternal in heaven.
Your word is a lamp to guide me
and a light for my path.

Treat me according to your constant love,
and teach me your commands.
I am your servant, give me understanding,
so that I may know your teachings.
Your teachings are wonderful;
I obey them with all my heart.
The explanation of your teachings gives light
and brings wisdom to the ignorant.

Psalm 119:89, 105, 124–125, 129–130

Some More Information

How the Books of the Bible are Organised

The sacred or inspired writings were organised into one book by special compilers or editors. An editor is someone who prepares something for publication, or receives it so that it is suitable for a particular book. An editor may also compile or collect a number of articles, stories or writings and put them in a particular order in a book.

God inspired people to gather the inspired writings together and put them in order. He gave these collectors, or editors, a special understanding so that they would know which writings to include in the 'Scriptures' and which to leave out. They often included more than one account of the same event or events, because the messages in the two accounts were both important (For example Genesis 1:1–2:4 and Genesis 2:5–25 are two accounts of creation.)

The Old Testament was being put together, or compiled, by the Jewish people for hundreds of years before Jesus was born. New writings were added and the different 'books' re-arranged as the centuries went by. The Old Testament, as we have it today, is organised into four main sections:

1. *The Pentateuch* — The first five books of the Bible. ('Pentateuch' means 'five scrolls'.)
2. *The Historical Books* — Joshua, Judges, Ruth, Samuel, Kings, Chronicles, Ezra, Nehemiah, Tobit, Judith, Esther and Maccabees.
3. *The Widsom Books* — Job, Psalms, Proverbs, Ecclesiastes, The Song of Songs, Wisdom and Ecclesiasticus.
4. *The Prophets* — Amos, Isaiah, Jeremiah and so on.

The New Testament was put together by the early Christian Church, and it is organised into three sections:

1. *The Gospels and Acts of the Apostles* — Matthew, Mark, Luke and John. (The Acts are a continuation of Luke's Gospel.)
2. *The Letters* — written by important Church leaders like Peter, Paul and John, to different Christian groups who had to live their faith in different situations.
3. *Revelation* — a mysterious book which uses many symbols to explain what the Kingdom of God will be like at the end of time.

THE CALL TO FAITH

CHAPTER 17

▼

ABRAHAM

The Call
Abram lived with his father Terah and his wife Sarai in the city of Ur. The family moved to Haran, where Terah died. Then the Lord spoke to Abram: 'Leave your native land, your relatives, and your father's home, and go to a country that I am going to show you. I will give you many descendants, and they will become a great nation.'

Abram left immediately with his wife Sarai and his nephew Lot whose father was dead. He took with him all his wealth and all his slaves, and set out for the land of Canaan.

When they arrived in Canaan, the Lord appeared to Abram and said to him, 'This is the country that I am going to give to your descendants.' Then Abram built an altar and worshipped the Lord. Then he moved on towards the southern part of Canaan.

Abram was a nomad, moving from place to place in search of grazing and water for his huge flocks of sheep, goats, cattle and other animals. Near Bethel he built an altar, and worshipped the Lord.

The Promise

Then Abram had a vision, and heard the Lord say to him, 'Do not be afraid, Abram. I will save you from danger and give you a great reward.'

But Abram answered, 'Sovereign Lord, what good will your reward do me, since I have no children? My only heir is Eliezer of Damascus. You have given me no children, and one of my slaves will inherit my property.'

Then he heard the Lord speaking to him again: 'This slave Eliezer will not inherit your property; your own son will be your heir.' The Lord took him outside and said, 'Look at the sky and try to count the stars; you will have as many descendants as that.'

Abram put his trust in the Lord, and because of this the Lord was pleased with him and accepted him.

The Sign of the Covenant

When Abram was ninety-nine years old, the Lord appeared to him and said, 'I am the Almighty God. Obey me and always do what is right. I will make my covenant with you and give you many descendants.' Abram bowed down with his face touching the ground, and God said, 'Your name will no longer be Abram, but Abraham, because I am making you the ancestor of many nations. You must no longer call your wife Sarai; from now on her name is Sarah. I will bless her and will give you a son by her. I will keep my promise to you and to your descendants in future generations as an everlasting covenant. I will be your God and the God of your descendants. I will give to you and to your descendants this land in which you are now a foreigner. The whole land of Canaan will belong to your descendants forever, and I will be their God.'

God said to Abraham, 'You also must agree to keep the covenant with me, both you and your descendants in future generations. You and your descendants must all agree to circumcise every male among you. From now on you must circumcise every baby boy when he is eight days old, including slaves born in your homes and slaves bought from foreigners.'

Abraham bowed down with his face touching the ground, but he began to laugh when he thought, 'Can a man have a child when he is a hundred years old? Can Sarah have a child at ninety?'

God said, 'Your wife Sarah will bear you a son and you will name him Isaac. I will keep my covenant with him and with his descendants forever. It is an everlasting covenant.' When God finished speaking to Abraham, He left him.

On that same day Abraham obeyed God and circumcised all the males in his household, including the slaves born in his home and those he had bought. Abraham was ninety-nine years old when he was circumcised.

Now Abraham and Sarah were very old. Sarah had stopped having her monthly periods. So Sarah laughed to herself and said, 'Now that I am old and worn out, can I still enjoy sex? And besides, my husband is old too.'

Then the Lord asked Abraham, 'Why did Sarah laugh and say, "Can I really have a child when I am so old?" Is anything too hard for the Lord? As I said, nine months from now Sarah will have a son.'

The Lord blessed Sarah, as he had promised, and she became pregnant and bore a son to Abraham when he was old. The boy was born at the time God had said he would be born. Abraham named him Isaac, and when Isaac was eight days old, Abraham circumcised him, as God had commanded. Abraham was a hundred years old when Isaac was born. Sarah said, 'God has brought me joy and laughter. Everyone who hears about it will laugh with me.' Then she added, 'Who would have said to Abraham that Sarah would nurse children? Yet I have borne him a son in his old age.'

The Test

When Isaac was a young boy, God tested Abraham; he called to him, 'Abraham!' And Abraham answered, 'Yes, here I am!'

'Take your son,' God said, 'your only son, Isaac, whom you love so much, and go to the land of Moriah. There on a mountain that I will show you, offer him as a sacrifice to me.'

Early the next morning Abraham cut some wood for the sacrifice, loaded his donkey, and took Isaac and two servants with him. They started out for the place that God had told him about. On the third day Abraham saw the place in the distance. Then he said to the servants, 'Stay here with the donkey. The boy and I will go over there and worship, and then we will come back to you.'

Abraham made Isaac carry the wood for the sacrifice, and he himself carried a knife and live coals for starting the fire. As they walked along together, Isaac said, 'Father!' He answered, 'Yes, my son?'

Isaac asked, 'I see that you have the coals and the wood, but where is the lamb for the sacrifice?'

Abraham answered, 'God himself will provide one.' And the two of them walked on together.

When they came to the place which God had told him about, Abraham built an altar and arranged the wood on it. He bound his son and placed him on the altar, on top of the wood. Then he picked up the knife to kill him.

But the angel of the Lord called to him from heaven, 'Abraham, Abraham!' He answered, 'Yes, here I am.'

'Don't hurt the boy or do anything to him,' He said. 'Now I know that you fear God, because you have not kept back your only son from him.'

Abraham looked round and saw a ram caught in a bush by its horns. He went and got it and offered it as a burnt offering instead of his son.

The angel of the Lord called to Abraham from heaven a second time, 'I make a vow by my own name — the Lord is speaking — that I will richly bless you. Because you did this and did not keep back your only son from me, I promise that I will give you as many descendants as there are stars in the sky or grains of sand along the seashore. Your descendants will conquer their enemies. All the nations will ask me to bless them as I have blessed your descendants — all because you obeyed my command.'

Abraham died at the ripe old age of 175. He was buried in Machpelah Cave in the field east of Mamre. It was the field that Abraham had bought some years earlier as a burial ground for Sarah. This was the only part of the Promised Land that Abraham ever owned. It was his descendants over 400 years later, who inherited what God had promised.

(Adapted from Genesis 11:27–25:10)

Some Notes on the Story

Abraham: This name sounds like the Hebrew words for 'ancestor of many nations'.

Covenant: This was a special agreement between God and Abraham. God promised to give the Land of Canaan to Abraham's descendants, and Abraham *promised to trust in God.*

The Sacrifice of Isaac: Child sacrifice was very common in the religions of the time in the Middle East. So Abraham would not have thought of God's request as strange, even though he was heartbroken.

Questions

1. What is your reaction to these stories? Does anything surprise you or shock you?
2. What kind of a person was Abraham?
3. What kind of a person was Sarah?
4. What picture of God do you get from these stories?
5. What do you think is the most important moment in Abraham's life? Why?
6. Every story in Scripture has a message or a meaning. What meaning or message is there in the life-story of Abraham?

A Person of Faith

Abraham's story tells us about the origins of God's chosen people. It tells us that God chose someone from Mesopotamia, and called him to start a new life. God promised him that his descendants would become a great nation, and that the name of Abraham would be famous forever. Because Abraham trusted and obeyed God, God's promise was fulfilled. Abraham's descendants became the People of Israel, God's Chosen People.

Abraham's story also describes the journey of faith that we must travel, if we want to get to know God and live with God forever.

Young people have to decide how to answer the call they received in Baptism.

> God called Abraham to believe in Him and to follow His plan. God also calls us through other people, through the stories in the Scriptures and through the events in our lives. This call asks us to believe in God and to trust in Him. God asks us to follow His plan in our lives, to love God and each other, to be just in our relationships and even to do good to those who hate us.

Like Abraham, we have a choice. We can ignore God's call, or we can do what God asks of us. Many young people are born into Christian families. They hear God's call through their parents and through their religion class in school. Each young person has to decide whether to answer this call or not — to trust in God and do what God asks, or to say no to God's plan.

Just like Abraham, we have no guarantee that our faith journey will be an easy one. It is only when we do what God asks of us that we will discover the truth as Abraham did. There will be times in our lives when we will see for certain that our faith in God is worthwhile, when good things happen to us, and we realise how much God helps us in different ways. For example, a student might ask God to help him to study and to concentrate on his work so that he will do well in an exam. In spite of the temptations from television or friends, the student manages to keep to his study plan and does very well in the exam. This student would feel very grateful to God and would realise just how much God has helped him.

At other times we will be tested, we will feel unsure and even heartbroken. Times of suffering are often times when our faith is tested. When someone we love falls sick and dies, in spite of our prayers, we can find it very hard to have faith, and trust in God. The example of Abraham shows us that we can still trust in God no matter what happens, and that one day God will show us the meaning of what we do not understand now. This is what it means to be a person of faith—to keep on trusting in God no matter what happens.

Prayer helps us to trust God.

Exercises

1. Pick out the words and phrases which show that Abraham trusted God completely.
2. (a) How do you think you might have responded to God's call to leave your home forever, if you had been Abraham?
   (b) How would you have reacted when God asked you to give up what you loved most in the world?
3. Give some examples to show how teenagers can have faith in God, by doing what God asks of them.
4. Have there ever been times when you have felt certain that your trust in God was worthwhile? Explain.
5. Have you ever found it difficult to have faith in God? Explain.

Assignment

Write a story about a person who had faith in God. You can base the story on the life of a real person, or make it up yourself.

Reflection: 'To have faith is to be sure of the things we hope for, to be certain of the things we cannot see. It was by their faith that people of ancient times won God's approval.'
Hebrews 11:1–2

Action: In your prayers, ask God to give you greater faith, and to help you to show this faith in your actions.

Psalm: Praise the Lord!
    Happy are those who fear the Lord,
        who greatly delight in his commandments.
    Their descendants will be mighty in the land;
    the generation of the upright will be blessed.

    It is well with those who deal generously and kindly,
        who conduct their affairs with justice.
    For the righteous will never be moved:
    they will be remembered forever.
    They are not afraid of evil tidings;
    their hearts are firm, secure in the Lord.

Psalm 112: 1–2, 5–7

THE PROMISED LAND

CHAPTER 18
▼

The Promised Land! A land flowing with milk and honey! Not flowing with gold and silver, however. God never promised to make the people fabulously wealthy. Instead, God promised them a fertile land where they could be comfortable and at home. In this land God would teach them how to live as His people, and prepare them for the Saviour of the world.
(*Note: all of the following dates are approximate*)

The Promise

1850 B.C. *Abraham* was the first to be told about the Promised Land. His descendants would own this land one day. Abraham's son *Isaac* and his grandsons *Esau* and *Jacob* settled down in Canaan.

God gave Jacob a new name, *Israel*. The descendants of Israel and his twelve sons were called *Israelites*, or the *Twelve Tribes of Israel*.

1750 B.C. *Joseph*, Israel's favourite son, was sold as a slave by his brothers and sent to Egypt, where he became the Prime Minister through the power of God. Joseph's family went to live in Egypt as honoured guests when there was a famine in Canaan. After a time, however, the Israelites became the slaves of the Egyptians and lived in misery.

1250 B.C. God called *Moses* to rescue the Israelites and lead them back to the Promised Land. The shortest way to the Promised Land was along the coast, but this was too dangerous, so the Israelites headed south-east into the wilderness of the Sea of Reeds (sometimes called the Red Sea). The Israelites got through the sea safely, but the Egyptians got caught by the returning tide.

The Twelve Tribes of Israel.

The Wilderness

1250 B.C. God made a *Covenant* with the Israelites at Mount Sinai and gave them the Law.

God gave instructions for a special tent to be built. This was to be God's 'home' with the people. The Tent is also called the *Tabernacle*.

Inside the Tabernacle was the '*Covenant Box*' or '*Ark of the Covenant*', a sign of God's presence with the people.

In spite of this the Israelites were afraid to try and take over the Promised Land when they reached it. They said:

'Why should we go there? We are afraid. The men we sent tell us that the people there are taller and stronger than we are, and that they live in cities with walls that reach the sky. They saw giants there.'
(Deuteronomy 1:28)

The Israelites wandered in the desert wilderness for forty years before they were ready to trust in God and enter the Promised Land.

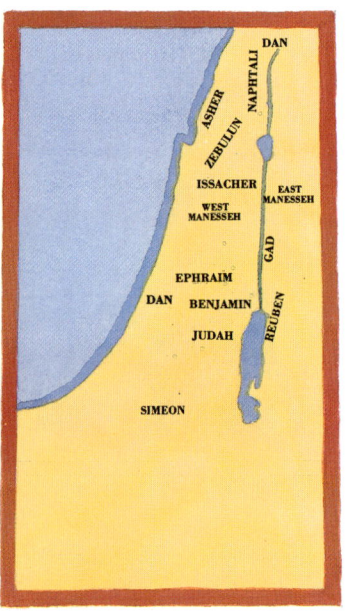

The Land

1200 B.C. When Moses died, *Joshua* became the new leader. He was a great military commander who had complete trust in God. According to the Book of Joshua, the Israelites defeated the Canaanites and began to divide up the land among the different tribes.

The Tabernacle

The *Levites* were one of the twelve tribes of Israel. Their special job was to take care of the Tabernacle. A special group of Levites, called *priests*, offered the sacrifices to God. The rest of the Levites had less important jobs connected with the worship of God, for example, composing and singing hymns for the great feasts. The Levites were also the teachers of the Law of God.

The Levites did not own any land. Forty-eight towns in the land were set aside for them, and everyone had to give a tenth of all their harvests and livestock to support the Levites.

The Ark of the Covenant was first brought to Shechem. Later it was kept at Shiloh. Eventually, in the time of David, it was brought to Jerusalem. The people gathered at the place where the Ark was kept to celebrate important festivals, like the Passover.

The Judges

1150 B.C. The Israelites had to defend their new land from many attacks. The Moabites, the Ammonites, the Amelekites and others all wanted to rule the land. When the Israelites remained faithful to God, they always defeated their enemies.

However, some of the Israelites forgot their Covenant with God, and began to worship the idols of the Canaanites. When the Israelites were unfaithful to God in this way, they could not defeat their enemies. God called special people to be leaders or *'Judges'* of the people at this time. They helped the people to defeat their enemies and reminded the people of God's Covenant. *Deborah* helped the Israelites to defeat Jabin, a Caneanite king. Gideon helped them to defeat the Midianites.

Samson was a judge, but he never led the Israelites into battle. He was famous for fighting the Philistines single-handed. Even when they captured him and blinded him, he managed to destroy the temple of their god, Dagon, with his bare hands.

The Kings

1020 B.C. The last judge, *Samuel*, was told by God to anoint *Saul* as the first king of the Israelites. Under Saul, the Tribes of Israel became more united. God protected them, and prevented them from being conquered by more powerful nations, especially the Philistines.

1000 B.C. God chose David, a young shepherd boy and gifted musician, to be the next King of Israel.

One famous story tells how young David killed a Philistine giant, Goliath, who was nine feet tall.

When David became king, he made Jerusalem his capital city. He was Israel's greatest king, who conquered Syria, Moab, Ammon and Edom and made Israel into an empire.

Although he was not perfect, David was faithful to God and to the Covenant. When he brought the Covenant Box, the sign of God's presence, from Shiloh to Jerusalem, he danced with all his might to honour the Lord. His wife Michal thought this was undignified for a king. God was pleased with David, and Israel was not attacked by a foreign power during his forty-year reign.

961 B.C. When David died, his son *Solomon* became king. Solomon made the nation even stronger by making treaties with surrounding nations, and marrying foreign princesses. He built the *Temple in Jerusalem*, and placed the Ark of the Covenant in it, in the *Holy of Holies*.

He also built places of worship where his foreign wives could worship their own gods, and soon he himself began to worship other gods.

The Divided Kingdom

922 B.C. When Solomon died, his son *Rehoboam* became king. However, many of the people were fed up with having an expensive king who imposed heavy taxes. *Jeroboam*, one of Solomon's officials, led the northern tribes in a rebellion against Rehoboam. He set up a separate kingdom called *'Israel'*. The southern kingdom was called *'Judah'*. Jeroboam set up new centres of worship for the northern kingdom, now that it was cut off from Jerusalem in the south. From now on the people of the south considered themselves to be the proper 'people of God', because they continued to worship at Jerusalem. They were suspicious of the northerners and regarded them as heretics. The two kingdoms were never united again. Later the people saw this as a punishment for Solomon's idolatry. But worse was to follow.

860 B.C. The *prophets* were called by God to remind the people of the Covenant, and to lead them back to God. *Elijah*, *Elisha*, *Amos* and *Hosea* warned the northern kingdom, Israel, what would happen if they did not repent, but the king and people took no notice.

721 B.C. A divided country was very hard to defend against invasion. Israel was conquered by the Assyrians around 721 B.C. Many of the people were deported to exile in *Assyria*, and some Assyrians were brought as colonists to the northern kingdom.

715 B.C. Prophets like *Isaiah* and *Jeremiah* warned the southern kingdom, Judah, to return to God's way. The people refused to listen.

The Exile

586 B.C. The Babylonians conquered Jerusalem, the capital of Judah, and the southern kingdom was devastated. Many Israelites were taken into captivity in *Babylon*.

These were the darkest days in Israel's history, since the slavery in Egypt. The hearts of the exiles were broken when they remembered Jerusalem, or Zion, now in ruins.

The Israelites would meet in groups in their exile to study and to pray together. Later in their history, their meeting places would be called *synagogues*.

The prophets reminded them that the exile was their punishment for sin, but that God would forgive them, and keep faithful to the Covenant.

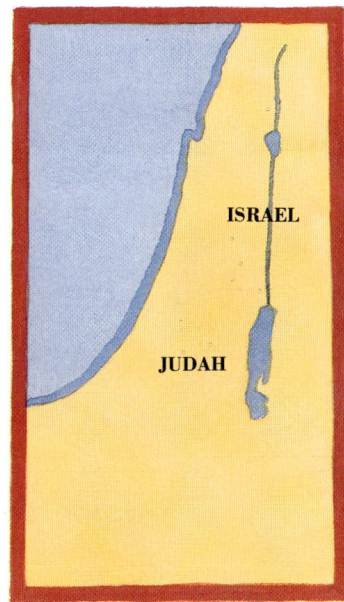

The Return

538 B.C. Eventually the exiles were allowed to return home. This was like a second escape from Egypt, another *Exodus*. The people rebuilt the Temple, and renewed their Covenant promises in a special ceremony. The people of *Samaria* never returned to worship at the Temple in Jerusalem. Many of them married foreigners, and they were despised by the other descendants of ancient Israel.

The Israelites were still part of a foreign empire and not allowed to govern themselves. They concentrated on religious affairs.

Through the Biblical writers, God continued to teach the people that they were still a great nation because they were God's people, even though they did not have political power. They continued to meet in synagogues and to worship at the Temple. Many continued to pray for a *Saviour*, a Messiah who would 'restore the kingdom' to the Israelites.

After the return from exile, the Israelites became the 'People of a Book'. *The Law*, following the law and studying the law became the most important thing in the life of a Jew.

Thousands of laws were made by the leaders, to try and help the people to put the law into practice in every tiny detail of their lives. In this way they hoped to do what God wanted and to show their love and respect for Him. People who were experts in the law were called *scribes* or *lawyers* or *rabbis*.

The Greeks

333 B.C. The land became part of the Greek Empire of Alexander the Great in 333 B.C. It was known as *Palestine* by this time. The Israelites were influenced by many Greek ideas. For example, the Scriptures were translated from Hebrew into Greek. However, the Israelites still tried to remain faithful to the Covenant and the Law.

After Alexander's death, Palestine was ruled by one of his generals, as part of an empire based in Antioch in Syria. At first the Israelites were allowed to follow their own religion, but later the Greek *Syrians* tried to force them to worship other gods.

Some Jews abandoned their religion, but others refused. Some of them used passive resistance against their oppressors and many died rather than worship idols. They were called the '*Hasidim*' or the 'pious' people.

Others revolted against their oppressors. *Mattathias*, a priest from Modein, his sons and their followers used a form of guerrilla warfare against the Syrians. These fighters became known as the Maccabees, after the third son *Judas*, who was nicknamed '*Maccabeus*' or the 'Hammer'.

Exactly three years after the first pagan sacrifices had been made on the old altar of the Temple, the Maccabees set up and dedicated a new altar. Every year since, the Jews have celebrated the *Feast of Dedication*, or *Hanukkah*, to remember this event.

The Romans

63 B.C. After the Maccabean revolt, the Israelites became practically independent for the next eighty years. However in 63 B.C. they were conquered by the Roman general, *Pompey the Great*, and became part of the *Roman Empire*. The Romans allowed *Herod Antipater* and his family to rule Palestine for them. His grandson, *Herod Antipas*, was the ruler of Galilee at the time of Jesus.

The Romans allowed the Jews to have religious freedom and to follow their own religious authorities. The Council of Priests, called the *Sanhedrin*, had a lot of power in religious affairs and could also act as judges for their people. They could decide if someone was guilty or not, and give punishments, but it seems that they were not allowed to execute anyone.

The Sadducees

Most of the people in the *Sanhedrin* were *Sadducees*, from wealthy priestly families. They wanted to keep their power, and so they were in favour of obeying the Romans and not causing any trouble. Sadducees believed in the Torah, the first five books of the Old Testament, but they did not believe in the later teachings.

The Pharisees

Another group of Jews were called *Pharisees*. They were mostly ordinary Jews, not priests, who tried to keep the law of God very strictly. They believed that anyone who did not follow the thousands of tiny rules about the right way to act, eat, wash, pray and so on, was a sinner. They were not interested in politics, but they believed that one day God would send the Messiah who would restore the kingdom of David. They accepted both the Torah and the later writings of the Old Testament. This meant that they believed in the resurrection of the body, and judgment after death. *St Paul* was a Pharisee before he became a Christian.

The Zealots

Another group of Jews, called the *Zealots*, tried to continue the war of independence started by Judas Maccabeus. They believed that God would set up the kingdom through war, and they were ready to fight. They refused to pay taxes to the Romans and started many revolts against them. Simon, one of Jesus' disciples, was probably a Zealot before he followed Jesus.

The Essenes

The *Essenes* were a small group of Jews who believed that the rest of Jewish society was evil; they even accused the Pharisees of being too soft in the way they followed the law! Most Essenes opted out of ordinary society and lived in well organised groups in the wilderness. They lived very simply and spent much of their time praying and studying the Scriptures. They believed that God would set up the kingdom very soon, in a dramatic way.

The Kingdom of God

About 24 A.D. *Jesus*, a carpenter from Nazareth, began to preach in Galilee. 'The right time has come,' he said, 'and the *Kingdom of God* is near! Turn away from your sins and believe the Good News!' The Sadducees and Pharisees were suspicious of this 'trouble-maker'. The Zealots lost interest when Jesus refused to let them crown him as king, to lead the rebellion against the Romans. Many people believed in Jesus, but even his closest followers found it hard to understand that the Kingdom of God was not a political state, like the Kingdom of David. Jesus taught them that the Kingdom of God was something greater than the Promised Land, it was greater than the whole world. Everyone could be a part of God's Kingdom if they said 'yes' to God's invitation.

After his resurrection, Jesus said to his disciples:
'I have been given all authority in heaven and on earth. Go, then, to all peoples everywhere and make them my disciples . . .'

EXERCISES

1. Make a list of the most important people and events in the history of the Israelites and the Promised Land. (You could do this in the form of a time-line.)
2. What does this history tell us about God? What does it tell us about people?
3. Does this history have any message or meaning for people today? Explain your answer.

The History of Salvation

The people of Israel believed that God had chosen them to be the People of God. In fact, they believed that they only became a people, or a nation, because God chose them. They were not chosen because they were special, or important, or clever. They felt that God had deliberately chosen a poor, scattered people so that God could make them great.

> When they looked back at their history, the Israelites could see God at work, saving them, rewarding them, punishing and scolding them. They believed that God was the Lord of History. Their history showed them that when they were faithful to their Covenant with God, they prospered, they were happy and content. When they turned their back on God and the Covenant, trouble followed. Inspired writers put the traditions and histories of the people into writing, to preserve them for the people of the time and for future generations. They hoped that by reading and listening to these Scriptures, the people would realise how God was at work in their lives, and turn back to God with faith.

Some of the history of salvation, or the history of God's saving acts in the lives of the people, makes strange reading for us, unless we understand the background of the people at the time. For example, the God of the Old Testament often seems very vindictive to us, cruel and harsh at times towards the people. We know that God is a God of love, and sometimes the God of the Old Testament does not seem to be very loving.

In order to understand this, we have to remember that the history of the Old Testament is the story of a people who were gradually getting to know God. Through the prophets and in His saving actions, God slowly told the people more and more about Himself. Finally, God sent Jesus, to show us more fully than ever before who God is and who God wants us to be. The people of the Old Testament knew that God was completely good, and therefore that He hated evil. That is why we read in the psalms, for example:

'He will pay them back for all their sins;
he will silence their wickedness.
Yahweh our God will silence them.'
Psalm 94:23 (Jerusalem Bible)

Another psalmist even prayed that God would take revenge on his enemy in the following way:

'May his children be homeless vagabonds,
beggared and hounded from their hovels;
may the creditor seize his possessions
and foreigners swallow his profits!'
Psalm 109:10–11 (Jerusalem Bible)

As far as these writers were concerned, people who committed evil and turned their backs on God deserved everything they got. However, many other parts of the Old Testament, including many psalms, tell us that God is full of forgiveness, mercy and compassion towards even the worst sinners:

'The Lord is merciful and loving,
slow to become angry and full of constant love.
He does not keep on rebuking;
he is not angry for ever.
He does not punish us as we deserve
or repay us for our sins and wrongs.
As high as the sky is above the earth,
so great is his love for those who
honour him'.
Psalm 103:8–11

When we read about God's 'anger and hatred,' we should remember that this refers to God's opposition to evil. God is angry when people are treated unjustly. God hates cruelty and meanness. Many passages in both the Old and New Testaments show that, although God hates evil, He loves people and wants to forgive them. In the Old Testament it is clear that God punishes people so that they will return to Him, and not because He is mean and nasty.

> Today, we are inclined to forget how important it is to turn away from evil. We can be tempted to ignore the fact that evil destroys our lives. The history of the people of Israel in the Old Testament, with its strong language and its reminder that evil brings punishment, can encourage us to make efforts to fight our own sinful tendencies and try to live a life of love.

Exercises

1. Are there any passages in Scriptures or events in the history of the Old Testament which seem to show God in a bad light? Explain.
2. Try to explain why the writer might have described God and His actions in this way.
3. Are there any other passages in the Scriptures which give us another view of God? Explain.
4. Do you think you could learn all there is to know about God from just one or two passages from the Scriptures? Explain your answer.

The Bible Group: an Owner's Manual (Fr William Riley, 1983)

... we should remember the purpose of the Old Testament: it is meant to take people from a situation far from God and to lead them, step by step, to Him — to prepare people for the full message of God made known in Jesus. Though I may not like to admit it, there is a lot which is non-Christian in me, a lot which needs something to prepare me to hear the word of Jesus in a particular corner of my own life. The Old Testament can speak to that part of me when the New Testament would fall on deaf ears. The love commandments of the New Testament are wonderful, but they can be empty platitudes* if I still need to learn the lessons of social justice and human dignity from the Old Testament.

* *meaningless statements*

Questions

1. According to this passage, what is the purpose of the Old Testament?
2. Do you find anything difficult in the teachings of Jesus? Explain.
3. Is it possible to really love another person and still treat that person unjustly? Explain.

Reflection: 'The Lord your God is bringing you into a fertile land — a land that has rivers and springs, and underground streams gushing out into the valleys and hills; a land that produces wheat and barley, grapes, figs, pomegranates, olives and honey. There you will never go hungry or ever be in need. Its rocks have iron in them, and from its hills you can mine copper. You will have all you want to eat, and you will give thanks to the Lord your God for the fertile land that He has given you.'
Deuteronomy 8:7–10

Action: Make a series of wall charts or posters showing the history of the people of Israel. Display them around the school.

Psalm: With our own ears we have heard it, O God—
    our ancestors have told us about it,
    about the great things you did in their time,
    in the days of long ago;
    how you yourself drove out the heathen
    and established your people in their land;
    how you punished the other nations
    and caused your own to prosper.

    Your people did not conquer the land with their swords;
    they did not win it by their own power;
    it was by your power and your strength,
    by the assurance of your presence
    which showed that you loved them.

    You are my King and my God;
    you give victory to your people,
    and by your power we defeat our enemies.

    I do not trust in my bow
    or in my sword to save me;
    but you have saved us from our enemies
    and defeated those who hate us.
    We will always praise you
    and give thanks to you forever.

            Psalm 44: 1–8

PROPHETS

CHAPTER 19
▼

DIARY: PRIVATE AND CONFIDENTIAL.
ALL RIGHTS RESERVED, NO PHOTOCOPYING.

Thursday

Yesterday I fell over some concrete blocks and broke my arm. Unfortunately it was my right arm, and I'm left-handed. Luckily Miss O'Connor thinks I'm right-handed, so I don't have to do any written work in English until my arm is better. My Dad asked Mr Ryan if I could get any compensation from the builders. Mr Ryan said he didn't think so, because the blocks had been locked away in our neighbour's shed when I fell over them.

Everyone on our street seems to be getting blocks, bags of cement and heaps of sand delivered. Mr Ryan says it's because of the subsidence. All the houses on our side of the street have it. It means that some of the walls are sinking slowly into the ground. Most of our neighbours have already built new walls or put up cement props to keep up the old ones. My dad says they're a crowd of fools. He says it's all a plot by the builders to make more money.

Friday

Mr Ryan had an architect round to his house today, to see what had to be done. Afterwards he sent her round to check our house for us. My dad said he wasn't paying any dressed-up, smart-aleck woman to find things wrong with *his* house. Mrs Keenan said that Mr Ryan was paying her fee. So Dad let her survey the house. She said that the back wall showed signs of severe stress. If it wasn't fixed it would fall down in three months. Dad laughed at her all the way to her car. He told her to stay at home and take care of her family, and not waste her time doing a man's job. Mrs Keenan just said, 'I'll send you my report, Mr MacMonagle,' and drove off.

Monday

Mr Ryan has the builders in next door. Mam told him yesterday what the architect said, and told him she was really worried about the back wall. So he sent one of the builders over to talk to Dad. The builder was a big man, a lot bigger than Dad. Dad was very polite to him, and brought him round the back to look at the wall. I had nothing better to do, so I followed them. (It's hard to play football with a broken arm.)

The builder looked at the wall and said that if a cat sneezed in its direction it would fall down. He advised Dad to have it seen to as soon as possible. 'I'm all booked up for the next few months, but I could recommend someone if you like,' he added. Dad said, 'You don't say?' and 'Really' and 'Imagine that'. When the builder had gone, Dad told me to go round to Mr Ryan and tell him to mind his own business in future. I told Mr Ryan that Dad thought there was nothing much wrong with the back wall. 'I see,' said Mr Ryan with a sigh. 'I'm thinking of sleeping in the sitting room for a few days,' I said. 'It's at the front of the house, but my bedroom is at the back.' I knew then that Mr Ryan was having difficulty keeping his temper. He began walking around the room muttering things like 'Blundering fool' and 'He'll kill someone with his carelessness'. Then he sat down again, and looked at me. 'Not to worry, Joseph,' he said, 'we'll think of something.'

Wednesday

Christopher Ryan called today. He's Mr Ryan's son. He's an engineer with a big construction firm in the city. Dad wasn't in when he called, but Mam was delighted to see him, and made him have tea and biscuits. She asked him to take a look at the back wall. While Christopher was examining it, Dad came home. He came out the back to see what we were doing. When he saw Christopher measuring the huge crack beside the kitchen window, he went mad. He grabbed Christopher under the chin and pushed him up against the wall. Mam shouted at him to stop, but Dad took no notice. 'What-do-you-think-you're-doing?' yelled Dad, banging Christopher's head off the bricks at every word. Mam and I rushed in to help Christopher. Then something hit me on the head and everything went black. When I woke up I was in hospital (with Christopher in the opposite bed). Apparently the wall couldn't take the strain, and it began to break up because of the hammering it was getting. Both Christopher and I have concussion, but Dad didn't get a scratch. The nurse is taking away my diary now. She says I have to rest.

Friday

When I got home from hospital this morning the builders were already working on the back wall. Mr Ryan is lending Dad the money to pay them. I don't know what Christopher thinks about it, his dad lending money to the man who attacked him. I suppose if he's anything like Mr Ryan he'll just forgive and forget.

It would be nice if Miss O'Connor would do the same. My mam got a note from her yesterday, asking why I can do all my other written work but not my English with my broken arm. I wonder how she found out? Mam says I have to catch up on all my English written work by Monday. It's just not fair.

QUESTIONS

1. What is your reaction to this story?
2. What kind of person is Mr MacMonagle?
3. What kind of person is Mr Ryan?
4. Why do you think Mr Ryan sent other people to talk to Mr MacMonagle rather than going himself? Do you think he did the right thing?
5. Why did Mr MacMonagle reject the advice of the architect, the builder and Christopher?
6. How do you think Mr MacMonagle feels about Mr Ryan now?

Prophets

The word 'prophet' comes from the Greek word 'prophetes', which means 'one who speaks in place of another', or a spokesperson. The builder, the architect and Christopher acted like prophets, speaking on behalf of Mr Ryan. They pointed out to Mr MacMonagle that his house was in a dangerous condition. They explained what would soon happen if nothing was done to improve the house. Unfortunately for Mr MacMonagle (and Joseph and Christopher) their prophecies came true. If Mr MacMonagle had listened to the messages of the three prophets, the accident need never have happened.

> In the Old Testament, a prophet was someone who was called to be a spokesperson for God, to give God's message to the people. Moses was a prophet, who brought God's message of freedom to an enslaved and suffering people. Through Moses, God established a special relationship with these, God's Chosen People, sealed by the Covenant at Mount Sinai. People like Elijah, Isaiah and Jeremiah, who spoke to the people in God's name, can be called prophets.

QUESTIONS

1. What do you usually associate with the word prophet? In what way is this similar to the Old Testament view of a prophet? Is it different in any way? Explain.
2. Give examples from modern life of people who could be called prophets. Why would you call each of them a prophet?
3. What do you know about any of the prophets in the Bible? Briefly explain.

Prophets in the Old Testament

The Old Testament contains the writings and recorded speeches of prophets such as Amos, Hosea, Isaiah, Micah and Jeremiah. Each of these prophets were called by God to remind the people of their Covenant with God and the promises they had made. Each of the prophets was inspired by God to see the religious meaning of what was happening in the country at the time, and to warn the people of what would happen to them if they did not repent and turn back to God.

The basic message of the prophets was that without God, and without their special relationship with God, the people of Israel had no future. If they were unfaithful to the Covenant they were cutting themselves off from God.

Although the prophets were speaking to the people of their time, and talking about what was happening then, their prophecies have important messages for us today also. Through the prophetic writing of the Old Testament, God tells us about our relationship with God and with each other, and warns us of the consequences of living without love and justice.

Amos

Amos was a shepherd from the town of Tekoa in Judah, the Southern Kingdom of the Promised Land. At the time of Amos, the country was divided in two — Israel in the North and Judah in the South. Amos was called by God to prophesy at Bethel, in the Northern Kingdom of Israel. He told the people that they would be defeated by a foreign power and many of them would be carried off into exile. This would happen because they had sinned and refused to keep their Covenant with God.

The people, and especially the leaders, were outraged because they were very happy with their lives. The economy was doing well and everyone took part in the festivals to worship God with prayers and sacrifices. Amos pointed out to them that the economy was only making the rich richer and the poor poorer. He said that their society was full of injustice against the poor and the oppressed. He told them that God was disgusted by their worship and their feasts because it was all hypocrisy. Amos said that God wanted to be worshipped with justice and good deeds, and not just with words and burnt offerings.

Amaziah, the chief priest at the sanctuary of Bethel, ordered Amos out of the kingdom, saying he was a public menace. Amos was lucky to escape with his life.

Shortly after Amos was deported, the Northern Kingdom was destroyed and the people taken into exile by the Assyrians.

EXERCISES

Look up the references to find the answers to each of the following questions.
1. Who told Amos what to say to the people of Israel? Amos 1:1; 7:12–15

2. In what ways have the people sinned? Amos 2:6–8; 5:10–13; 8:4–6
3. How will the people be punished? Amos 3:10–4:3; 6:14; 7:10–17
4. How will God treat the people after they have been punished? Amos 9:11–15
5. Do you think Amos has any message for us today? Explain, with reference to the passages mentioned above.

ASSIGNMENT

(a) Read the following 'Letter to Amos', which might have been written by the people of the society he was speaking to in God's name.

(b) Write a letter to these people, in response to their letter, stating whether you agree or disagree with the points they have made, and why.

Letter to Amos

Dear Mr Amos,

Your intemperate criticisms of the merchants of Bethel show that you have little understanding of the operations of a modern business economy. You appear not to understand that a businessman is entitled to a profit. A cobbler sells shoes to make as much money as he can. A banker lends money to get a return on his loan. These are not charitable enterprises. Without profits, a tradesman cannot stay in business.

Your slanders also reveal a lack of appreciation for the many contributions made to our land by the business community. Visitors to Israel are greatly impressed by the progress made in the past few decades. The beautiful public buildings and private homes are a proud monument. Increasing contacts with foreign lands add to the cultural opportunities open to our citizens. Our military strength makes us the envy of peoples already swallowed up by their enemies.

Despite the great gains during Jereboam II's reign, there is some poverty. That we admit. But is it just to blame us for the inability of some people to compete? You say that the peasants were cheated out of their lands. Not so! They sold their property. Or in some cases, it was sold for back taxes. Some peasants put up the land as collateral on a loan, then failed to meet the payments. No one was cheated. The transactions to which you refer were entirely legal. Had you taken the trouble to investigate the facts, your conclusions would have been more accurate.

The real reason for poverty is lack of initiative. People who get ahead in this world work hard, take risks, overcome obstacles. Dedication and determination are the keys to success. Opportunities don't knock, they are created by imagination and industry.

Our success can be an inspiration to the poor. If we can make it, they can too. With the growth of business, Israel grows. More jobs, better pay and increased opportunity for everyone. The old saying contains more than a germ of truth: What's good for General Chariots is good for the country.

Yours for Israel.

Taken from *'Far-out ideas for Youth Groups'* by Wayne Rice and Mike Yaconelli

The Work of Justice (*Irish Bishops' Pastoral*)
The message of all the prophets is the same. For centuries the Church has introduced Lent on Ash Wednesday with the words of Isaiah about what is required for our fasting to be more sincere. We have to set about 'breaking unjust fetters . . ., letting the oppressed go free . . ., sharing your bread with the hungry and sheltering the homeless poor' (Isaiah 58:6–10).

Another prophet, Jeremiah, is used by the Church as a special source for her message of repentance and conversion. He insists that true religion demands conversion, conversion of the heart and conversion of our lives. He warns that, unless we 'amend our behaviour and our actions' and cease to exploit the poor, merely coming to the Temple of the Lord will not save us. (Jeremiah 7:1–11)

(Paragraphs 8 and 9)

QUESTIONS

1. What is the message of the prophets?
2. What is the real fasting described in Isaiah 58:6–10?
3. According to Jeremiah, what is real religion?
4. How would teenagers show that they have real religion?
5. Do you think the prophets are telling us that we do not need to go to the 'Temple' or church at all? Explain your answer.

Reflection: '... Jesus went to a town called Nain, accompanied by his disciples and a large crowd. Just as he arrived at the gate of the town, a funeral procession was coming out. The dead man was the only son of a woman who was a widow, and a large crowd from the town was with her. When the Lord saw her, his heart was filled with pity for her, and he said to her, "Don't cry." Then he walked over and touched the coffin, and the men carrying it stopped. Jesus said, "Young man! Get up, I tell you!" The dead man sat up and began to talk, and Jesus gave him back to his mother.

They all were filled with fear and praised God. "A great prophet has appeared among us!" they said, "God has come to save his people!"'

Action: Make up a play about a modern-day prophet, who gives the people a message from God. Include the people's response to the prophet in your play. Act out the play for the rest of the class or for other classes in the school.

Psalm: Listen, my people, to my teaching,
    and pay attention to what I say.
    I am going to use wise sayings
    and explain mysteries from the past,
    things we have heard and known,
    things that our fathers told us.
    We will not keep them from our children;
    we will tell the next generation
    about the Lord's power and his great deeds
    and the wonderful things he has done.

    He gave laws to the people of Israel
    and commandments to the
    descendants of Jacob.
    He instructed our ancestors
    to teach his laws to their children,
    so that the next generation might learn them
    and in turn should tell their children.
    In this way they would also put their trust in God
    and not forget what he has done,
    but always obey his commandments.
    They would not be like their ancestors,
    a rebellious and disobedient people,
    whose trust in God was never firm
    and who did not remain faithful to him.

            Psalm 78:1–8

PSALMS AND FESTIVALS

CHAPTER 20

Imagine the following situation. Two young people from your local community, a brother and sister, are going home from work when their car is involved in an accident. The two of them are seriously injured and are rushed to hospital. Everyone in your class knows them and is shocked by the event. They are in Intensive Care, so no one except the immediate family can visit them. You would all like to be able to do something for them, but there does not seem to be much you can do. Everyone contributes some money towards sending them flowers. But you all want to do something more. Someone suggests that you might pray for them, both as individuals and as a class. In order to help the class to pray as a group, you decide to compose a prayer which the class can pray together for the young people in Intensive Care.

1. Working on your own, compose a prayer which you think would be meaningful for your class to pray in a similar situation. Choose a situation which is of concern to the whole class at this time. You might compose a prayer for people in your own community, or elsewhere, who are in need of your prayers.
Some of the following suggestions might help you to compose your prayer:
(a) To whom are you praying? What is your image of God to whom you are praying?
(b) Do you need help with your prayer? Do you want God to help you to pray well?
(c) What is the reason for your prayer? What do you want God to do? Whom do you want God to help?
(d) What is your relationship with the people for whom you are praying? What do you know about their lives? What kind of people are they? What would you like them to be able to do or achieve in their lives? Why do you think life is precious to them?
(e) Do you have any questions or comments to make to God about what has happened?

    (f) How will you conclude your prayer? (The prayer may be composed in the form of prose, poetry, drama or painting.)
2. Think about how you might help the class to pray well using this prayer. Consider the following points:
    (a) Could the prayer be sung, or could there be music in the background as it is being prayed?
    (b) What kind of lighting would be appropriate to the prayer — darkness, candlelight, daylight, bright lights or a combination of different forms of light and shade?
    (c) Should the prayer be said silently by each person; or prayed together aloud in unison; or should one person say the prayer aloud for the class; or should different groups in the class say different parts of the prayer aloud?
    (d) What signs or symbols would be appropriate to use before, during or after the prayer? (The Sign of the Cross; standing, kneeling or other postures; objects, pictures or photographs representing the people for whom you are praying; symbols of the importance and value of life; or symbols of the presence of God among you.)
3. Share your prayer and your ideas about how it might be prayed with the rest of the class.
4. Plan to use some or all of your prayers for people who need your prayers, perhaps during a class prayer service, or at any time when the class prays together.

The Psalms

Sometimes when we pray we use informal words which are unplanned or spontaneous. At other times we use formal or set prayers. This can be particularly useful when we want to pray as a community. It can give us a feeling of solidarity* to use the same words together, and helps us to show that we are called as a community to praise and thank God and ask for His help.

There are many examples of prayers in the Bible, in both the Old and New Testaments. Some of these prayers are the spontaneous prayers of individuals speaking to God at a particular time in their lives. For example, when Jeremiah is being persecuted and tormented because he speaks God's word, he prays: 'Whenever I speak, I have to cry out and shout, "Violence! Destruction!" Lord, I am ridiculed and scorned all the time because I proclaim your message' (Jeremiah 20:8). Many of the prayers of the Bible are formal and were used as part of the worship of the community. The psalms are this kind of prayer.

Solidarity means being united with people, having the same aims or interests.

> The psalms are the 'prayer-book' of the Bible. Some of the psalms praise and thank God for His goodness and love; others ask for God's help in time of trouble. Many of the psalms are seen as great literature. For example, Psalm 23 is one of the greatest poems ever written. Some of the psalms are prayers for individual people, personal prayers to God which were later used as community prayers. Most of them are community prayers, from the whole people of Israel to God. Many of these psalms were specially composed for use in the festivals and worship of the people in the Temple at Jerusalem. The psalms were meant to be sung, and accompanied on musical instruments like the lyre, harp and drums.

Exercises

1. Read Psalm 79 and answer the following questions:
   (a) Who is praying?
   (b) For whom is the person/people praying?
   (c) What has happened?
2. Compare your prayer for help with Psalm 79. In what ways are they similar? In what ways are they different?
3. Match the following themes (Column A) with the correct Psalm (Column B).

A	B
(i) Praise of God	(a) Psalm 88
(ii) The community calls for help	(b) Psalm 60
(iii) Prayer for the King	(c) Psalm 117
(iv) Thanksgiving to God	(d) Psalm 97
(v) Praise to God, the King of Israel	(e) Psalm 30
(vi) Individual lament, or cry for help	(f) Psalm 45

Assignment

Make up a psalm of praise to God, following the same pattern as you did in the prayer for help at the beginning of the chapter.

The Calendar of the Israelites

The psalms were a vital part of the worship of the Israelites, particularly during the great festivals of the year. The following calendar gives an outline of the annual seasons and festivals in the lives of the Israelites. Some of the festivals, such as the Passover, were celebrated in different forms as far back as their nomadic days in the wilderness after the Exodus. Other festivals began much later in their history. For example, Hanukkah, the Feast of Dedication, was celebrated from 164 B.C. when the Temple was re-dedicated to God after the Maccabean revolt. Most of the festivals celebrate God's saving actions for the people, but many also celebrate God's continuing goodness to them, blessing them with fertile soil, plenty of rain and good harvests.

Festivals

The most important festivals were Passover, Pentecost and Tabernacles, the three pilgrimage festivals. Every male over the age of twelve had to go to Jerusalem to celebrate these feasts.

Celebrating the New Year in a Jewish home.

New Year

The Jewish New Year began in Autumn, either Tishri (September) or Marchesvan (October), depending on the year. The beginning of the New Year was called Rosh Hashanah. This was the time when the Israelites celebrated the fact that God created everything, and that God is the king of the whole universe. On New Year's Day the shofar horn was blown one hundred times, to remind the people that God was calling them to repent of their sins and return to God's love.

To mark the end of the Day of Atonement, the shofar horn is also blown.

The Day of Atonement (Yom Kippur)

Atonement means being 'at one' with someone. This festival was a special annual ceremony in which the people confessed their sins and asked for God's forgiveness. In this way they became 'one' with God again, and re-dedicated themselves to the Covenant.

Tabernacles

This was also called the Feast of Ingathering, because it was an autumn festival celebrating the fruit harvest. For seven days the people lived in temporary shelters (or 'booths') made of branches. This was partly because, during the fruit harvest, the people made these shelters in the orchards and vineyards and lived there while they gathered in the harvest. It also reminded the people of the years their ancestors had spent as nomads in the wilderness, after the escape from Egypt, when they had lived in tents. At the end of this festival, the people prayed for rain, so that the new agricultural year would be good.

A family celebrates the Feast of Tabernacles.

Julian Calendar	Israelite Calendar	Agricultural Season	Religious Festivals	God's Saving Acts
September	Tishri	Ploughing	New Year Yom Kippur Tabernacles	God is King; forgiveness; wandering in the desert.
October				
November	Marchesvan	Rainy Season		
	Kislev		Festival of Lights	Re-dedication of the Temple
December				
	Tebet	New Spring growth		
January				
	Shebat	Harvesting the figs		
February				
	Adar	Harvesting the flax	Purim	Israelites saved from genocide by Esther
March				
	Nisan	Lambing season Barley	Passover Unleavened Bread	The first Passover. Escape from Egypt
April				

Lighting the candles at Hanukkah.

Hanukkah

This feast celebrated the time when the Temple in Jerusalem was re-dedicated to God, after the Maccabean revolt. It had previously been used for the worship of idols by the Syrians. This feast lasted for eight days. On the first night of the feast, a lamp or candle was lit in each house. Another lamp was lit on each of the following nights. The light was a symbol for the light of the law.

Julian Calendar	Israelite Calendar	Agricultural Season	Religious Festivals	God's Saving Acts
April	Iyyar	General Harvest		
May				
	Sivan	Tending the vineyards	Pentecost	The Covenant at Sinai
June				
July	Tamuz	Harvesting the grapes		
	Ab	Summer fruit		
August				
	Elul	Harvesting the olives		
September				

Children dress up and act the story of Purim.

The Feast of Purim

This feast celebrated the time when Esther, the Jewish wife of a Persian king, managed to save the Jewish people from being destroyed by one of her husband's officials.

Passover and Unleavened Bread

The Passover celebrates the escape of the Israelites from slavery and death in Egypt. The feast of Unleavened Bread celebrated the earliest harvest of the year, the cutting of the barley. The first cuttings of the crops (and the first-born animals) were given to God in thanksgiving. The people ate the new bread made without leaven (which makes bread rise) because the leaven was dough from a previous baking. For the feast they ate 'flat' bread made only from the new grain.

The blessing of Matzah (unleavened bread) at the Passover meal.

Decorating the synagogue for the celebration of Pentecost.

Pentecost

Pentecost was celebrated seven weeks after Unleavened Bread. This was why it was called the feast of 'Weeks'. (Seven weeks make a week of weeks.) It was originally the harvest festival, celebrating the cutting of the wheat crop. Later it was linked with the Covenant which God made with the people at Mount Sinai.

As well as celebrating these festivals, the Israelites also celebrated the Sabbath every week, from sunset on Friday to sunset on Saturday. They also celebrated at the time of crisis — war, drought, famine and so on. The leaders of the people would declare a special day of prayer, which often included fasting, to beg God to help the people.

Exercises

1. Do you see any similarities between our year and the Israelites' year? What are the differences?
2. Look up the Book of Esther in your Bible. Read especially Esther 2:5–9:32.
   (a) What feast is based on these events?
   (b) How did the feast get its name?
   (c) How were the Jews (Israelites) told to celebrate the feast?

The Bible Group: an Owner's Manual (Fr William Riley)
'The psalms have been referred to as the whole Old Testament put into prayer; you can certainly find all the great themes and the more important ideas of the Old Testament somewhere in the one hundred and fifty psalms. The psalms use history and legend, the questions raised by Israel's wise men, the challenge of the prophets, and even the love of the Law. While some of the Old Testament was written as literature and some as law and some as record, the psalms were written to be *used* in acts of worship, pieces of living liturgy.'

Questions

1. Try to find psalms which refer to each of the following themes of the Old Testament:
   (a) the history of the people
   (b) the problem of suffering
   (c) the call to repent, and turn back to God
   (d) the law of God.
2. Briefly describe how we use the psalms today in the Liturgy of the Word.
3. Do you think you could use the psalms as personal prayer? Explain.

Reflection: 'Speak to one another with the words of psalms, hymns and sacred songs; sing hymns and psalms to the Lord with praise in your hearts.' Ephesians 5:19

Action: Pay special attention to the psalm the next time you go to Mass. Try to pray the Response to the psalm and really mean it with all your heart.

Psalm: Praise the Lord!
　　　　Praise God in his Temple!
　　　　Praise his strength in heaven!
　　　　Praise him for the mighty things he has done.
　　　　Praise his supreme greatness.

　　　　Praise him with trumpets.
　　　　Praise him with harps and lyres.
　　　　Praise him with drums and dancing.
　　　　Praise him with harps and flutes.
　　　　Praise him with cymbals.
　　　　Praise him with loud cymbals.
　　　　Praise the Lord, all living creatures.

　　　　Praise the Lord!
　　　　　　　　　Psalm 150

SCRIPTURE—THE NEW TESTAMENT

JESUS

CHAPTER 21

ONE SOLITARY LIFE

Here is a man
who was born of Jewish parents
the child of a peasant woman. . . .
He never wrote a book.
He never held an office.
He never owned a home.
He never had a family.
He never went to college.
He never travelled two hundred
miles from the place
where he was born.

He never did one of the things
that usually accompany greatness.
He had no credentials
but himself. . . .

While still a young man,
the tide of popular opinion
turned against him.
His friends ran away.

One of them denied him. . . .
He was nailed to a cross
between two thieves.
His executioners gambled for
the only piece of property
he had on earth . . . his coat.
When he was dead
he was taken down
and laid in a borrowed grave
through the pity of a friend.

Nineteen wide centuries
have come and gone
and he is the centrepiece
of the human race and the
leader of the column of progress.
I am far within the mark
when I say that all the armies
that ever marched,
and all the navies
that were ever built . . .
have not affected the life of a man
upon earth
as powerfully as has that
One Solitary Life.

          Author unknown

Questions

1. Do you agree with the author that Jesus has had a more powerful effect on people than anyone else in history? Why/Why not?
2. How do you account for the fact that Jesus is still remembered almost 2,000 years after he lived on earth?
3. Has Jesus had any effect on your life? Explain your answer.

Jesus

If anyone had told Pontius Pilate, the governor of Judea, that the Roman Empire would no longer exist in five hundred years' time, he would probably have been shocked and dismayed. But he would have known that empires do rise and fall. After all, the Romans had taken over most of the empire of Alexander the Great, so Pilate knew what could happen to empires.

However, if someone had told Pilate that in two thousand years' time, millions of people all over the world would be the followers of Jesus of Nazareth, he would have been stunned. If he was told that these 'Christians' not only remembered Jesus, but believed that he was still alive and helping his followers, Pilate would have said that this was impossible.

Pilate knew that at the time of Jesus' crucifixion only a few thousand people (at most) had even heard of Jesus of Nazareth. He was a Jewish preacher, a holyman, a 'Prophet' according to his friends and a rebellious troublemaker according to his enemies. In fact, Pilate might recall that, at the time of his death, Jesus had any amount of enemies, but precious few friends. The idea that this man, who had died as a common criminal, would be worshipped by millions of people in two thousand years' time was ridiculous.

Yet we know that the 'impossible', the 'ridiculous', has really happened. Nearly two thousand years later, people pray to the Risen Jesus, love him, and try to follow his teachings in their lives.

If we just think about Jesus' life, his words and actions in Palestine, it is not hard to see why he is still important to us. He was a powerful speaker who told stories with a real punch. Yet many people have been good preachers, but we do not remember them as we remember Jesus. Other people have been healers, and could perform miracles just as Jesus did, so it is not these alone that make him special. Other people have been killed for their beliefs as he was, and so it is not just his suffering and death that give him a special place in our lives.

There are three main reasons why Jesus is so important to Christians.

1. Jesus has a special message.
One of the reasons why Jesus is still important to us is that his message to us, his teaching about God and about people is different from what anyone else has ever taught. Much of Jesus' teaching was based on what God had already told us in the Old Testament. Jesus himself said:

'Do not think that I have come to do away with the Law of Moses and the teachings of the prophets. I have not come to do away with them, but to make their teachings come true.' (Mt. 5:17)

What was new and different in Jesus' teaching was that he took the teaching of the Old Testament and brought it to fulfillment. What had been hinted at in the Old Testament, Jesus made clear and open for all to see. For example, he said:

'You have heard it was said, "Love your friends, hate your enemies." But now I tell you: love your enemies and pray for those who persecute you, so that you may become the sons of your Father in Heaven.'

The Old Testament teaching made it clear that God asks us to 'love our neighbour as ourselves'. Jesus' teaching made it clear that 'neighbours' included our enemies, as well as our friends.

2. *Jesus has a special authority.*

The second reason why Jesus is important to us is because of the kind of person he is. As the Gospel of Matthew notes 'he wasn't like the teachers of the law; instead he taught with authority' (Mt. 7:29). The people were amazed and excited by the *way* Jesus taught his new message. When he spoke to them, they felt as if he could see everything about them, as if he knew them inside out. As the Samaritan woman said to her neighbours, 'Come and see the man who told me everything I have ever done' (Jn. 4:29). John's Gospel also tells us that 'There was no need for anyone to tell him about them, because he himself knew what was in their hearts' (Jn. 2:25). Jesus obviously made a big impact as a person on everyone he met. Even those who hated him recognised that he had an inner power which was even more important than his ability to work miracles, to make speeches.

Jesus cured the servant of the Roman centurion even though the Romans were the enemies of the Jewish people.

3. *Jesus is alive today.*

The third and most important reason why he makes a difference in our lives is because he is alive today. When Jesus was raised from the dead and sent the Holy Spirit to the apostles, they realised that he was not just a good man, sent by God to do powerful deeds. Gradually his followers realised that Jesus was God made man, the Son of God. This is the wonderful news that has made him the centre of life for his followers for nearly two thousand years. The

At the Easter Vigil we celebrate the fact that Jesus is truly alive.

> marvellous words and actions of Jesus of Nazareth are God's word to us, God's saving acts in the life of the people. When Jesus suffered and died, he showed us that God really shares in our suffering, and that even death cannot separate us from God. Because Jesus is both God and man, his resurrection shows us that one day we too can rise from the dead, through the power of God.

This is why people today still pray to the Risen Jesus, and try to learn about him and get to know him through the Scriptures. We believe that he gives us God's love and forgiveness, and makes it possible for us to love God and love each other.

EXERCISES

1. Look up the Scripture references below to help you answer the following questions:
   (a) In what way was Jesus' teaching similar to what the people had heard before? In what way was it different?
   Mt. 5:21–48; 6:1–4; 7:1–5; 23:23–28; Luke 12:41–44; 12:22–31.
   (b) What kind of person was Jesus, and what effect did he have on people? Mark 6:1–6; Mt. 16:21–24; Mt. 22:15–22; Mt. 22:23–33; Mark 11:15–19; Mark 3:1–6.
   (c) According to the Gospels, what does Jesus tell us about himself? Lk 4:16–21; Mt. 7:24–27; Mt 9:1–8; Mt. 28:16–20 Jn 4:5–42; Jn 6:25–69.
2. Try to explain why the authorities and leaders of the people wanted to kill Jesus.
3. If Jesus was born into our society today, do you think people would want to kill him, or have him assassinated? Explain.

GROUP WORK

1. Get into groups.
2. Each group should take one of the following Scripture passages and make up a drama based on the incident described.
   (a) Luke 16:19–31
   (b) Luke 19:1–9
   (c) John 13:1–17
   (d) John 11:1–44
   (e) Mark 14:32–42
   (f) Luke 24 24:1–12, and 36–44.
3. Act out each drama for the rest of the class.

Assignment

Write a brief review of each of the plays, and explain what message they give you about Jesus.

Reflection: 'For God loved the world so much that he gave his only Son, so that everyone who believes in him may not die, but have eternal life.' John 3:16

Action: Ask your parents, or some other adults whose opinion you value, who they believe Jesus is, and what they think about him.

Hymn of Praise
Before the world was created,
the Word already existed;
he was with God
and he was the same as God.
From the very beginning
the Word was with God.

Through him, God made all things;
not one thing in all creation
was made without him.
The Word was the source of life,
and this life brought light to mankind.

The light shines in the darkness,
and the darkness has never put it out.

The Word became a human being and,
full of grace and truth,
lived among us.
We saw his glory,
the glory which he received
as the Father's only Son.
    John 1: 1–5, 14

THE KINGDOM OF GOD

CHAPTER 22
▼

Everywhere Jesus went, he announced the Good News that the Kingdom of God was coming soon. This is one of the stories which Jesus told to show people what the kingdom would be like.

'The kingdom of heaven is like this. Once there was a man who went out early in the morning to hire some men to work in his vineyard. He agreed to pay them the regular wage, a silver coin a day, and sent them to work in his vineyard. He went out again to the market place at nine o'clock and saw some men standing there doing nothing, so he told them, "You also go and work in the vineyard, and I will pay you a fair wage." So they went. Then at twelve o'clock and again at three o'clock he did the same thing. It was nearly five o'clock when he went to the market place and saw some other men still standing there. "Why are you wasting the whole day here doing nothing?" he asked them. "No one hired us," they answered. "Well, then, you also go and work in the vineyard," he told them. When evening came, the owner told the foreman, "Call the workers and pay them their wages, starting with those who were hired last and ending with those who were hired first." The men who had begun work at five o'clock were paid a silver coin each. So when the men who were the first to be hired came to be paid, they thought they would get more; but they too were given a silver coin each. They took their money and started grumbling against the employer. "These men who were hired last worked only one hour," they said, "while we put up with a whole day's work in the hot sun — yet you paid them the same as you paid us!"

"Listen friend," the owner answered one of them, "I have not cheated you. After all, you agreed to do a day's work for one silver coin. Now take your pay and go home. I want to give this man who was hired last as much as I have given you. Don't I have the right to do as I wish with my own money? Or are you jealous because I am generous?"

And Jesus concluded, 'So those who are last will be first, and those who are first will be last.' (Matthew 20:1–16)

Notes on the story
1. The kingdom of heaven: Matthew's Gospel talks about the kingdom of 'heaven' rather than the Kingdom of 'God' because the Gospel was written for Jewish Christians. They followed the Jewish tradition and often avoided saying the word 'God' out loud.
2. It was the custom in Palestine at the time of Jesus for people who needed work to go to the marketplace and wait to be hired for the day.
3. One silver coin was seen as a fair wage for a day's work at the time. It would enable a worker to provide the basic necessities for the family for one day. If a person earned less than one silver coin, or earned nothing at all, then the family would suffer.

QUESTIONS

1. What is your reaction to this story?
2. What kind of person was the owner of the vineyard?
3. Do you have sympathy with the men who had worked all day long? Explain.
4. Why do you think the vineyard owner paid the last workers a silver coin each, even though they had only worked for one hour? Do you think he did the right thing? Explain.
5. Does anything or anyone change by the end of the story? Explain.
6. What do you think is the most important moment in the story? Why?
7. What do you think is the most important message or meaning in this story?
8. Jesus told this story to explain something about the Kingdom of God. What do you think this story tells us about how people will be treated in the Kingdom of God?

The Kingdom of God
When Jesus first began to preach in Galilee, this is what he said:
> 'The right time has come! The Kingdom of God is near! Turn away from your sins and believe the Good News!' (Mark 1: 15)

This was wonderful news to the people who believed it. For hundreds of years they had been waiting for God to send the Messiah who would set up the Kingdom of God. In this kingdom, there would be no evil and no oppression because God would rule everyone with justice and love. (See Isaiah 29: 18–19)

The Jews naturally believed that they would have first place in the kingdom because they were God's Chosen People. The pharisees, scribes and other people who obeyed the law in every detail were confident that they would be the most important people in the kingdom. They were sure that prostitutes and tax collectors, as well as the poor and ignorant people who neither knew nor kept the law properly, would have no place in the kingdom.

However, Jesus' message about the Kingdom of God was very different. He announced that God's kingdom was *for* the poor, the broken-hearted, the sick, the oppressed and the sinner. Jesus said:
> 'The Spirit of the Lord is upon me, because he has chosen me to bring good news to the poor. He has sent me to proclaim liberty to the captives and recovery of sight to the blind; to set free the oppressed and to announce that the time has come when the Lord will save his people.' (Luke 4: 18–19)

The only thing which people had to do to be part of the Kingdom of God was to turn away from their sins and believe in the good news of the kingdom. The prostitutes and the tax collectors knew that they were sinners and that they needed God's forgiveness. They were delighted to hear that God's kingdom was for them.

The scribes and the pharisees were disgusted. They had no intention of 'turning away from their sins' because they saw themselves as good people, not sinners like the prostitute or the tax collector. Jesus told the scribes and the pharisees that they were the worst kind of sinners because they were hard-hearted and unloving. He warned them that the Kingdom of God was for people who knew they needed God's healing, mercy, love and forgiveness. It was not for people who thought they were perfect already. This was astonishing news to everyone.

They had thought that the kingdom would be a reward for people who were good. It was a shock to realise that the kingdom was a generous gift from God to anyone who was willing to accept it.

> Jesus had many stories about the Kingdom of God and all of them showed that God's kingdom is different from any ordinary kingdom. People of all nations are welcome and not just the Chosen People. It is far harder to be part of God's kingdom if you are rich. The most powerful and important people in the kingdom are those who serve everyone else and put themselves last. Justice, mercy, love and compassion for *everyone* are the most important values in the kingdom.

EXERCISES

1. Look up the Scripture passages given below and find out the answers to the questions.
    (a) When will God set up the kingdom? (The Parable of the Ten Girls, Matthew 25: 1–13)
    (b) What kind of people will be in the kingdom? Who will be left out? (The Parable of the Great Feast, Luke 14: 15–24)
    (c) When will we know for certain who is and who is not part of God's kingdom? (The Parable of the Weeds, Matthew 13: 24–30)
    (d) How can we show that we want to be part of God's kingdom? (The Parable of the Good Samaritan, Luke 10: 30–37)
2. Write a *modern* parable about the Kingdom of God using events and ideas from your everyday life.

Preparing for the Kingdom
We do not know when the Kingdom of God will come. However, Jesus warns us, just as he warned the people of his time, to be prepared when the kingdom does come. In order to prepare for the kingdom, we must behave like people who want to be part of God's kingdom. We must build up our relationship with God and other people. We must turn away from sins such as selfishness, greed and hatred. We must be just and loving to all people. We must be compassionate to the poor, the downtrodden and the suffering. If we live life simply, without too much wealth or too many possessions, we will find it easier to be a part of God's kingdom.

A 48-hour fast in aid of homeless people.

A field-worker from the Bonda mission advises the members of a co-op about planting maize.

As Christians, we are called upon to spread the good news of the Kingdom of God. We must let everyone know that God loves them and freely offers them a place in the kingdom.

> During his life on earth, Jesus showed by his actions as well as his words that the Kingdom of God was close at hand. His miracles were important signs that the kingdom was near. He lived among the poor and down-trodden. He made friends with sinners who were despised by everyone else. He healed the sick and fed the hungry. He spoke out against injustice and oppression.
>
> We too are called upon to show by our actions that the Kingdom of God is near. For example, we can allow ourselves to feel compassion and sympathy for others. We can make personal sacrifices in order to help them. We can say or do something, no matter how small, to relieve the suffering, misery and oppression of others. All instances of love, compassion, justice and freedom in the world around us are signs of the Kingdom of God.

EXERCISES

1. Give examples to show how the following people or groups could prepare for the coming of the Kingdom of God.
   (a) a fifteen-year-old student
   (b) a family
   (c) a class
   (d) a school
2. Is there anything which makes it difficult for people to prepare for the kingdom?
3. Can you see any signs of the Kingdom of God in the world today? Explain.
4. Sometimes we can feel discouraged when our efforts seem to make little difference to the sadness and misery in the world. Some people say, 'We can do so little — what good will it do?' Each of the following parables about the Kingdom of God can give people hope and encourage them to keep trying. Look at each parable and briefly explain the message or meaning of the parable.
   (a) The Parable of the Mustard Seed, Mark 4: 30–32
   (b) The Parable of the Growing Seed, Mark 4: 26–29
   (c) The Parable of the Yeast, Luke 13: 20–21

The Parable of the Mustard Seed

The Parable of the Growing Seed

The Parable of the Yeast

Assignment

Choose five major events taking place in the world today. Which of these events show people working for God's kingdom? Do any of them show people working against God's kingdom? Explain.

Reflection: 'The Kingdom of heaven is like this. A man happens to find a treasure hidden in a field. He covers it up again, and is so happy that he goes and sells everything he has, and then goes back and buys that field.' Matthew 13:44

Action: Examine your life to see what action, if any, you are taking at present which is helping to prepare you for God's kingdom. With the rest of your class, decide on some way in which you will work together towards God's kingdom.

Psalm: I will praise you, Lord, with all my heart;
I will tell of all the wonderful things you have done.
I will sing with joy because of you.
I will sing praise to you, Almighty God.

. . . the Lord is King forever;
he has set up his throne for judgment.
He rules the world with righteousness;
he judges the nations with justice.

The Lord is a refuge for the oppressed,
a place of safety in times of trouble.
Those who know you, Lord, will trust you;
you do not abandon anyone who comes to you.
Psalm 9: 1–2, 7–10

THE BEATITUDES

CHAPTER 23
▼

VOL 9. NO. 102

the fastest growing magazine for teenagers!

TEENAGE WORLD
SUPER COMPETITION

WIN THE PRIZE OF YOUR DREAMS, WORTH £10,000

What do you think makes Teenagers happy? We at Teenage World really want to know? All you have to do to win a super prize is to fill in the spaces below with your Top Ten Ways to be happy. If your list is chosen by our panel of judges, then you can choose any prize you like to the value of £10,000!

Fill each of the spaces below with a full sentence, and send the entry form to Teenage World with your name and address before the end of next month. Good Luck!

MY TOP TEN WAYS TO BE HAPPY!

1.
2.
3.
4.
5.
6.
7.
8.
9.
10.

NAME_____
ADDRESS_____
_____

The Beatitudes

> The Beatitudes are Jesus' guidelines for perfect happiness. The word 'beatitude' means 'happiness' or being blessed. The Beatitudes are based on the idea that real, lasting happiness comes from things that will last forever, and which can never be taken away from us.

Some things can make us happy in the short term. Winning a competition, getting new clothes, doing well in an exam, or finding something we have lost can make us feel happy. But this kind of happiness does not last very long. New clothes get old and ragged, and the exam or competition may seem less important as time goes by. Real happiness lasts. For example, when two people really love each other, they make each other feel very happy. If one of them dies, the other person will feel very sad and lonely. However, as time goes by, the partner who is left will begin to remember the love of the other person and the good times they had together. This memory will make the person feel happy. The love between the two people will always be important and will always bring happy memories. This kind of happiness is long-term happiness and it can never be taken away.

The Beatitudes show that real happiness often comes from suffering and sorrow, as well as from love, peace and joy. In God's kingdom, everyone will live according to the Beatitudes. We can prepare for the kingdom by trying to put the Beatitudes into practice in our everyday lives.

Jesus said:

'Happy are those who know they are spiritually poor. The kingdom of heaven belongs to them!'
You will be happy if you know that you need God more than anything else because this means that you will be part of God's kingdom.

'Happy are those who mourn; God will comfort them!'
You will be happy if you allow yourself to feel sad about what is unjust and sinful in the world because God will comfort you.

'Happy are those who are humble; they will receive what God has promised!'
You will be happy if you are humble and gentle because you will be blessed with God's promise.

'Happy are those whose greatest desire is to do what God requires; God will satisfy them fully!'
You will be happy if your greatest wish is to have right relationships with God and other people because God will give you your wish.

'Happy are those who are merciful to others; God will be merciful to them!'
You will be happy if you are merciful and forgiving to other people because God will be merciful and forgiving to you.

'Happy are the pure in heart; they will see God!'
You will be happy if you keep your mind fixed on God because you will be able to see God at work in the world.

'Happy are those who work for peace; God will call them His children!'
You will be happy if you work for peace and justice in the world because God will proudly call you one of His children.

'Happy are those who are persecuted because they do what God requires; the kingdom of heaven belongs to them!'
You will be happy if you are persecuted for doing what God wants because you will be part of God's kingdom.

(adapted from Matthew 5: 3–10)

Questions

1. What is your reaction to the Beatitudes?
2. Do you think Jesus is right when he says that following these guidelines will make you really happy?
3. In what way are the Beatitudes similar to your guidelines for happiness? In what ways are they different?

Exercises

1. What value is important in each of the Beatitudes?
2. Examine each of the following situations. In each case explain:
   (a) What Beatitude applies to the situation?
   (b) Which of the people in the situation has the greater chance of real happiness in the long term? Why?

(i) Lucy is unpopular with some of her friends at school because she refuses to go shoplifting with them. Her friend Ellen does not want to shoplift either, but she wants to keep her friends, so she gives in to their pressure.

(ii) Rachel, Maureen and a few of their friends were playing around with a football in the school grounds at the weekend, and broke a window. They all ran away. On Monday, Rachel went to the principal and said she had been involved in breaking the window. She offered to help pay for it. She did not say who was with her at the time. On the way home from school, Maureen and the others beat her up for 'telling' and warned her not to give them away.

(iii) Joe and David are both doing important exams in a few months' time. Joe always asks his older sister to check his work if she has time, to see how he can improve it. He also says a prayer before starting his study, asking God to help him do well. David says he has enough brains to do well without asking anyone's help.

(iv) James and Susan are very close. They study together, go to football matches and concerts together, and spend a lot of time with each other's families, chatting and watching television. Robert and Jennifer also go out together. Robert says there is no point in talking seriously to a girl, because she will only go and tell all her friends what you said. He goes out with Jennifer because it looks good to have a girlfriend.

(v) Cormac is a bully at home and at school. He always wants his own way and will fight anyone to get it. His brother Finn refuses to allow Cormac to bully him. He stands up for himself — and for any of Cormac's victims — because he is not afraid of his brother. However he does not fight Cormac, because he does not believe in fighting.

(vi) There are two rival gangs in Carol's school. They hate each other, and violence often breaks out at lunch-time and after school. Carol does not belong to either gang, but she has friends in both. She is trying to get them to make friends — inviting a few members of both gangs to her house for the evening; trying to talk to them and get them to talk to each other. Laura says Carol will probably end up losing all her friends because of her interfering. Laura thinks, if they want to fight, let them fight.

(vii) When his little brother wrecked Mark's new bike, Mark was really angry at first. But when he cooled down, he told his brother that it was all right. When the bike was fixed he even let his brother ride it again. Mark's friend Tony thought he was daft. Tony said he would have given *his* brother a good hiding if he ever damaged Tony's bike, and he would never have let him touch it again, much less ride it.

(viii) Watching TV programmes about the problems of poor people in developing countries always makes Ruth feel sad, and sorry that she cannot do more to help the people. Anne refuses to watch this kind of programme, and always chooses something entertaining to watch on TV.

Faith Alive (Edited by Rowanne Pasco and John Redford, 1988)

. . . if we keep trying to model our lives along the lines of the Beatitudes — if we keep trying to be more detached from this world,* if we try to have true sorrow for our sins, if we try to spread peace, to be chaste and keep our hearts intent on God, thirsting for God, if we try always to forgive others and put up with the wrongs done to us — then even in this life we shall know something of the joys of heaven.

(Taken from Chapter 19)

* *detached from this world*—this means not being too preoccupied with money, status and power in our everyday lives.

QUESTIONS

1. What does the writer mean by saying that we are all sinners? Do you agree or disagree? Explain.
2. What kinds of things should teenagers try to be 'detached' from in order to follow Jesus' teaching?
3. Give an example to show how a person could be truly sorry for a sin.
4. How could the following people spread peace: students; teachers; parents; children?
5. What does it mean to be chaste?
6. When the writer talks about putting up with wrongs that are done to us, do you think this means doing nothing about injustice and evil? Explain your answer.
7. Give examples to show how following the Beatitudes could make a person happy now, and not just in the long term.

Reflection: 'You are the salt of the earth; but if salt has lost its taste, how can its saltiness be restored? It is no longer good for anything, but is thrown out and trampled under foot. You are the light of the world. A city built on a hill cannot be hid. No one, after lighting a lamp, puts it under the bushel basket, but on the lamp-stand, and it gives light to all in the house. In the same way, let your light shine before others, so that they may see your good works and give glory to your Father in heaven.'
Matthew 5: 13–16 (N.R.S.V.)

Psalm: Who has the right to go up the Lord's hill?*
    Who may enter his holy Temple?
    Those who are pure in act and in thought,
    who do not worship idols or make false promises.
    The Lord will bless them and save them;
    God will declare them innocent.
    Such are the people who come to God,
    who come into the presence of the God of Jacob.
                          Psalm 24: 3–6

* *the hill in Jerusalem on which the Temple was built*

JESUS' RESURRECTION

CHAPTER 24

In your opinion, which of the following statements best describes the resurrection of Jesus?

1. Jesus became a ghost after his death, and appeared to the disciples.
2. The disciples were overcome with grief so that they had hallucinations in which they imagined they saw Jesus.
3. Jesus was brought back to life exactly as he had been before his death.
4. After his resurrection Jesus was the same person as before, but he was alive in a new way.
5. Someone stole Jesus' body and pretended that he was alive again.
6. Jesus never really died; he recovered from his terrible injuries and lived with the disciples.

When you have chosen your statement, read the following Scripture passages to check your answer.
1. Luke 24:36–44
2. Mark 16:9–14
3. John 20:11–29; 1 Corinthians 15:3–7
4. Luke 24:13–35
5. Matthew 27:62; Matthew 28:1–15
6. John 19:31–37

The Resurrection

A tomb in Israel, similar to the one in which Jesus was buried.

> No one saw the resurrection. This means that no one knows exactly what happened on the third day after Jesus was crucified. The reason we know that *something* happened is that the tomb was empty, Jesus' body was no longer there, and Jesus himself appeared several times to his followers. The accounts of how Jesus appeared to his followers make it clear that although he was the same Jesus whom they had known for years, he was changed, transformed in fact. He was not a ghost, because he had a body and could eat with them. Yet his body was different from the body he had before. His new body could go through locked doors and appear to several hundred people at once. When he appeared, some of his followers did not recognise him at first, until he said or did something which made them realise who he was.

Some people have suggested that the apostles might have made up the story of Jesus' resurrection for some reason. If this was true, it is difficult to understand why they did not make up *one* story about the resurrection, and stick to it. Instead we have an account in each Gospel, as well as an account in St Paul's first letter to the Corinthians, all of which give different descriptions of the finding of the empty tomb and the appearances of Jesus. (St Paul does not mention the empty tomb at all.) The very fact that the followers of Jesus were happy to accept these different accounts shows that they were completely convinced that Jesus was truly risen from the dead, and so they had no need to make up one single account to 'prove' it. The differences in the accounts point to the fact that many different people met the Risen Jesus and believed in him.

Apart from the testimony of the people who actually met the Risen Jesus after his resurrection and before the Ascension, we can also discover the truth of the resurrection in our own lives. Jesus is alive today, and we can get to know him through other people, especially the poor and the oppressed. Jesus speaks to us whenever we read or listen to the Scriptures. We can also get to know Jesus by praying to him and by celebrating the sacraments. When we celebrate the Eucharist, we meet the Risen Jesus in a special way when he gives himself to us in Holy Communion.

EXERCISES

1. The earliest account we have of Jesus' appearances after the resurrection was written in a letter by St Paul to the Christians living in Corinth.
   (a) Read I Cor 15:3–7.
   (b) What is the great news preached by Paul?
   (c) Who had met the Risen Lord, according to Paul?
   (d) Could Paul's message about the resurrection be checked by the people of Corinth?
2. St Paul goes on to explain that because Jesus has been raised from the dead, all of his followers will also be raised from the dead. Some of the people in Corinth were wondering what kind of body they would have if they were raised to life after death.
   (a) Read St Paul's reply in I Cor 15:35–43 and I Cor 15:51–54.
   (b) According to St Paul, what is the connection between our present body and the body we shall have after the resurrection?
   (c) Explain the similarities and the differences between the 'earthly' body and the immortal body.
   (d) According to St Paul, why is it impossible to describe exactly what the immortal body will look like?

GROUP WORK

As a class, produce a resurrection newspaper, that is, a newspaper as it might appear on Monday morning, after the resurrection.
1. Get into groups of three to five.
2. Each group should choose one of the following areas to work on.
   (a) Cover story, and headline for the front page.
   (b) Interviews with Jesus' followers — Mary Magdalen, Peter, his mother etc.
   (c) Report by on-the-spot reporter at the empty tomb, and interview with the guards placed there by Pilate.
   (d) Interviews with the authorities — Pilate, King Herod, the High Priest etc.
   (e) Editorial letters — expressing both belief and disbelief in the resurrection.
   (f) Review of the life and death of Jesus, the events that led to his execution by the authorities.

(g) Report from a 'Roving reporter' among the crowds in Jerusalem, especially with people whom Jesus cured, who heard him speak, who condemned him from the crowd on Friday.
3. Put your stories and reports in 'column' form (typewritten if possible), and include some 'photographs', maps and diagrams.
4. One person should be chosen from each group to be part of an overall editorial group at the end, deciding the exact layout of the paper.
5. Display your newspaper in a prominent position.

The Resurrection in my life

Jesus' resurrection shows that death is not the end of life. Jesus said:
  'I am the resurrection and the life. Those who believe in me, even though they die, will live, and everyone who lives and believes in me will never die.' John 11: 25–26 (N.R.S.V.)
This means that whoever believes in Jesus and follows his example and teaching will live forever with God.

Jesus' resurrection also shows that good is more powerful than evil. Jesus was tortured and brutally killed, but he was not defeated. He rose from the dead as he said he would. This shows that God can bring new life and hope, even out of terrible suffering and evil. Injustice, hatred, greed and oppression are still present in our world and in our lives, but they can never overcome the power of love, justice, generosity and self-sacrifice.

> The resurrection is the most important sign of the kingdom. It shows that evil can be overcome by the power of God. It strengthens our hope that, one day, God will set up the kingdom, and evil will no longer have any place in our lives. All Christians hope that this will happen soon, and so we continue to pray to God as Jesus taught us:
>   'Your kingdom come,
>   Your will be done on earth, as it is in heaven.'

Death is not the end of life . . .

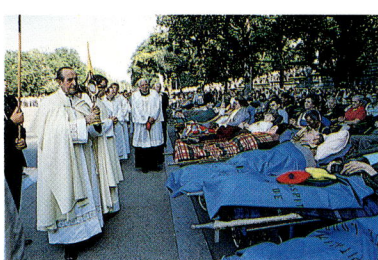

God can bring new life and hope, even out of suffering.

EXERCISES

1. Give examples from nature to show that death is not always the end of life.
2. Give some examples to show that good is more powerful than evil.
3. Do you look forward to the coming of the kingdom? Explain.

Assignment

Pretend you are writing a letter to someone who has never heard of Jesus. They want to know something about your faith. Write your understanding of the life, death and resurrection of Jesus, and what it means in your life.

Reflection: 'On that same day two of Jesus' followers were going to a village named Emmaus, about eleven kilometres from Jerusalem, and they were talking to each other about all the things that had happened. As they talked and discussed, Jesus himself drew near and walked along with them; they saw him, but somehow did not recognise him. Jesus said to them, "What are you talking about to each other, as you walk along?"

They stood still, with sad faces. One of them, named Cleopas, asked him, "Are you the only visitor in Jerusalem who doesn't know the things that have been happening there these last few days?"

"What things?" Jesus asked.

"The things that happened to Jesus of Nazareth," they answered. "This man was a prophet and was considered by God and by all the people to be powerful in everything he said and did. Our chief priests and rulers handed him over to be sentenced to death, and he was crucified.

"And we had hoped that he would be the one who was going to set Israel free! Besides all that, this is now the third day since it happened. Some of the women of our group surprised us; they went at dawn to the tomb, but could not find his body. They came back saying they had seen a vision of angels who told them that he is alive. Some of our group went to the tomb and found it exactly as the women had said, but they did not see him."

Then Jesus said to them, "How foolish you are, how slow you are to believe everything the prophets said! Was it not necessary for the Messiah to suffer these things and then to enter his glory?" And Jesus explained to them what was said about himself in all the Scriptures, beginning with the books of Moses and the writings of all the prophets.

As they came near the village to which they were going, Jesus acted as if he were going farther; but they held him back, saying, "Stay with us; the day is almost over and it is getting dark." So he went in to stay with them. He sat down to eat with them, took the bread, and said the blessing; then he broke the bread and gave it to them. Then their eyes were opened and they recognised him, but he disappeared from their sight.

They said to each other, "Wasn't it like a fire burning in us when he talked to us on the road and explained the Scriptures to us?"

They got up at once and went back to Jerusalem, where they found the eleven disciples gathered together with the others and saying, "The Lord is risen indeed! He has appeared to Simon!"

The two then explained to them what had happened on the road, and how they had recognised the Lord when he broke the bread.' Luke 24:13–35

Action: Look for signs of new life and hope in nature, in yourself, and in other people during the coming week.

Hymn of Praise
Christ Jesus,
    who though he was in the form of God,
    did not regard equality with God
    as something to be exploited,
but emptied himself,
    taking the form of a slave
    being born in human likeness.
And being found in human form,
    he humbled himself
    and became obedient to the point of death—
even death on a cross.

Therefore God also highly exalted him
    and gave him the name
    that is above every name,
so that at the name of Jesus
    every knee should bend,
    in heaven and on earth and under the earth,
and every tongue should confess
    that Jesus Christ is Lord,
    to the glory of God the Father.
        Phil. 2: 6–11 (NRSV)

THE LAST THINGS

CHAPTER 25

Jesus told the following story to explain what God asks us to do during our life on earth.

The Final Judgment

Characters: Narrator; King (Jesus); Good People; Bad People

Narrator: When the Son of Man comes as King, and all the angels with him, he will sit on his royal throne, and the people of all the nations will be gathered before him. Then he will divide them into two groups, just as a shepherd separates the sheep from the goats. He will put the righteous people on his right and the others on his left. Then the King will say to the people on his right:

King: Come, you that are blessed by my Father! Come and possess the kingdom which has been prepared for you ever since the creation of the world. I was hungry and you fed me, thirsty and you gave me a drink; I was a stranger and you received me in your homes, naked and you clothed me; I was sick and you took care of me, in prison and you visited me.

Narrator: The righteous will then answer him:

Good People: When, Lord, did we ever see you hungry and feed you, or thirsty and give you a drink? When did we ever see you a stranger and welcome you in our homes, or naked and clothe you? When did we ever see you sick or in prison and visit you?

Narrator: The King will reply:

King: I tell you, whenever you did this for one of the least important of these brothers of mine, you did it for me!

Narrator:	Then he will say to those on his left:
King:	Away from me, you that are under God's curse! Away to the eternal fire which has been prepared for the Devil and his angels! I was hungry but you would not feed me, thirsty but you would not give me a drink; I was a stranger but you would not welcome me into your homes, naked but you would not clothe me; I was sick and in prison but you would not take care of me.
Narrator:	Then they will answer him:
Bad People:	When, Lord, did we ever see you hungry or thirsty or a stranger or naked or sick or in prison, and would not help you?
Narrator:	The King will reply:
King:	I tell you, whenever you refused to help one of these least important ones, you refused to help me.
Narrator:	These, then, will be sent off to eternal punishment, but the righteous will go to eternal life.

(based on Matthew 25: 31–46)

Questions

1. What are your thoughts and feelings about this story?
2. Who is the 'Son of Man,' the King?
3. How will the 'Son of Man' decide who will be part of the Kingdom of God?
4. Does anything surprise you or seem unusual to you in this story? Do you have any questions about it?
5. What signs or symbols does Jesus use in the story?
6. Why are both the 'Good' and the 'Bad' people surprised by what the King says? Does this help you to understand how people who have never heard of Jesus will be judged?
7. What do you think is the main message or meaning of this story?

The Last Things

The story which Jesus told about the final judgment makes it clear that all of us will have to account to God for the way we live our lives. What will happen to us in the next life depends on the choices we make every day of our lives — to love or to be selfish, to care for or to ignore people in need, to think of others or to think only of ourselves. We know that God is all-merciful and loving, always ready to forgive. We know that God gives us the Spirit to help us to put into practice the values of the Kingdom of God in our lives. He wants everyone to live forever with Him and gives us every opportunity and help to choose eternal life.

The Bible uses a lot of colourful images to describe the 'end of the world'. Both Jesus in the Gospel and the writer of the Book of Revelation refer to natural disasters and calamities like earthquakes, floods and wars which will happen before or at 'the end' of time. At the same time, Jesus tells us that no one knows the day or hour when the end-time will come; he says it will be like a thief in the night, so we must be ready at all times. So wars and famines, earthquakes and other upheavals are like metaphors, telling us that the end of time will be a time when everything will change utterly, and the change will be more dramatic than even an earthquake or a war.

Natural disasters completely disrupt people's lives — nothing is as it was before.

Heaven

Heaven means living forever with God in absolute happiness. It is a gift which God offers to everyone. Every day, we are given the opportunity to choose heaven, to choose God's love. When we choose to love other people, especially 'the least important ones', we are saying 'Yes' to God's gift of love.

We do not know exactly where or what heaven is. We do know that it means being happy with God forever. It probably also means being reunited with the people we loved during our earthly life. The Book of Revelation gives this description of heaven: 'Now God's home is with people. He will live with them and they shall be His people. God Himself will be with them and He will be their God. He will wipe away all tears from their eyes. There will be no more death, no more grief or crying or pain. The old things have disappeared.' (Rev. 21:3–4)

Purgatory

Some people who have died are not ready to meet God face to face. These people have tried to love God during their lives on earth, but they are very aware of all the times that they failed to love God and other people. They may not feel worthy to be with God forever.

God gives these people an opportunity to reflect on how much God loves them. They have a chance to realise that God truly forgives all their sins and wants them to be with God forever. This is what we call 'purgatory', when people are purified or cleansed of all their shame and doubt, and the effect that their sins have had on them as people.

We do not know where purgatory is. We do not know how long it takes for people to be purified, or if it takes place in an instant. All we know is that purgatory is another sign that God loves us and wants to help us.

Hell

The 'eternal punishment' which Jesus speaks of, and which we call 'hell', is a punishment which we can bring on ourselves by deliberately rejecting God's invitation to love and choosing selfishness and evil throughout our lives. Hell should not be thought of as a punishment for one isolated action, or thoughtlessness or not realising what we are doing. People *choose* to be in hell, freely and with full knowledge of what they are doing. When people constantly choose to be selfish, unjust and heartless towards others, and do what *they* want regardless of how it affects other people, they are choosing hell. Hell means being forever alone, without God, without love, without hope. This is where selfishness leads.

Jesus' teaching and the rest of the Scriptures show that heaven and hell are part of our lives now and not just at the end of time. When we live as God's children, in peace, love and justice, we are in some way already in heaven. When we deliberately choose selfishness, injustice and cruelty, we are in some way already in hell.

EXERCISES

1. Who is it who decides whether each of us will be part of God's kingdom or not? Explain your answer.
2. Give other examples, apart from those given by the King, of how we can show we want to be part of God's kingdom.
3. How does the idea of purgatory show us that God is merciful and loving?
4. We know that many people are in heaven — Mary and the saints, for example. We do not know for certain if anyone is in hell. Do you think that anyone would deliberately choose to be in hell? Explain your answer.

GROUP WORK

Each group will need poster paper and markers/crayons/paints.

1. Get into groups of three or four.
2. Each group should take one of the following Scripture references and read the passage carefully.

   (a) 1 Thess. 4:15–18
   (b) Luke 12:15–21
   (c) Deut. 30:15–20
   (d) Rev. 21:1–6
   (e) John 11:20–27
   (f) Romans 8:18–23
   (g) Col. 1:15–20
   (h) 1 Thess. 5:1–11
   (i) 2 Thess. 1:3–10
   (j) 2 Tim. 2:3–10

3. Draw/Paint a picture or design a poster which gives the main message or meaning of your Scripture readings using images, not words. Plan your picture/poster as a group before starting on it, and make sure that every member of the group is involved in some way with the finished product.
4. Present your picture/poster to the rest of the group. If necessary, briefly explain the thinking behind the picture.

Reflection: 'One of the criminals hanging there hurled insults at him: "Aren't you the Messiah? Save yourself and us!"

The other one, however, rebuked him, saying, "Don't you fear God? You received the same sentence he did. Ours, however, is only right, because we are getting what we deserve for what we did; but he has done no wrong." And he said to Jesus, "Remember me, Jesus, when you come as King!"

Jesus said to him, "I promise you that today you will be in Paradise with me."' Luke 23:39–43

Action: Try to live today as if it were your last day on earth, and tomorrow you will be called to account for your life.

Psalm: Praise the Lord, my soul!
>All my being, praise his holy name!
>Praise the Lord, my soul,
>and do not forget how kind he is.
>He forgives all my sins
>and heals all my diseases.
>He keeps me from the grave
>and blesses me with love and mercy.
>He fills my life with good things,
>so that I stay young and strong like an eagle.
>
>. . . for those who honour the Lord,
>his love lasts forever,
>and his goodness endures for all generations
>of those who are true to his covenant
>and who faithfully obey his command.
>>*Psalm 103: 1–5, 17–18*

THE SACRAMENTS

CHRISTIAN INITIATION

CHAPTER 26

Becoming a Christian
(Rome, late 4th century A.D.)

It is a dark, cold night, shortly before dawn. In the main church building the rest of the Christian community is celebrating the *Easter Vigil* with prayers, readings from Scriptures and hymns. Soon the whole community will celebrate the Eucharist together, when the sun comes up as a powerful reminder of Jesus' resurrection from the dead. Separated from the rest of the community, the people who will be baptised tonight stand shivering in the cold entrance hall that leads to the place of Baptism, the 'baptistry'. A number of *deacons* and *deaconesses* wait with them, as well as their sponsors.

The *catechumens*, as they are called, have been looking forward to this moment for years. Their preparation for Baptism has not been easy. They have learned about the Christian message, they have studied the Scriptures, and, guided by their teachers, they have tried to put Jesus' teaching into practice in their lives. Each Sunday they have taken part in the Liturgy of the Word with the rest of the Church, but they have always had to leave before the Liturgy of the Eucharist. (Only people who are full members of the Christian community may celebrate this most important of all the actions of the Church.) For the last few weeks they have prayed and fasted with special fervour to prepare themselves for this night, this day when their entire lives will be transformed.

The whole Christian community has prayed for them and is praying for them now, getting ready to welcome them with joy.

Suddenly the *bishop* comes into the hall, and tells the catechumens, 'Take off your clothes.' They obey him quickly, and while they are naked the deacons screen the men from the female catechumens and the deaconesses do the same for the women. Many of them are feeling faint from fasting, and the floor is very cold under their bare feet, but in spite of everything the catechumens are full of anticipation. They feel a great sense of awe and mystery. They know that tonight they will die with Christ, and will rise to new life with him, but they do not know exactly how this will happen. The younger ones are a little afraid, and all are curious to know what will happen when they go inside the doors of the baptistry for the first time in their lives.

The bishop orders them to face towards the west, where the sun dies swallowed up in darkness, and demands that they denounce the King of Shadows, darkness and death. Each of the catechumens comes forward in turn to reject *Satan* and all his works and all his empty promises. Then the bishop tells them to turn to the east, where the sun rises. Each of them loudly proclaims that they accept the *King of light and life* who has trampled down death by his own death. As each one finishes, he or she is anointed with olive oil by a deacon or deaconess.

When all the catechumens have been anointed, the baptistry doors are thrown open. Brilliant golden light spills out into the shadowy hallway. Following the bishop, his assistants (the presbyters), the catechumens, deaconesses, deacons and sponsors crowd into the most glorious room most of them have ever seen. Green, gold, purple and white mosaic covers the room from the marble floor to the high ceiling. It sparkles like jewels in the light of the many oil lamps. Vines are growing out of the floor and climbing the walls. The ceiling is decorated with pictures of the apostles, and at the very highest point there is a picture of Jesus being baptised by John at the River Jordan.

In the middle of the floor there is a *pool of water*. More water is gushing noisily into it from the mouth of a stone lion crouching on top of a pillar at the side of the pool. The bishop stands beside it, with his assistants on either side. The room is warm and humid. A deacon gets into the warm water of the pool, which has been heated in a furnace.

The bishop begins to pray — something about the Spirit and the waters of life and death — and then strikes the water a few times with his staff, like *Moses* in the desert striking the rock from which water flowed. Then a young male catechumen of about fifteen is led down into the pool by the deacon. The oil on the boy's body spreads out in shining swirls. The deacon positions the boy near the water cascading from the lion's mouth. The bishop leans over his staff and says loudly, *'Euphemius! Do you believe in God the Father, who created all of heaven and earth?'*

After a nudge from the deacon beside him, the boy murmurs that he does. And just in time, for the deacon, who has been doing this for fifty years and is the boy's grandfather, wraps him in his arms, lifts him backwards into the rushing water and forces him under the surface. The old deacon smiles through his beard at the wide brown eyes that look up at him in shock and fear from beneath the water (the boy has purposely not been told what to expect). Then he raises him up, coughing and spluttering. The bishop waits until he can speak again, and leaning over a second time, tapping the boy on the shoulder with his staff, says *'Euphemius! Do you believe in Jesus Christ, God's only Son, who was conceived of the Virgin Mary, suffered under Pontius Pilate, and was crucified, died and was buried? Who rose on the third day and ascended into heaven, from whence he will come again to judge the living and the dead?'* This time the boy replies like a shot, 'I do,' and then holds his nose, as he is held under the water for a second time . . . *'Euphemius! Do you believe in the Spirit, the master and giver of life, who proceeds from the Father and the Son, who is to be honoured and glorified equally with the Father and the Son, who spoke by the Prophets? And in one Holy, Catholic and Apostolic Church which is the communion of God's holy ones? And in the life that is coming?'* 'I do.' When he comes up the third time, his grandfather guides him up the steps leading out of the pool. There another deacon dries Euphemius with a warm towel.

One of the bishop's assistants, a senior presbyter, pours perfumed oil from a glass pitcher over the boy's damp head until it soaks his hair and runs down over his upper body. The fragrance of this enormously expensive oil fills the room as the old presbyter murmurs: *'God's servant, Euphemius, is anointed in the name of the Father, Son, and Holy Spirit.'* Everyone replies with a thunderous *'Amen.'* Euphemius then puts on a new *white linen tunic*. The fragrant *chrism* seeps into it. He is given a *burning oil lamp* and told to go and stand by the door and keep quiet. Meanwhile the other baptisms continue. A deaconess takes the place of Euphemius' grandfather when the women are being baptised.

When every catechumen has been baptised, the clergy strike up the Easter hymn, *'Christ is risen from the dead, he has crushed death by his death and bestowed life on those who lay in the tomb.'* This melody is constantly repeated, together with the psalm verse, 'Let God arise and smite his enemies,' as the whole baptismal party — tired, damp, thrilled and oily — walk out into the blaze of Easter morning and go next door to the church, led by the bishop. There he bangs on the closed doors with his staff; the doors are flung open, the endless vigil is halted, and as the baptismal party enters, everyone takes up the Easter hymns. The fragrance of chrism fills the church. Everyone crowds around the newly baptised (or neophytes) to welcome them, to touch their chrismed hair and rub its fragrance on their own faces.

The bishop ascends the lower front steps of the ambo, then turns and opens his arms to the newly-baptised Christians, and once again everyone sings 'Christ is risen.' He then affirms and reads their prayer after baptism, for all the faithful to see. *He lays his hand on each head*, and signs each oily forehead once again in the form of a cross while saying loudly, 'The servant of God is sealed with the Spirit.' Everyone replies '*Amen*.' Then, for the first time, the former catechumens give and receive *the kiss (or sign) of peace*.

While this continues, bread and wine are laid out on the holy table. When things quieten down, the bishop prays a long *Eucharistic prayer* over them. Then the neophytes receive the *Body and Blood of Christ* for the first time with the rest of the faithful. Afterwards each of them drinks from two other special cups — one containing *baptismal water*, the other containing *milk and honey*, symbols for the Promised Land.

Over the following weeks and months, the new Christians will learn more about their faith and its mysteries. They have begun a new life which Christians are still living today more than fifteen centuries later.

Questions

1. What is your reaction to this account?
2. Do you have any questions about it? Ask your teacher and the rest of the class to help you find the answers.

Exercises

1. Briefly outline the stages which the catechumens went through in order to be initiated into the Christian community in Rome in the late fourth century A.D.
2. The catechumens received three sacraments as part of their initiation. Identify them in the account given above.

3. How were you initiated into the Christian community?
4. What are the similarities and the differences between your initiation and the initiation of Euphemius?

Original Sin

Every person is capable of being good, kind and loving. Everyone is special and unique, with gifts and abilities which make us feel proud of ourselves. This is the bright side of every person, the side we want other people to know.

Every person also has a dark side, a tendency to do the wrong thing. Everyone is capable of being mean, cruel and sinful. This is the side of ourselves that we hide from other people. Sometimes we even try to hide it from ourselves, and pretend that everything we do is always good and right. However, when we are honest with ourselves, we can see that we do have a dark side. Even before we are old enough to deliberately commit a sin, we have a tendency or the potential in us to commit sin. It is a part of human nature.

> The dark side of ourselves is very powerful. It can prevent us from loving God and loving each other. We use the term 'original sin' to describe the dark side of our nature — our tendency to give in to temptation and commit sin. It is called 'original', because it is part of human nature from the very beginning, and it is part of us even before we ourselves have committed a sin. It is called 'sin' because it prevents us from loving God and loving each other, just as deliberate sins do.

We know that everything God created is very good. We also know that God made human beings in God's own Image. God did not intend us to have a dark side. God intended us to be perfect human beings. However, from the beginning, people decided to use their freedom to turn away from God's love, and commit sin. When they did this, they came under the power of sin and evil. One sin led to another, and they began to blame one another. They were no longer perfect. They now had a dark side. From then on, everyone was born with a dark side, a tendency to give in to temptation and commit sin.

> God sent Jesus to save us from the power of sin and evil in ourselves. This means that although our dark side still exists, and we are still tempted to sin, we are also free to reject sin and live as God wants us to. Through the Sacrament of Baptism, Jesus frees us from the power of original

sin. The saving power of Jesus defeats the power of our dark side, and gives us the freedom to be loving towards God and others. As children of God, we are filled with the Spirit of hope and love. Baptism is an important sign to the whole world that Jesus is the Saviour of the world, and that the power of love is stronger than the power of evil.

EXERCISES

People receiving Baptism in the Jordan river.

1. What evidence is there to show that human beings have a dark side?
2. Give examples to show how love can defeat evil.
3. Do you think that Christians are *better* than other people? Explain your answer.
4. Do you think that Christians have a greater *responsibility* than other people? Explain your answer.

Gift and Responsibility
1. Examine the following list of gifts. Make a note of the ones which you feel you have been given (and add any which may not have been included here):

I am — hardworking.
I am — a good listener.
I am — able to explain my point of view.
I am — a peacemaker.
I am — healthy.
I am — able to pray.
I am — cheerful.
I am — responsible.
I am — a good friend.
I am — patient.
I am — able to make sacrifices.
I am — not lacking the basic necessities of life.
I am — able to take criticism.
I am — sensitive to other people.

I am — able to cheer people up.
I am — good at study.
I am — good at sport.
I am — a reader.
I am — able to control myself.
I am — generous to others.
I am — kind to animals.
I am — happy when alone.
I am — a leader.
I am — happy in a crowd.
I am — able to see someone's point of view.
I am — interested in world events.
I am — concerned about other people.
I am — just in my actions.

2. Our gifts are not given to us for our own benefit only. As Christians, we should use our gifts to care for other people, build up the community, and spread the word of God by our words and actions.

Draw the following grid into your copy, and fill it in, using the gifts you noted above for the first column.

My Gifts	How I can use these gifts		
	At home	With my friends	To spread God's Word of Love

3. Do you think you use your gifts as fully as you should? Why/Why not?

Rite of Christian Initiation of Adults (1986)

Baptism . . . forms us into God's people. This first sacrament pardons all our sins, rescues us from the power of darkness, and brings us to the dignity of adopted children, a new creation through water and the Holy Spirit. Hence we are children of God.

By signing us with the gift of the Spirit, confirmation makes us more completely the image of the Lord and fills us with the Spirit, so that we may bear witness to Him before all the world.

Finally, coming to the table of the Eucharist, we eat the flesh and drink the blood of the Son of Man so that we may have eternal life and show forth the unity of God's people.

(Taken from *Christian Initiation*, General Introduction)

QUESTIONS

1. How does Baptism change us?
2. Give some examples to show how we can show that we are made in the image of the Lord.
3. What does the Spirit enable us to do? Give examples to explain your answer.
4. How does the Eucharist show that the people of God are united?
5. What is the connection between the Eucharist and Eternal Life?

EXERCISES

1. What effect has your Christian initiation had on your life? Do you think of yourself as:
   (a) a 'new creation'
   (b) a child of God
   (c) an image of the Lord
   (d) a witness to Jesus
   (e) a part of God's people
   (f) having the gift of eternal life?
2. Pick a title from the list given, which best describes how you see yourself as a Christian. Explain why you have chosen this title.

Discussion: Am I glad to be a Christian?

Reflection: 'The apostles in Jerusalem heard that the people of Samaria had received the word of God, so they sent Peter and John to them. When they arrived, they prayed for the believers that they might receive the Spirit. For the Spirit had not yet come down on any of them; they had only been baptised in the name of the Lord Jesus. Then Peter and John placed their hands on them, and they received the Holy Spirit.' Acts 8:14–17

Action: Ask your parents or guardians why they had you baptised. Find out who your sponsors were (if you do not already know) and ask them (directly, or by letter) why they agreed to be your sponsors.

Psalm: I love the Lord because he hears me;
>   he listens to my prayers.
>   He listens to me every time I call to him.
>   The danger of death was all round me;
>   the horrors of the grave closed in on me;
>   I was filled with fear and anxiety.
>   Then I called to the Lord,
>   'I beg you, Lord, save me!'
>
>   The Lord saved me from death;
>   he stopped my tears and kept me from defeat.
>   And so I walk in the presence of the Lord
>   in the world of the living.
>   *Psalm 116: 1–4, 8–9*

THE EUCHARIST

CHAPTER 27
▼

Note your responses to the following statements in your copy. Write 'A' if you agree totally with a statement. Write 'D' if you completely disagree with it. If you are not sure, or if you agree/disagree only partly with the statement, write '?', and *briefly* note your reasons.

1. I enjoy celebrating the Eucharist with my community.
2. I find Mass boring.
3. You don't have to celebrate the Eucharist to pray to God.
4. Everyone should celebrate the Eucharist on Sunday.
5. Celebrating the Eucharist helps you to be a better person.
6. God speaks to us in the Liturgy of the Word.
7. My parents make me go to Mass.
8. You can meet Jesus in a special way in the Eucharist.
9. I don't understand what the Eucharist is all about.
10. If the government made it a crime to celebrate the Eucharist, I would still try to celebrate it.

GROUP WORK

1. Get into groups of three or four.
2. Share your responses to each of the above statements in turn.
3. Try to come to some agreement as a group about each statement.
4. Report your conclusions to the whole class.
5. As a class, make out a list of things
   (a) that you could do and
   (b) that other people could do to help you celebrate the Eucharist in a more meaningful way.

The Eucharist

From the very beginning of the Christian community, Christians were looked on with suspicion. Strict Jews were horrified by the Christian belief that Jesus was God, and people like Paul (before his conversion) dragged Christians from their homes and had them beaten up or put in prison. The authorities in the Roman Empire disapproved of Christians because they would not worship the emperor as a god — this was seen as treason. There were also rumours going around that Christians performed unspeakable rituals — they were cannibals, some said, killing and eating the children of Roman citizens. In the time of the Emperor Nero, Christians were blamed for the great fire that destroyed the city of Rome. Many Christians were fined, flogged, imprisoned, executed, thrown to the lions to be eaten alive, or burned to death for their imagined crimes, and in particular for the crime of being a Christian.

Christians met secretly in the Catacombs.

In spite of the terrible dangers, the Christian community continued to follow Jesus. They willingly risked their lives in order to celebrate the Eucharist, which they believed to be the most important event in their lives. This love of the Eucharist and the willingness to risk anything to celebrate it can usually be seen whenever Christians are persecuted. In the Penal times in Ireland, when it was against the law to be a Catholic, and priests were hanged, drawn and quartered if they were caught, the people still celebrated the Eucharist at Mass Rocks in out-of-the-way places. In parts of Latin America today, where the Church is seen as a dangerous influence, and where priests, religious brothers and sisters and lay people are often murdered by 'death squads', people will travel for miles to celebrate the Eucharist.

The attitude of these Christians often seems very different from ours. They see it as a privilege to celebrate the Eucharist, while we sometimes see it as a chore, a burden. We sometimes complain that Mass is 'boring', that it should be more 'entertaining'. Persecuted Christians do not expect to be entertained when they celebrate the Eucharist. Instead, they celebrate the Eucharist:
- *to come closer to God and to each other,*
- *to hear the Word of God,*
- *to take part in Jesus' sacrifice on the cross, which is re-enacted or re-lived in the Eucharist,*
- *to take part in the sacred meal and receive the Body and Blood of Jesus in Holy Communion.*

A Eucharistic celebration on the site of a Mass Rock from Penal times in Ireland.

When these Christians celebrate the Eucharist together, they give each other courage and hope because they are a community and not just isolated individuals. *As Jesus offers up his life on the cross, they offer up their lives too, with all the dangers, difficulties, joy and happiness that they experience.* They praise and thank God for all the gifts they have, especially love. The Eucharist they celebrate is the same Eucharist we celebrate. Their experiences can help us to see more clearly the true meaning of the Eucharist and its importance in our lives.

Exercises

1. How do you think a persecuted Christian would respond to each of the sentences given at the beginning of the chapter?
2. What are the similarities and the differences between your response as a class, and their response?
3. Try to explain why the Eucharist is so important in the life of the Christian community. You should include the following points:
   (a) What do we give thanks for in the Eucharist?
   (b) What do we remember and re-live (or re-enact) in the Eucharist?
   (c) How does God unite us with each other and with God in the Eucharist?
   (d) In what way can our lives be affected or changed when we celebrate the Eucharist?

Questions

1. Who are the 'faithful'?
2. List the ways in which the faithful should allow the Eucharist to affect their lives.
3. Does the celebration of the Eucharist have any effect on your life? Explain.

Reflection: 'On Saturday evening we gathered together for the fellowship meal. Paul spoke to the people and kept on speaking until midnight, since he was going to leave the next day. Many lamps were burning in the upstairs room where we were meeting. A young man named Eutychus was sitting in the window, and as Paul kept on talking, Eutychus got sleepier and sleepier, until he finally went sound asleep and fell from the third storey to the ground. When they picked him up, he was dead. But Paul went down and threw himself on him and hugged him. "Don't worry," he said, "he is still alive!" Then he went back upstairs, broke bread, and ate. After talking with them for a long time, even until sunrise, Paul left. They took the young man home alive and were greatly comforted.' Acts 20:7–12

Action: Plan to celebrate the Eucharist together as a class, in a very meaningful way. Use readings, prayers, hymns, posters and music to remind yourselves that the Eucharistic celebration is a special privilege.

Psalm: O God, you are my God,
and I long for you.
My whole being desires you;
like a dry, worn-out and waterless land,
my soul is thirsty for you.

Let me see you in the sanctuary;
let me see how mighty and glorious you are.
Your constant love is better than life itself,
and so I will praise you.

I will give you thanks as long as I live;
I will raise my hands to you in prayer.
My soul will feast and be satisfied,
and I will sing glad songs of praise to you.
Psalm 63: 1–5

RECONCILIATION

CHAPTER 28

A community has to work hard to build up good relationships between people. When anyone is left out, taken for granted, treated unjustly or hurt in any way, relationships can be damaged. The community should take the time to help people become reconciled to one another again. The whole community benefits when people feel appreciated and respected.

The following activity could help your class community to build up their relationships with one another and to become reconciled with one another.

A Class Celebration
In order to celebrate this service you will need a metal bin or bucket and matches. Each person will need 8–10 separate slips of paper and a pen. Appoint two people as readers before you begin.

Repentance
1. Get into groups of eight to ten people, sitting in a circle in silence.

2. Write down each of the following statements on a separate slip of paper.
    - I am sorry for not listening properly to you.
    - I am sorry for being rude to you.
    - I am sorry for taking you for granted.
    - I am sorry for forgetting to say thank you.
    - I am sorry for forgetting to say well done.

   Fill in the other slips of paper with some of these sentences, or make up other appropriate sentences. You should have enough slips to give one to each member of your group, except yourself. (Keep one slip blank for later.)

3. Take a few moments to decide which statement you want to give to each of the people in your group. Put the person's name on their slip of paper. Then sign your own name.

4. *Reading from Scripture*
   First Reader: The first reading is from the Letter of James:
   So then, confess your sins to one another and pray for one another, so that you will be healed. The prayer of a good person has a powerful effect. (James 5: 16).

5. One at a time, each member of the group stands up and hands the slips of paper around to the rest of the group.

6. When everyone has read their sentences privately, the whole class says the act of contrition slowly and quietly:
   O My God, I thank you for loving me. I am sorry for all my sins, for not loving others and for not loving you. Help me to live like Jesus and not to sin again. Amen.

Forgiveness
1. The 'Sin-bin' is passed around the class and each person puts the slips of paper they have received into it, as a sign that they want to forgive the people who have hurt them in any way.

2. The slips of paper are then burnt in the bin, while everyone sings 'Lord, have mercy', to show that we all need God's forgiveness.

   > Lord, have mercy, Lord, have mercy.
   > Lord, have mercy on us all. (Repeat)
   >
   > Christ, have mercy. Christ, have mercy.
   > Christ have mercy on us all. (Repeat)
   >
   > Lord, have mercy. Lord, have mercy.
   > Lord, have mercy on us all. (Repeat)

   From the 'Israeli' Mass

3. *Gospel Reading*
   Second Reader: This is a reading from the Gospel of Matthew:
   Then Peter came to Jesus and asked 'Lord, if my brother keeps on sinning against me, how many times do I have to forgive him? Seven times?'
   'No, not seven times,' answered Jesus, 'but seventy times seven . . .' (Matthew 18:21–22)

Appreciation

1. Write down one (or more) reasons why it is good to be a member of this class, on a blank slip of paper. Put all the slips into a box or bag.

2. The teacher (or students) should read out the comments to the whole class.

3. Conclude by singing 'We are One in the Spirit'.

   We are one in the Spirit,
   We are one in the Lord;
   We are one in the Spirit,
   We are one in the Lord;
   And we pray that all unity
   may one day be restored.

   Chorus
   And they'll know we are Christians
   By our love, by our love;
   Yes, they'll know we are Christians
   By our love.

   All praise to the Father
   From whom all things come;
   and all praise to Christ Jesus
   His only Son,
   and all praise to the Spirit
   Who makes us one.

   Repeat *Chorus*.

QUESTIONS

1. How did you feel during this celebration?
2. Do you think it was worthwhile? Why/Why not?
3. According to this exercise, what different things are involved in being reconciled with other people?

The Sacrament of Reconciliation

All Christians, by reasons of their baptism, have the vocation to spread God's love in the world. When we ignore the needs of other people and when we refuse to be loving, we sin. Sin can mean deliberately being hurtful and mean to other people, but it can also mean deliberately refusing to help or love another person in some way. Being thoughtless or careless about others is not usually a serious sin, but it is often a sign that we are not fully living up to our vocation as Christians.

Real love and caring builds up the Christian community in the home, at school, in the neighbourhood and in the world. It brings people closer together. People who are loved feel good about themselves, closer to God and better able to bring God's love to others.

Reconciliation is all about bringing the Christian community closer together and closer to God. When reconciliation takes place, people are sorry for hurting one another and harming their relationships with each other as a community. They are able to forgive those who have hurt them and bear no grudge against them. *Reconciliation heals the hurt that people feel and makes it possible for them to really love each other again, without any barriers.* One of the ways in which we show that we are reconciled is to try to build up the community by encouraging people, praising them and showing them by our actions that we think they are worthwhile people.

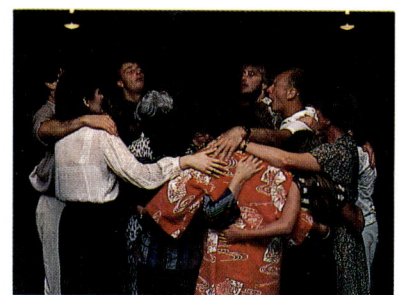

In the Sacrament of Reconciliation, we have a special opportunity to meet with the Risen Jesus and celebrate all the efforts we are making towards reconciliation in our class, in our families and in the wider community. We receive God's forgiveness for our sins, and we are filled with the strength to go on trying to build up the community so that we can all spread the news of God's love together. A community torn apart by selfishness, greed, injustice, violence or hatred cannot be a sign to the world of God's love. When we genuinely try to be reconciled and to love one another in the community, then God's love can be seen at work in the world.

EXERCISES

1. Give examples to show how you can build up the class community.
2. Do you think your class is a sign of God's love to the world? Explain your answer.

3. Give examples to show how the class community can be harmed by sin.

Assignment

Write a brief report explaining how celebrating the Sacrament of Reconciliation could help a parish to become reconciled as a community.

Reflection: 'You are the people of God; he loved you and chose you for his own. So then, you must clothe yourselves with compassion, kindness, humility, gentleness and patience. Be tolerant with one another and forgive one another wherever any of you has a complaint against someone else. You must forgive one another just as the Lord has forgiven you. And to all these qualities add love, which binds all things together in perfect unity.' Colossians 3:12–14

Action: Organise a reconciliation service for the members of the class, their families and friends. Remember to include the elements of sorrow for sin, forgiveness, the Word of God and the building up of the community through praise and thanks to one another and to God. This service could include the Sacrament of Reconciliation, or it could be a preparation for it.

Psalm: Happy are those whose sins are forgiven,
whose wrongs are pardoned.

. . . I confessed my sins to you;
I did not conceal my wrong-doings.
I decided to confess them to you
and you forgave all my sins.

So all your loyal people should pray to you
in times of need;
when a great flood of trouble comes rushing in,
it will not reach them.
You are my hiding place;
you will save me from trouble.
I sing aloud of your salvation
because you protect me.
Psalm 32: 1, 5–7

MARRIAGE

CHAPTER 29

▼

Angela and Stephen are a young married couple with one baby daughter Anne. They describe what being married means for them.

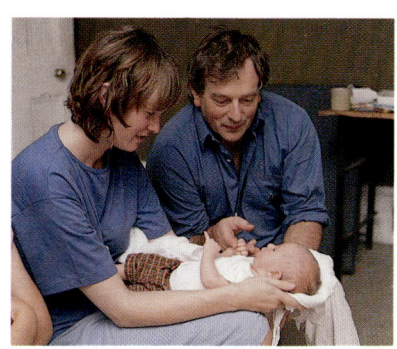

Angela
'I feel I am a more relaxed and happy person since I got married. I know that Stephen really loves me as I am and that makes me feel secure or safe in some way. I trust him and he trusts me completely. He believes in me and encourages me to have more confidence in myself. I work part-time with deprived young people and it can be stressful at times. It really helps to talk about what is happening at work with someone who really listens, who really cares about what I do.

I feel I have greater freedom now than I had before. I'm not afraid to try new things or to risk making mistakes. I don't worry so much about what other people think of me.

I have always been interested in needlework, especially tapestry, but I always treated it as a hobby. Stephen really admires my work and encourages me to spend more time at it because he knows how important it is to me. He will often take Anne out shopping, or to the park, so that I can do my tapestry. I am even thinking of setting up my own business soon, which I would never have done without his encouragement.

I feel I have a responsibility to share our love with other people, especially Anne. It's like the ripples in a pond that spread out from the centre. Being married to Stephen makes me realise how powerful love is, how it can change you and help you to grow and develop as a person. I want to love my family and friends, so that they can share in my happiness.

My marriage has brought me closer to God. Because Stephen loves me the way he does, I can understand better now how Jesus loves me. I feel that Stephen shows me what kind of person Jesus is, and what my relationship with him can be like.'

Stephen

'For me, marriage means living my life for the sake of Angela and Anne. Before I was married, I did what *I* wanted to do most of the time. I travelled abroad, had lots of different experiences. When I got married I didn't really realise how much I would have to give up in order to share my life with Angela.

We make all our decisions together, which isn't always easy — what is best for both of us is not always what *I* think I want! We have a lot less money now, especially since Anne was born, so foreign travel is out of the question for the time being. So marriage, for me, involves making sacrifices.

However, I'm a much happier person now than I was before. All the sacrifices seem to be worthwhile. Every day when I come home someone is there who wants to listen to me and tell me about her day, who wants and needs to get to know more about me, and who wants me to know her.

It is great to be able to share everything with Angela — our thoughts and feelings, our opinions and dreams. Even doing the washing-up, making the dinner or changing nappies are things we share happily because we are doing them for each other, as part of our life together.

Angela has taught me a lot about myself. I am a very impatient person, both with myself and with other people. I expect to be able to do everything instantly and perfectly. I think I have become less demanding and more tolerant because of Angela's influence.

One of the great things I have learned is to prize small things. When we were on our honeymoon in Venice, I would point out how magnificent some great building was, and Angela would point and say, "Look at the beautiful cat over there!" It's one of the things we laugh about now.

Angela has given me a lot of confidence in myself. I used to be full of self-doubt about my talents and abilities. Angela's interest and encouragement helps me to believe in myself.

I think that being married has brought me closer to God. God wants the best for all of us, and Angela and I want the best for each other. In a way we are "Godly" for each other. Being married has helped me to understand the meaning of being a Christian. Happiness is not the aim of marriage, any more than it is the goal of life. But happiness comes when you do what is right, when you really try to love each other as much as you can.'

Questions

1. What is your reaction to Angela and Stephen?
2. What kind of a person is Angela? Stephen?
3. In what ways has Angela changed because of her marriage to Stephen?
4. What does Angela's account tell you about Stephen?
5. In what ways has Stephen changed because of his marriage?
6. What does Stephen's account tell you about Angela?
7. (a) Are there any similarities between their statements about their marriage?
   (b) Are there any differences? Explain.
8. Is God an important part of their marriage? Explain your answer.
9. Do you think Angela and Stephen have a happy marriage? Explain, giving examples.

Marriage

Most teenagers are not thinking of getting married in the near future, although they may be interested in forming relationships with people of the opposite sex. However, most teenagers have some ideas about marriage and what it is like. Everyone knows some married people. Many teenagers actually live with a married couple — their parents or guardians. Apart from this, many songs, films, television programmes, magazines and books are all about people falling in love, getting married, having children, living happily ever after, or hating each other. Even stories which are mainly about war or alien beings from outer space usually have a 'love interest' somewhere in the script.

Many people in your class will be married in fifteen years' time. Many of you will have children. Over the next few years, you have the chance to prepare for a happy marriage. Trying to be loving and unselfish is a good way to start. It is also good to reflect on your own ideas about marriage and what you think it will involve. When you eventually meet someone you would like to marry, the two of you can plan together the kind of marriage you would like to have.

Exercises

1. Give some examples of married couples whom you have seen on television, in a film or in a book.

2. Choose one of your examples and explain:
   (a) Do you think this couple has a good marriage?
   (b) Is their marriage true to life?
   (c) Would you like to have this kind of marriage when you are an adult?
3. What do you think are the good things about being married?
4. What kinds of problems do you think married people face today? Choose one of these problems and briefly outline how a couple might try to solve this problem.
5. Where do you think you got your ideas about marriage?

Christian marriage is always witnessed by the community.

The Sacrament of Marriage

Christian marriage is a covenant between a woman and a man, by which they promise to love each other in a special way forever. Their love is an exclusive sexual love which makes the marriage relationship different from any other relationship. Because of their love for each other they want to be united, and share one life together physically, mentally and emotionally. This does not happen automatically on their wedding day. Becoming united with another person in heart and mind takes real love and sacrifice. Even people who have been married for years can have serious disagreements, family problems and other worries. Patience, kindness, politeness, unselfishness, calmness, forgiveness, honesty and faithfulness are some of the virtues which married people need in order to be able to live together in peace and grow more united.

> In the Christian community, when a man and a woman decide to marry each other, they have a special opportunity to receive God's blessing on their relationship in the Sacrament of Matrimony. On their wedding day, the couple publicly make their covenant with one another in the presence of a priest and two witnesses. Their families and friends are usually present also. The priest represents the Church which gives a special blessing to the newly married couple. For the rest of their lives, each of them will represent Jesus to one another. Each will try to love the other as Jesus loves. Through the priest, the community prays that the couple will be faithful to each other, that they will bring joy and happiness to each other, and that they will accept with love the children God may send them.

Christian marriage is a *vocation*. The two partners are called to spread the Good News of God's love by showing that love in their relationship with one another, and with their children.

When a woman and a man love each other in good times and in bad times, 'for richer, for poorer, in sickness and in health' all the days of their life, they are showing the whole world what real love means. An important part of this vocation is to teach their children how to love, by encouragement and example. The relationship between a husband and wife is also a powerful sign of the love God has for us — a passionate, self-sacrificing, life-saving and faithful love which will never end.

Exercises

1. In what ways is a Christian marriage relationship different from any other relationship? In what ways is it similar?
2. Do you think marriage is an important vocation? Why/Why not?
3. Look up the following Scripture passages. In each case, explain what the passage tells us about marriage and sexuality:
   (a) Genesis 1:26–31
   (b) Song of Songs 1:15–17, 4:9–11
   (c) Song of Songs 8:6–7
   (d) Romans 12:9–18
   (e) Colossians 3:12–17
   (f) Matthew 19:3–6

Rite of Christian Marriage

1. INTRODUCTORY RITE AND LITURGY OF THE WORD

This proceeds as usual at the beginning of Mass. The readings are chosen by the couple and the priest from the list provided by the Church. Some of these readings are given above in Exercise 3. Others include Mt. 5:1–12 (the Beatitudes); Jn 2:1–11 (the Wedding Feast at Cana); and I Cor 12:31–13:8 (true love).

2. RITE OF MARRIAGE

(a) *Introduction.* The priest addresses the bride and groom:
My dear friends, you have come together in this church so that the Lord may seal and strengthen your love in the presence of the Church's minister and this community. Christ abundantly blesses this love. He has already consecrated you in Baptism and now he enriches and strengthens you by a special sacrament so that you may assume the duties of marriage in mutual and lasting fidelity. And so, in the presence of the Church, I ask you to state your intentions.

Lighting the marriage candles

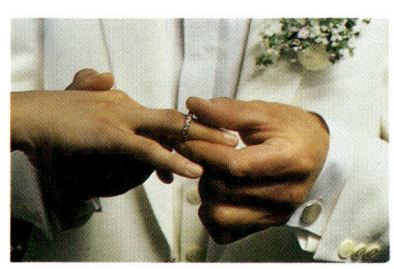

(b) *Statement of Intentions*. Priest questions the couple:

N. and N., have you come here freely and without reservation to give yourselves to each other in marriage?

Will you love and honour each other as man and wife for the rest of your lives?

Will you accept children lovingly from God, and bring them up according to the law of Christ and his Church?

(The couple answer each question separately.)

(c) *Consent*. The priest invites the couple to declare their consent.

Priest: Since it is your intention to enter into marriage, join your right hands, and declare your consent before God and His Church.
(They join hands.)

Groom: I, N., take you, N., to be my wife. I promise to be true to you in good times and in bad, in sickness and in health. I will love you and honour you all the days of my life.

Bride: I, N., take you, N., to be my husband. I promise to be true to you in good times and in bad, in sickness and in health. I will love you and honour you all the days of my life.

(d) *Reception of Consent*. The priest receives their consent for the whole Church:

You have declared your consent before the Church. May the Lord in his goodness strengthen your consent and fill you both with his blessings. What God has joined, men must not divide.

People: Amen.

(e) *Blessing and Exchange of Rings*. At this point in the ceremony, the rings are blessed and lovingly exchanged by the couple. The ring is a symbol for eternal love.

3. LITURGY OF THE EUCHARIST. The marriage Mass continues as usual with a few minor changes.

(a) After the Lord's Prayer, the priest faces the couple and gives a beautiful *nuptial blessing*. He praises God for His divine plan for creation in His image and likeness, for the beauty of marital love and marriage which symbolises Christ's love for His Church. Then he prays specifically for the couple that they might love and cherish each other for life.

(b) The rite concludes with a special blessing:

May God, the almighty Father,
give you His joy
and bless you in your children. *Response:* Amen.

May the only Son of God have mercy on you
and help you in good times and in bad. *Response:* Amen.

May the Holy Spirit of God
always fill your hearts with his love. *Response:* Amen.

And may Almighty God bless you all,
the Father,
the Son, and the Holy Spirit. *Response:* Amen.
(Adapted from *The Sacraments and You*, by M. Pennock)

QUESTIONS

1. What is meant by the 'duties' of marriage?
2. Pick out the phrases which make it clear that the priest does not 'marry' the couple, but that they confer the sacrament on each other.
3. Describe the symbols which are used as part of a marriage rite, including the ones mentioned in this account. Do you think these are good symbols for marriage? Why/Why not?
4. Invent a 'new' symbol for marriage. Explain it to the rest of the class.

ASSIGNMENT

1. (a) Interview some married people (both men and women) to find out their views on marriage. What do they think is good or difficult about being married? What do they remember about their wedding day? Do they see their marriage as a vocation?
(b) Record the answers on a tape, video or in written form. Present your findings to the rest of the class.
(c) Note the similarities and the differences in the responses. Did newly married couples have different ideas than those who had been married many years? Did men and women have different points of view? Did the people you interviewed bring up any of the points mentioned in this chapter?
(d) Write a report on 'Marriage in our Local Community' based on your findings.

Group Work

1. As a class, make out a list of topics which you feel engaged couples should learn about and discuss on a pre-marriage course. (For example, budgeting, coping with disagreements, sharing the housework, how many children they will have, where they will live, what kind of social life they will have etc.)
2. Get into groups of four or five. Each group should take one of the topics mentioned by the class and prepare a short talk about it, to give to a group of people on a pre-marriage course. The aim of your talk should be to get the engaged people thinking about the topic and to remind them of any difficulties they may face.
3. Each group should choose one or two people to give the talk to the rest of the class.
4. When it is your turn, pretend that the rest of the class consists of a number of engaged couples, and you are giving them a pre-marriage course. Read out the talk your group has prepared. Allow time for questions from the 'engaged couples'. (The rest of your group may help you to answer these questions.)
5. When every talk has been given, as a class make up a list of 'Ten Commandments' for a happy marriage, based on the 'talks', and on what you have learned in this chapter.

Discussion: Boy/girl relationships help you to prepare for marriage.

Reflection: 'No one has ever seen God, but if we love one another, God lives in union with us, and His love is made perfect in us.'
1 John 4:12

Action: Examine the ways in which marriage is shown on television — in films, advertisements and other programmes. Note how these views of marriage are often very different from the Christian view of marriage.

Psalm: O Lord, I will always sing of your constant love;
I will proclaim your faithfulness forever.
I know that your love will last for all time,
that your faithfulness is as permanent as the sky.

How happy are the people who worship you with songs,
who live in the light of your kindness!
Because of you, they rejoice all day long,
and they praise you for your goodness.
Psalm 89: 1–2, 15–16

HOLY ORDERS

CHAPTER 30

Father John is a curate in a parish in Co. Wexford. He describes what being a priest means to him:

'My Christian vocation is all about my relationship with people. I am a person called to be a leader in the Christian community. This involves being with people, recognising and encouraging their gifts, helping them to see and believe in their own worth and value. My vocation involves being with people in times of sorrow and joy, helping them to see the love of God at work in the events of their lives.

This does not mean I work alone or in isolation. In fact it frequently means working with parishioners who are already supporting and ministering to each other in different ways; for example, in the Society of St Vincent de Paul, in Bereavement Groups or small prayer groups. I see the parish as a wheel — the spokes all meet in the middle to form the axle. The priest acts as the axle, or the focus for the community.

A very important part of being a priest is allowing other people to influence me and challenge me so that I can continue to grow and develop as a person and as a priest.

All of the experiences of life are gathered together in the Liturgy. My vocation involves leading the people in prayer and worship. I believe that through the sacraments I can lead the people in bringing our experiences of pain and happiness to God. I can also bring God's blessing and love and healing to the people through the sacraments.'

UESTIONS

1. What is your reaction to Father John's account of his priesthood?
2. What kind of a person do you think he is?
3. Give examples of the kind of work Father John does. Do you know of any other work that priests do in a parish?

Every Christian is part of the 'priesthood' of all believers.

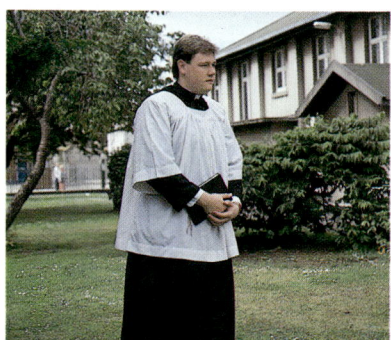

A deacon.

Archbishop Desmond Connell of Dublin.

4. Father John is a curate in a parish, an assistant to the parish priest. Do you know of any other 'jobs' that priests can have, apart from working in a parish? Explain.
5. Have you ever met a priest who impressed you or influenced you in any way? Explain your answer.

The Sacrament of Holy Orders

A priest is someone who speaks to God on behalf of others, and who brings the Word, love and forgiveness of God to them. Everyone who is baptised is a 'priest' in this way. All Christians are called to worship God and to pray for the whole world. We are called in a special way to pray on behalf of the poor, the outcast and the oppressed. We are also called to bring the Good News of Jesus Christ to others, in our words and in our actions. In all of these ways, every Christian is part of the 'priesthood' of all believers. As St Peter says:

' . . . you are the chosen race, a royal priesthood, a holy nation, God's own people, in order that you may proclaim the mighty acts of him who called you out of darkness into his marvellous light.' (Peter 2: 9)

> God calls some people to be 'ministerial' priests — bishops, priests and deacons. These are known as 'orders' of the Church. That is why the sacrament by which a person is ordained is called 'Holy Orders'. The vocation of an ordained priest is to help the community, by preaching the Gospel, leading and guiding the people and celebrating the sacraments, especially the Eucharist.
>
> The priest is called in a special way to represent Christ in the community. He tries to be the servant of everyone, especially the poor and the oppressed. Priests do not marry so that they will be free to give themselves and their time to the whole community.

EXERCISES

1. In what ways can you act as a 'priest' in your life?
2. What are the main differences between the vocation of an ordained priest and the vocations of the rest of the Christian community? Are there any similarities?
3. Make a list of the ways in which people need ordained priests.
4. The pope is called 'the servant of the servants of God'. Try to explain what this means to you.

5. Look up the following Scripture passages. In each case, briefly explain what the passage tells you about the ministerial priesthood.
   (a) Mt. 28:16–20
   (b) Acts 6:1–6
   (c) Acts 14:23
   (d) I Tim. 3:8–13

The Rite of Ordination for a Priest

1. *Introduction*
   The introductory rites of a typical Mass take place the same as usual up to the homily.
2. *The Call to Priestly Ministry*
   The deacon of the Mass calls each candidate by name. The response is: 'Present'. The candidates go before the bishop who receives them after a properly designated priest testifies that they have been trained and are worthy of receiving the sacrament. The bishop then addresses the people and the candidates on the meaning of priesthood.
3. *The Assent to Serve*
   The bishop now questions the candidates on their willingness to serve.

   Bishop: My sons, before you proceed to the order of the presbyterate*, declare before the people your intention to undertake this priestly office.
   Are you resolved, with the help of the Holy Spirit, to discharge without fail the office of priesthood in the presbyterial order as conscientious fellow workers with the bishops in caring for the Lord's flock?

   Candidates: I am.

   Bishop: Are you resolved to exercise the ministry of the Word worthily and wisely, preaching the Gospel and explaining the Catholic faith?

   Candidates: I am.

   Bishop: Are you resolved to consecrate your life to God for the salvation of His people, and to unite yourself more closely every day to Christ the High Priest, who offered himself for us to the Father as a perfect sacrifice?

   Candidates: I am, with the help of God.

   Bishop: Do you promise your ordinary obedience and respect?

   Candidates: I do.

* *presbyterate — the priesthood*

4. *Ordination*
   When the prayers are concluded, the candidates go and kneel before the bishop who lays hands on them. Then all priests present lay their hands on the candidates. The bishop now says the consecratory prayer. Part of the prayer is reproduced here.

Bishop: Almighty Father,
grant to these servants of yours
the dignity of the priesthood.
Renew within them the Spirit of holiness.
As co-workers with the order of bishops,
may they be faithful to the ministry
that they receive from you, Lord God,
and be to others a model of right conduct.

May they be faithful in working with the order of bishops,
so that the words of the Gospel may reach the ends of the earth,
and the family of nations,
made one in Christ,
may become God's one, holy people.
We ask this through our Lord Jesus Christ, your Son,
who lives and reigns with you and the Holy Spirit,
one God, for ever and ever.

Response: Amen

The ordination ceremony continues with the dressing of the new priests in chasubles*, anointing of the hands with chrism, the presentation of a chalice filled with wine and the exchange of a sign of peace.

5. *Liturgy of the Eucharist.*
   In the Liturgy of the Eucharist which follows, the newly ordained priests celebrate Mass for the first time, led by the bishop who ordained them.
   (Adapted from *The Sacraments and You* by M. Pennock)

* *Chasuble* — a large decorated garment worn over the white alb when the priest is celebrating the Eucharist

Questions

1. In what ways are priests called to serve the people?
2. Describe the symbols that are used as part of the rite of ordination. Do you think these are good symbols for the priesthood? Why/Why not?
3. Invent a new symbol for the priesthood. Explain it to the rest of the class.

Assignment

Interview one of your local priests. Ask him how he sees his vocation, how he spends his day, what kind of social life he has. Report your findings to the class, and compare your conclusions.

Reflection: Jesus 'appointed some to be apostles, others to be prophets, others to be evangelists, others to be pastors and teachers. He did this to prepare all God's people for the work of Christian service . . .' Ephesians 4:11–12

Action: Invite some people who are training to be priests to come and talk to your class, and answer any questions you may have.

Psalm: May the Lord answer you when
    you are in trouble!
  May the God of Jacob protect you!
  May he send you help from his Temple
    and give you aid from Mount Zion.
  May he accept all your offerings
    and be pleased with all your sacrifices.
  May he give you what you desire
    and make all your plans succeed.
  Then we will shout for joy over your
    victory
  and celebrate your triumph by
    praising our God.
  May the Lord answer all your
    requests.
                    Psalm 20: 1–5

THE CHRISTIAN COMMUNITY — THE CHURCH

THE HISTORY OF THE CHRISTIAN COMMUNITY

CHAPTER 31

It has been nearly 2000 years since Jesus called the first community of his followers together. In different times and in different places, Christians have tried to get to know Jesus better and to follow his teachings in their lives. Some of these people were saints, and their lives are examples to us all. Many Christians made mistakes, through ignorance or greed. Sometimes we can even be shocked by the events which took place and the ways in which people behaved.

The following account mentions some of the most important people and events in the history of the Church in Palestine and in Europe.

The Early Church

27–30 A.D. While Jesus was preaching, teaching and healing in Galilee, Judea and in Jerusalem itself, he gathered a *community of disciples* around him. Many tried to put his teachings into practice in their own lives, while going about their daily work in the usual way. Others followed him from place to place. Among these were the *twelve apostles* whom Jesus had chosen as his special companions.

Jesus gave the apostles a special authority to preach his gospel. Before he ascended into heaven he told them, 'Go, then, to all peoples everywhere and make them my disciples; baptise them in the name of the Father, the Son and the Holy Spirit, and teach them to obey everything I have commanded you.' (Matthew 28:19–22)

30 A.D.

In spite of this command, the apostles were too frightened to do what Jesus said until *the day of Pentecost, when they received the gift of the Holy Spirit*. On that day, the apostles, together with Mary the mother of Jesus, some of Jesus' relatives and many of the women who had remained faithful to him, were all filled with the Holy Spirit. From that day on, none of them was afraid to admit that they were followers of Jesus, and the apostles immediately began to preach in his name.

When anyone wanted to be a follower of Jesus and part of his community, the apostles baptised them with water as Jesus had said, and then they laid their hands on the newly baptised person so that the Holy Spirit would come upon them and fill them with love, courage and wisdom.

The believers shared everything in common, so that no one was in need. *They worshipped together in the Temple with the other Jews, and then met in each other's homes to celebrate the 'breaking of bread,' the special gift of himself that Jesus had left them as an 'everlasting Covenant'*. Soon there were small groups of 'Christians', as they became known, in most of the Jewish communities in the region.

Peter, the leader of the Christians, had a special vision given to him by the Holy Spirit which made him realise that the Good News of Jesus should be preached to Gentiles, as well as to Jews. However, it was *Paul* who was given the special vocation to travel all around the Mediterranean world and convert the Gentiles, after his own dramatic conversion on the road to Damascus. For this reason he is called the 'Apostle of the Gentiles'.

34 A.D.

The first Council or meeting of Christian leaders was held in Jerusalem. At this meeting, guided by the Holy Spirit, the apostles decided that anyone who wanted to follow Jesus did not first have to become a Jew as some had thought. Instead, they were to follow the law of Jesus, which was the fulfilment of the old law of Moses.

49 A.D.

The first Christians were seen as heretics and blasphemers by many Jews. Some Christians were stoned to death for their faith and most of them were treated with suspicion.

64 A.D.

The Romans also distrusted the Christians. When the city of Rome was swept by fire in the reign of the Emperor Nero, the Christians were used as scapegoats, tortured and killed. Eventually, all of the apostles (except perhaps John) and many other Christians were killed because of their faith in Jesus. *In spite of the terrible persecution, the Christian community grew larger and stronger.* The visits of the apostles and other preachers gave them great encouragement. In the same way, *the letters written by Paul, Peter and John, and the written accounts of the Gospel, helped to remind the people of Jesus and encouraged them to be faithful to him.*

When they met to celebrate the Eucharist, they would read parts of these letters and accounts of Jesus' words and actions, as well as sections from the Jewish Scriptures. *Eventually the Jewish Scriptures became known as the Old Testament, and the Gospels, Letters and Book of Revelation were called the New Testament.*

As the number of Christians grew larger, the apostles appointed overseers or *bishops* to carry on their work. The bishop was assisted by the *presbyters*, *deacons* and *deaconesses* and others who had special tasks in the community. The bishop and his assistants had the special task of serving the community by administering the sacraments, preaching and teaching the Good News of Jesus. *However, everyone in the community was called to serve in different ways, by loving each other and spreading the Good News by word and example.*

Each little group of Christians was called 'the Church', which means the people called together by God. All of the little communities together were also called 'the Church', and they all prayed for one another and helped each other in any way they could. The well-off communities in Rome and Corinth sent money and goods to the poorer community in Jerusalem, for example.

Christians gathered to celebrate the Eucharist.

Second Century

The community organised the catechumenate. This was a special time of study and prayer in which people who wanted to become Christians could learn about Jesus and his message. The catechumenate gave the catechumens an opportunity to realise what being a Christian meant in those difficult times. *No one could be baptised and initiated into the community until they had shown by their way of life and their faith that they were ready to follow Jesus.*

There were many local persecutions of Christians in the third century. Persecution of Christians was often ordered by the emperor.

Third Century

The Emperor Decius persecuted Christians in 250 A.D.

The Emperor Valerian persecuted Christians in 257 A.D.

Christians often had to meet in the Catacombs to escape discovery.

QUESTIONS

1. Why do you think people wanted to be Christians, even though they were persecuted?
2. Do you think you would have become a Christian if you had lived at this time? Explain.
3. What was the most important event in the early Church? Explain why you think so.

Christianity—The Religion of the Roman Empire

Fourth Century

The fourth century began with the great persecution by the Emperor Diocletian. But in *313 A.D. the Emperor Constantine, who was interested in the Christian religion, granted religious freedom to all Christians.*

Christians could now meet openly, preach freely and worship in public. Many great meeting places were built, so that the growing numbers of Christians could celebrate the Eucharist together. These 'churches' as they became known (because the 'Church', or people of God met there) were often splendidly decorated so that Christians could show their love and respect for God, but also to show the new importance of the Christian religion in the empire.

Whenever there were disputes or differences of opinion among the people about their faith or way of life, the bishops helped them to decide what was the right thing to do. In serious cases, the bishops met in a Synod, or council, to decide what was best for the whole Church community. In these matters, the Bishop of Rome (or the pope, as he became known) was the final authority. This was because he was the leader of the whole Church, as the successor to St Peter.

325 A.D.

The first ecumenical (or worldwide) council was held at Nicea. Every bishop was free to attend this meeting without fear of imprisonment or death. It is from this council that we get our creed, the statement of our Christian belief which we still proclaim today.

330 A.D.

Saints like Anthony and Basil founded some of the first monasteries in the desert. The monasteries consisted of people who wanted to devote their lives in a special way to the Gospel message. They lived a very simple life, with few possessions, fasting and praying together, sharing a common life and following the same rules

A monastery in the desert.

The western part of the empire was becoming weaker because of the invasions of various European tribes. Rome was considered unsafe, so Constantinople in Greece became the new capital of the empire. This caused problems for the Church community. The eastern bishops felt that the Patriarch of Constantinople should be equal to the pope, now that the emperor ruled from Constantinople. The pope and the western bishops did not agree. As the eastern and western parts of the empire grew further apart, and were ruled separately, so *the Christian community began to split more and more into two groups also.*

350 A.D.

The Emperor Theodosius made Christianity the official state religion of the whole empire. From now on it was dangerous to be a member of another religion. Eventually all other religions were completely outlawed. Now the Christians who had been persecuted for so long became persecutors themselves. Some of them burned synagogues and pagan places of worship. They imprisoned, fined and sometimes killed Jews and people who were not Christian.

380 A.D.

The empire was officially divided into East and West, two separate empires. The Christian community was still one Church, sharing the same beliefs, values and sacraments. However many of the customs were different between East and West; for example, the way in which they celebrated the sacraments and the rites they used were different. The official language of the East was Greek; in the West it was Latin. Also, the Western Church looked to the pope as their leader, while the Eastern Church gave similar respect to the patriarch of Constantinople.

395 A.D.

Christians began to build huge churches, such as the Basilica of St John Lateran in Rome.

1. What were the advantages of Christianity being the official religion of the empire?
2. Were there any disadvantages? Explain.
3. Would you have liked to be a Christian at this time? Why/Why not?

The Middle Ages

Over the next few centuries, the empire grew weaker and began to break up, especially in the west. The Christian community grew larger and stronger, partly because of its missionary activity. For example, Patrick converted the Irish (432 A.D.); Clovis, King of the Franks, and many of his people were baptised in 496 A.D.; St. Augustine of Canterbury converted the Anglo-Saxons of England (597 A.D.); St Boniface preached in the German-speaking lands (746 A.D.); St Cyril and St Methodius preached to the Slavic peoples (836 A.D.); and in 950 A.D. Poland was converted.

The Christian community also grew stronger because some of the power and authority which had belonged to the Roman emperor fell to the pope. *In this way the pope became a political leader as well as a religious leader, particularly after 476 A.D. when the Western Empire collapsed completely.*

During the Middle Ages, *monasteries* were a very important part of the Christian community. They were like little towns — indeed many towns grew up around them later. The life of the monastery was based on prayer. As well as the celebration of the Eucharist, the monks or nuns prayed together in the morning, at mid-day and in the evening. Many also got up to pray during the night, often more than once. The monasteries were centres of learning and education at a time when there was no public education in Europe at all. The monasteries were self-supporting. They grew and cooked their own food, made their own clothes, dishes and furniture. Many of them were very generous to the poor, to travellers and to pilgrims.

In 432, Patrick began converting the Irish to Christianity.

1054

There was a final break between the western and eastern parts of the Christian community when the patriarch of Constantinople refused to accept that the pope in Rome was the head of the Christian community. Both pope and patriarch denounced each other and cut off all ties between each other. This split was called a 'schism'. This word means that the split did not involve a dispute about the basic teaching of the Church.

St Francis of Assisi was born into a wealthy Italian family. When he grew up, he became aware of the terrible poverty and misery all around him. He believed that Jesus was calling him to be a monk, to preach to the poor, to show them God's love and to share their poverty with them, while building up the Church of God. He founded the *Franciscan Order*, and his friend *St Clare* founded the *Poor Clares*. Their example reminded people that God loves everyone, especially the poor and outcast. St Francis felt united with every living and natural thing — even 'Brother Sun', 'Sister Moon', 'Brother Wolf'. He saw God's love in the whole of creation.

1181

St Francis of Assisi.

1378-1417 The Great Western Schism

When Rome was attacked by foreigners, the pope moved for safety to *Avignon in France*. Later there was a row about who was the 'real' pope — the pope in Avignon, who said it was not safe yet to return to Rome; or the 'pope' in Rome. Later still a third 'pope' was elected to settle the dispute, but this only made things worse. *Eventually the leaders of the Church community agreed that Martin V was the only pope*. This schism did not affect the beliefs or way of life of ordinary Christians, but it brought the Church community into disrepute for fighting among themselves at such a high level.

The efforts of St Catherine of Siena, a very holy and learned woman, were of great help to the leaders of the Church when they were trying to heal the divisions in the Church leadership. She met with them and gave them good advice on how to deal with the situation.

1380

St Catherine of Siena.

QUESTIONS

1. In what ways did Christians make a contribution to the well-being of the societies in which they lived during the Middle Ages?
2. What do you think was the most important event or happening in the life of the Christian community at this time? Why?
3. Would you have liked to have been a missionary trying to convert the Germans or the Slavs at this time? Explain.

Reform of the Christian Community

By the late Middle Ages, it became obvious to many Christians that *the Church community needed to be reformed* in some ways. The Great Western Schism had shown that some Church leaders were more interested in having power than in serving the Christian community. Some Church leaders lived worldly, scandalous lives, and neglected their duty to look after their local community. Some bishops lived like political leaders, living on the money collected from the community, but hardly taking part in the life of the community at all.

Many priests were very badly educated and most of the people were not educated at all. This meant that they fell easily into superstition and unChristian ways without realising it. They still celebrated the sacraments and prayed together, but they needed to learn more about their faith to help them live it more fully in their lives.

Pope Alexander VI lived a scandalous life and poisoned many of his enemies.

1500

A Dutchman, Erasmus, wrote many books urging the Church leaders to reform the Church, improve the way it was run, remove unsuitable leaders and improve religious education.

Other reformers, like *Zwingli* in Switzerland, *Luther* in Germany and *Calvin* in France and Switzerland, wanted to go much further. They rejected the abuses in the Church community, but they also rejected some of the teachings of the Church, such as the authority of the pope and some of the sacraments. They wanted worship to be celebrated in the language of the people, not Latin; and they wanted all Christians to read and interpret the Bible for themselves.

Erasmus

The *Protestant Reformation*, as it was called, divided the Christian community into a number of groups, all of whom still shared many of the same beliefs and values but who disagreed on some very important points. Some countries, like England under Henry VIII, took advantage of the Reformation to set up national 'Churches', which would be under the control of the political ruler and free from the authority of the pope in Rome. In England, Henry VIII became the head of the Anglican Church, which had much the same beliefs and practices as the Catholic Church. This gave Henry more control over his people and also meant that the Church lands, money and property now belonged to Henry.

Martin Luther

The Council of Trent was held by the Christians of the Roman Catholic Church. *The aim of the Council was to remove the abuses in the Church community while remaining faithful to the traditional teachings of the Church.* The Council rejected the changes in belief brought in by the Protestant reformers, who were seen as heretics. The Catholic reforms included a better education in the faith for both priests and lay Christians; reform in religious orders and the lives of the clergy; and a greater effort to help the community to pray and work together so that they could come closer to God.

1545

King Henry VIII

The Council of Trent

QUESTIONS

1. Why do you think the Christian community needed to be reformed at this time?
2. Make a note of the different ways in which people tried to reform the Church.
3. The division of Christians into a number of different groups has often been called a tragedy. Do you agree? Why? Why not?
4. Is there any evidence to show that this period in our history still has an effect on our lives as Christians today? Explain.

The Age of Enlightenment

1600

St Vincent de Paul in France founded religious groups of men and women and also organisations for lay people. These groups wanted to help the poorest people in the community and show them that God loved them.

1620

Many Christians emigrated from Europe to colonise different parts of the world. Some of them went to escape persecution from other Christians at home, while others went to escape from poverty. Still others wanted to exploit the 'new' countries, hoping to become wealthy there. Most Christian groups preached the Gospel of Jesus in the new lands. In this way, *the Christian community gradually spread all over the world*, to India, Africa, North and South America, Australia and the Far East.

In spite of many set-backs and failures, Christians continued to try and follow Jesus in their lives and to improve and reform the Christian community. Some tried to do this by breaking away and forming separate communities based on different understandings of the Christian faith. Other outstanding Christians remained within the Catholic Church and continued to build up the community by their work and example.

St Vincent de Paul and the Sisters of Charity

1624–91

George Fox, the son of a Leicestershire weaver, began preaching in the mid-seventeenth century. He believed that Christ is an inward teacher, that there is an inward 'Light' in every person which makes it possible for them to respond to the guidance of the Holy Spirit in their lives. With his followers, George Fox held meetings in silence to 'wait upon the Lord'. People prayed spontaneously and had no organised liturgy. The Society of Friends, or Quakers as they became known, wore plain clothes, refused to use titles and treated everyone equally. They placed great emphasis on helping the suffering and especially reforming prisons.

1647–90

St Margaret Mary Alacoque was a French nun of the Order of the Visitation. During her lifetime she had many visions in which Jesus appeared to her and told her how much he loved people. He told her to spread devotion to his Sacred Heart, as a symbol of the great love of God for all human beings. This was at a time when many people thought of God only as a stern judge, so St Margaret Mary's message reminded people of

God's great love and the humanity of Jesus. In 1765, the Feast of the Sacred Heart was officially added to the Church's calendar.

John Wesley, a priest of the Anglican Church of England, had a spiritual experience in 1738 which changed his life. He wrote: 'I felt my heart strangely warmed. I felt I did trust in Christ, Christ alone for salvation; and an assurance was given to me that he had taken away my sins, even *mine*, and saved *me* from the law of sin and death.' He travelled throughout Great Britain and Ireland, preaching and gathering his followers into societies. John Wesley emphasised that everyone can be saved by believing in Jesus, and can know they are saved. His followers were known as 'Methodists' and later became a separate Church.

In Ireland, Catherine McAuley focussed on educating poor young girls and women. She also wanted to provide nursing care and medicine for the poor. Today her followers, the Sisters of Mercy, work in schools and hospitals all over the world. She was declared Venerable in 1989. This means that she is considered to be an example to the whole Church.

St John Bosco, an Italian, founded the Salesians to educate boys in their faith as well as in secular subjects. His mission was particularly directed to the poor who had no other hope of education. He himself was a very holy person and full of fun. He was a great favourite with the boys he taught.

The Sacred Heart, a symbol of God's love

1703–91

John Wesley preaching

1778–1841

Catherine McAuley

1815–88

UESTIONS

1. What do you find most interesting about this period of our history as a Christian community? Why?
2. In what ways did Christians contribute to the life of the society in which they lived at this time?

The Modern Age

The Industrial Revolution, the Enlightenment, the growth of scientific research and other factors meant that people lived and thought very differently in the 'new' world. The Christian community knew that its mission was still to spread the Good News of God's love by word and example, but they had to do this in a new kind of world. Far more people lived in cities instead of in the countryside so new parishes had to be set up, for example. Christians had to decide how to help the 'new poor' in the vast cities, whose problems were different from those of the poor in rural areas.

The Church leaders also had to work out the role they would play in the 'new' world. For centuries the pope had been a political and cultural leader as well as a religious leader. Now that most of Europe was divided into nation states, the pope no longer had political power.

1870

The bishops met at the First Vatican Council in Rome. They declared that:
1. *The pope's most important role is to be the pastor and teacher of the whole Church community.*
2. The pope is *infallible.* This means that he cannot make a mistake when he makes a solemn declaration about the Christian faith and Christian values.
3. *The Holy Spirit guides the pope* as the leader of the whole Church, so that the Church community will remain faithful to the teachings of Jesus.

The First Vatican Co...

1897

An unknown Carmelite nun, Thérèse of Liseux in France, died of tuberculosis at the age of 24. Over the next few years the Christian community began to learn about her life. She had done nothing spectacular — she had simply tried to do the 'ordinary things extraordinarily well'. This included prayer, taking part in the Eucharist, doing housework, being patient and kind in her relationships, putting other people first. She always thought of God as her Father and was very aware of how much God loved her. St Thérèse was canonised (officially declared a saint) in 1925.

St Thérèse of Lisieux

1941

Maximilian Kolbé died in the Auschwitz concentration camp. He had been imprisoned when the Germans took over Poland because he was a priest. In the camp he was a great comfort and help to the other prisoners. When some people escaped, the guards decided to kill some prisoners in retaliation, and to dissuade other people from trying to escape. Maximilian was not chosen to die, but he offered to take the place of another prisoner who was filled with grief at the thought of never seeing his family again. So Maximilian, along with the other condemned prisoners, was left to die of cold and starvation and thirst. Up until the end, over a week later, Maximilian prayed with the others, encouraged them to sing hymns and to die peacefully. He himself was the last to die and eventually was killed by the guards with an injection of poison. Maximilian Kolbé was canonised for his self-sacrifice, faith and love in 1983. The man whose life he had saved was present at the ceremony.

St Maximilian Kolbé

1948

Mother Teresa of Calcutta began working with 'the poorest of the poor', with only five rupees in her pocket. Today her Missionaries of Charity work all over the world, bringing the love of God to the suffering, the dying, the poor and the neglected. She sees the person of Jesus Christ in every leper, abandoned baby, dying man or woman. Her message to the world is to try to love *one* person who really needs you, rather than saying 'I can do nothing, the world's problems are too great.'

Mother Teresa

1962

Pope John XXIII, the son of a poor Italian farmer, called the bishops of the Church together for the Second Vatican Council. The aims of the council were:
1. to help the Christian community to adapt to the needs of the world around them so that it could be a better sign of God's love in the world; and
2. to work for Christian unity.
   Apart from the bishops, many observers were invited to attend the Council — some lay Catholics and also Orthodox, Anglican and Protestant Christians.

Pope John XXIII

Some important teachings of the Council are:
1. All people everywhere can come to know God, and the Catholic Church 'rejects nothing of what is true and holy' in different religions.
2. All people are entitled to religious freedom. The Council specifically condemned anti-semitism in any form, as well as the hatred or persecution of people because of their religion.
3. The Liturgical celebrations of the Church should be revised, so that the community could be more actively involved. The language used was to be the ordinary language of the people, rather than Latin alone, and the whole community was to spend more time studying and praying the Scriptures so that their faith would be renewed.
4. The lay-people of the Church, who share in the 'priesthood of all believers', were to take a more active role in the mission and life of the Church community.
5. The whole Church community should work and pray for unity among all Christians, recognising and respecting the sincerely-held beliefs of all Christians.
6. Christians have a responsibility to put their faith into practice in the world around them, and especially to work for peace, justice and the liberation of the poor.

1965

Pope Paul VI

Pope Paul VI visited the Holy Land in 1964 and met the *Patriarch of Constantinople, Athenagoras. In 1965, the two met again in St Peter's Basilica in Rome and officially made peace between the Orthodox and Catholic Christians.* A commission was set up to work towards complete unity between the two groups.

In the same year, *Pope Paul VI went to New York to attend the General Assembly of the United Nations.* He made a dramatic impact on the Assembly, calling for an end to war as a way to settle differences between nations.

Archbishop Oscar Romero of El Salvador in South America was very strong in his support of the poor and oppressed in his country. Because of this, he was shot dead in his cathedral just after celebrating the Eucharist. He is a present-day martyr who died because of his faith, which led him to love the poor.

At the present time, the Christian community all over the world is trying to put its faith into practice. The prayer and liturgical celebrations of all Christians give them the hope and courage to continue to spread the Good News of God's love, particularly to the poor and the oppressed.

Pope John Paul II travels all over the world speaking to members of the Christian community in every country and celebrating the Eucharist with them. He has a special love for young people and sees in them the future of the Church.

1980

Pope John Paul I

Pope John Paul II in Africa

QUESTIONS

1. What new challenges face Christians in the modern world?
2. In what ways are Christians contributing to the well-being of the world today?
3. What is your reaction to this brief account of the Christian community?
4. Is there anything in the account that makes you feel glad or proud to be a member of this community? Explain.
5. Is there anything in the account that saddens you? Explain.
6. In what ways do you think the Church community today is the same as the early Church community? In what ways is it different? Do you think the community will be changed in any way over the next few centuries? Explain.

EXERCISES

1. Pick out the three most important moments in the history of the Christian community, and explain *why* they are important.
2. Are there any important events or people left out of this account and which you think should be included? Explain, giving your reasons.

ASSIGNMENT

Write an account of a Christian (living or dead) who you think has made an important contribution to the Christian community.

The Vocation and Mission of the Laity (Pope John Paul II, 1989)

In a great many countries of the world, [young people] represent half of entire populations, and often constitute in number half the People of God living in those countries. Simply from this aspect youth makes up an exceptional potential and a great challenge for the future of the Church. In fact the Church sees her path towards the future in the youth . . . the Council has defined youth as 'the hope of the Church' . . . The words of St John in his first letter can serve as special testimony: 'I am writing to you, young people, because you have overcome the evil one. I write to you, children, because you know the Father . . . I write to you, young people, because you are strong and the word of God abides in you' (1: Jn. 2:13ff) . . . In our generation, at the end of the second Millennium after Christ, the Church also sees herself in the youth.

(Taken from Paragraph 46)

QUESTIONS

1. According to Pope John Paul II, why are young people important in the Church?

2. Give examples to show that young people:
   (a) have great potential
   (b) present a challenge to the Church community
   (c) can learn from the wider Church community.
3. According to St John, what qualities make young people particularly valuable as Church members?

PROJECT

As a class, research the history of your local parish community — when it was founded and by whom; the main events, movements, groups and individuals who are remembered by the community; and the life of the community today, and in particular the part played by young people. As well as researching books, pamphlets and other records, be sure to ask the members of your community for their memories.

People could work individually, in pairs or in small groups, focussing on *one* event, period, person, group or building.

The project should be displayed where everyone in the community can view it, for example in the parish church or community hall.

Reflection: 'You, too, are built upon the foundation laid by the apostles and prophets, the cornerstone being Christ Jesus himself. He is the one who holds the whole building together and makes it grow into a sacred temple dedicated to the Lord. In union with him you too are being built together with all the others into a place where God lives through his Spirit.'
Ephesians 2:20–22

Action: Interview some of the members of your local Church community, asking them: 'What does it mean for you to be a member of the Christian community?' Share your answers or findings with each other in class. What do your findings tell you about your local community?

Psalm: Give thanks to the Lord, because he is good,
and his love is eternal.
Let the people of Israel say,
'His love is eternal.'
Let the priests of God say,
'His love is eternal.'
Let all who worship him say,
'His love is eternal.'
Psalm 118: 1–4

THE MISSION OF THE CHRISTIAN COMMUNITY

CHAPTER 32

Examine each of the following situations carefully. Pick out the ones which you think the Church community should be involved in. Note whether, in your opinion, Christians should get involved in these situations:

    (a)   as individuals, working or acting privately;
    (b)   as a local group — parish, organisation etc.;
    (c)   as an official community, through the words and actions of the pope and bishops;
    (d)   in a number of these ways.

1. A particular group of people is being discriminated against and treated unjustly by the law in a certain country because they have a different culture and tradition than the majority of people in the country.
2. There is a general election taking place in a democratic country.
3. There is a referendum taking place in a democratic country to decide whether or not to make voluntary euthanasia legal.
4. The neighbours know that a particular woman is frequently beaten up by her husband, and she often goes to their houses looking for help, or for somewhere to stay for the night.
5. A sixteen-year-old girl is having a birthday party with her friends.
6. The teenagers in a certain town usually meet in a pub because there is nowhere else for them to socialise in the town.
7. A company which manufactures dangerous chemicals is looking for planning permission to set up a chemical factory near a town.
8. There is a very high rate of unemployment in an area of a city.
9. Many of the books and magazines in a local shop are pornographic.
10. There will be a big public celebration when the winner of two gold medals in the Olympics comes back to her home town.

Group Work

1. Get into groups of four or five.
2. Each person should call out the situations in which they feel members of the Church should be involved.
3. As a group, try to agree on which situations should be chosen.
4. Try to come to some agreement on which member or members of the Church community should get involved in the situations you have chosen as a group.
5. Briefly suggest what these persons, groups or leaders could actually do in each situation.
6. Each group reports back to the class. Note the similarities and the differences between the reports.

Assignment

Briefly outline the picture of the Church community which seems to come from the group reports. What is important to this community? What kinds of things does it do? What is the relationship between the Church community and the rest of the society, or the rest of the world?

> **The Mission of the Church Community**
> All Christians are given a special task or mission at Baptism. This mission is to spread the good news of God's love throughout the whole world and to prepare for the coming of the Kingdom of God. We are called upon to do this in many ways — through our words, attitudes and actions. It is not enough to *tell* other people that God loves them. We must *show* by what we do that we love other people and want to help them in all situations.

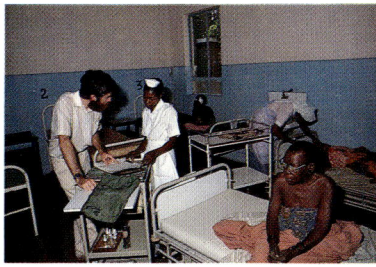

Missionaries at work in a hospital.

There are three main ways in which Christians can be missionaries, or bring God's love to the world.

1. *We can serve other people.*
   When we serve other people, we put their needs first. We do what we can to help them, without expecting great thanks or reward. A servant is someone who does a job without making a fuss. As Christians, it is our job to serve others as Jesus served the people of his time. When we spend time listening to people, helping them at home or in

We can help each other . . .

school, or thinking of ways to make their lives easier, we are showing in a practical way that God loves them and that the Kingdom of God is near.

2. *We can speak out against evil in the world.*
Each of us is called upon to 'stand for God' and speak the truth about the situations in which we find ourselves. When we know that something is unjust, or that someone's life is being threatened, or when any other evil is present in a situation, then, as Christians, we must try to do something about it. First, we must call attention to what is wrong in the situation. Secondly, we must take whatever action we can to remove the evil.

For example, if a third-year student knows that a first-year student is being bullied, the third-year student cannot keep silent. She or he can speak to the bully, or, if this is impossible, speak to the authorities in the school about the situation. He or she might take direct action by walking to and from school with the victim, or getting his/her friends together to protect the victim from further harrassment. The whole school community should make it clear that it will not tolerate bullying by taking quick action when it occurs.

Sometimes there are evil situations which an individual cannot tackle alone — such as world hunger or war. In these situations, all Christians must act together as a community to bring God's word of love to the situation.

When we speak out against evil and take action to defeat it, we are a sign to the world that God loves people and wants to free them from evil.

3. *We can pray for others.*
   When we pray for people, privately or as a community, we are placing their needs before God. We are showing that we know God is concerned about them and wants to help them. One of the main ways in which God shows love to people is through other people. When we pray for others, we ourselves become better able to love them and care for them.

   When we pray, we are opening ourselves to the power of God's love which can transform even the worst situation. Our prayer is a sign of how much we need God in our lives. It gives us the strength and courage we need to keep on serving others and speaking out against evil. Prayer is therefore a vital part of our missionary task.

A young people's day of prayer.

Exercises

1. Look back over the situations mentioned at the beginning of the chapter.
   (a) In each situation, give examples to show how Christians could be missionaries and bring God's love to each situation.
   (b) Could a teenager be a missionary in any of the situations? Explain.
2. Give examples of individual Christians or Christian groups/organisations who act as missionaries in any way.
3. Whom do you usually think of as missionaries? Why? Do they act as missionaries by (a) serving or (b) speaking and acting against evil, or (c) praying? Explain your answer.
4. How could each of the following people be a missionary by following their own vocation?
   (a) a single person working in a shop
   (b) a married person working on a farm
   (c) a religious brother or sister working in a nursing order
   (d) a nun or monk in a contemplative order, living a life of prayer, penance or work.
5. How could a teenager be a missionary:
   (a) at home
   (b) at school
   (c) in the local community?

Reflection: 'The end of all things is near. You must be self-controlled and alert, to be able to pray. Above everything, love one another earnestly, because love covers over many sins. Open your homes to each other without complaining. Each one, as a good manager of God's different gifts, must use for the good of others the special gift he has received from God. Whoever preaches must preach God's messages; whoever serves must serve with the strength that God gives him, so that in all things praise may be given to God through Jesus Christ, to whom belongs glory and power for ever and ever. Amen.'
1 Peter 4:7–11

Action: Decide on a task you will undertake as a class as part of your mission to your local community.

Psalm: Sing to the Lord, all the world!
Worship the Lord with joy;
come before him with happy songs!

Never forget that the Lord is God.
He made us, and we belong to him;
we are his people, we are his flock.

Enter the temple gates with thanksgiving;
go into its courts with praise.
Give thanks to him and praise him.

The Lord is good;
his love is eternal
and his faithfulness lasts forever.
Psalm 100

ECUMENISM

CHAPTER 33
▼

Ecumenism is the name given to the efforts that Christians are making to understand and respect each other, and to grow more united. There are many young people involved in ecumenism, as the following account shows.

Taizé

Every year, thousands of young people from all over the world travel to a small town in France called Taizé. Catholics, Protestants, Anglicans, Eastern Orthodox — young people of every faith. Some are workers; some are students; others are unemployed. They come to deepen their faith, to meet other young people from all over the world and to pray with the community of brothers who live in Taizé.

The community of Taizé was founded by Roger Louis Schutz-Marsauche, who is Swiss. He is called Brother Roger and he moved to Taizé in 1940, during the Second World War. His dream was to set up a community of people who would share a common life of prayer, work and recreation together. This community would be a sign of peace and reconciliation, witnessing to Christ by their prayers and actions. One of the most important aims of the community is to work for unity among Christians. Brother Roger says:

> 'It is true that we cannot solve here and now, all the . . . problems that have separated Christians through the centuries. What we can do is begin with a concrete act, by sharing all we can share, and above all, our lives'

The first brothers were all from two or three European countries, mainly France and Switzerland. Today there are brothers from twenty countries in Western and Eastern Europe, Asia, Africa and America. Living and praying together, from such different backgrounds, is a small but very real sign of reconciliation in the human family. It is also a sign of reconciliation in the Church, since the brothers come from many different Christian denominations, including Catholic, Lutheran, Anglican and Eastern Orthodox. Each brother continues to follow his own faith while sharing the common life.

The brothers did not plan for Taizé to become a place of pilgrimage, but they always made visitors welcome. When more

Young people come to Taizé from all over the world.

and more people came, they organised simple accommodation for them and tried to help them make the most of their time at Taizé.

Three times a day, the bells ring out. The discussion groups stop talking and the 'welcome area' closes down, the kitchen team leaves its pots and puts down its knives. Everyone — brothers and pilgrims alike — stops their activities and heads towards the Church of Reconciliation. Whether you are at Taizé for a week, a month or for life, everything is centred on prayer. For the new arrivals, it can be surprising or even frightening to discover that you are expected to attend prayer three times in a single day. According to one boy from Sweden: 'At home I go regularly to church on Sunday, but I was rather disturbed at the thought of going to church so many times in one week.' And what about those who never go to church at home!

However, by the end of the week, most young people are wondering how they could put into practice at home what they have discovered at Taizé. They love the prayer which includes the chanting of psalms, scripture readings, intercessions and so on. This takes place in many languages. During one time of prayer you may hear English, German, Swedish, Spanish, Italian, Portuguese — even Chinese and Japanese. Reading the Gospel in ten different languages gives people a sense of the world-wide nature of the Church.

Prayer is very important at Taizé.

The music of Taizé is famous. The community wanted to allow everyone to take part in the singing, but how could they do this when there were so many different languages spoken, and when most people only stayed for a few days? The solution was to use a few words, which people could easily learn, and to sing them over and over to the beautiful melodies composed by the brothers.

After the Bible readings, there is always a time of silence. This is followed by prayers for people all over the world — the persecuted, the forgotten, the suffering. At the end of the evening prayers, many of the young people remain in the church and the singing continues, sometimes for hours. Some of the brothers also remain. They listen to any young people who have something they wish to talk about, or who have personal difficulties which they want to discuss.

The young people gather in groups throughout the day to discuss important issues. Every afternoon at five, people stop for a cup of tea after a busy day of Bible introductions, small groups sharing, prayer, silent reflection and practical work. During tea, the 'intercontinental' meetings take place. This is a time for those who come from farthest away to share something of their country, their faith, their own hope and those of their people. They have come from South Africa and Zaire, from Chile and Peru, from Haiti and Thailand . . . It becomes a real challenge when, after a week spent in Taizé, they begin to reflect on how to continue when they return home. As the week comes to an end, regional meetings are organised. At the end of the morning Bible introduction for that day, a brother explains where the different nationalities will meet — the Spanish under the large tent; the Africans in front of the church; the Irish at the Yellow House. In these meetings, the young people plan how they will contribute to the life of their Church community at home, how they will build up their local parish and how they will work for justice, peace and reconciliation. An important part of this is making links between Christians of different denominations, praying and working together.

Sharing a meal at Taizé.

In order to continue the spirit of Taizé outside the place itself, a huge meeting of young people is held in a European city each year. In 1981, the meeting took place in London; in 1986 it was in Berlin; and in 1989, young people from both East and West met in the town of Pécs in southern Hungary.

During these meetings, the young people share in the life of the Christians of that city. They spend four or five days living, worshipping and reflecting together with the Christians there.

On the first day, until late at night, thousands of young pilgrims arrive in the city, invading the railway and underground stations before making their way to the parishes. They are heading for the places of welcome which have been set up, according to languages. Once they reach these welcome points, they are sent to the places where they will be staying. Those who arrive often do not speak a word of the language of their host country, so from the very beginning it is a journey of trust!

Long before this can happen, however, a long preparation time is needed. Shortly after Easter, those who are in charge of preparing the meeting go from one parish and community to another in the city that has been chosen. A conversation with the person in charge, a contact with the groups in the parish, a simple prayer service — things are underway. Little by little, a network of contacts grows up in the city. In each parish, families offer to welcome one, two or more pilgrims. Groups are formed to take charge of the welcome, to organise the families, to reflect on how to make the meeting a meaningful event for the parish. An important part of the preparation is looking for signs of hope in the community which can be shared with those who come to the meeting. By the time the meeting takes place, Christians generally discover that they have much more to share with those who arrive than they had thought. In London, one sign of hope was a shelter for homeless people run by the Methodists. The minister explained: 'Christ loves us just as we are, so we welcome those who come just as they are — tramps, alcoholics, prostitutes and so on. Our job is to love them.'

A similar gathering was held in Ireland in May 1985. On the first day of the meeting, five thousand participants filled three large churches in Dublin — the Catholic Pro-Cathedral, St Patrick's Church of Ireland cathedral, and a third church in a poor neighbourhood. When Brother Roger spoke in one of the churches, he could be heard simultaneously in the other two.

Several hundred young people came from Northern Ireland for the meeting. For some Protestants from the North, it was the first time they had entered a Catholic church. The Catholic archbishops and leaders of the other Churches took part in the prayers.

The young people who go to Taizé and try to live the spirit of Taizé back home in their own parishes realise that the purpose of ecumenism is not just to unite Christians. An important goal is to enable Christians to go out to other people to show the whole world that God loves them. When we are reconciled as Christians and when we share a wider faith together, then we can be a better sign of hope, love and reconciliation to the world.

(adapted from *The Story of Taizé* J.L. Gonzalez - Bolado)

QUESTIONS

1. What do you think about Taizé? Do you think you would like to go there some day? Why? Why not?
2. Do you think Taizé is a good example of ecumenism in action? Explain your answer.

EXERCISES

1. A number of groups such as those at the Corrymeela Centre, the Rostrevor Christian Renewal Centre and Columba House in Derry work for greater understanding between Christians in Ireland. Why do you think ecumenism is needed so urgently in Ireland?
2. Make a list of the ways in which your class can build bridges between Christians of different denominations in your local

At the Rostrevor Christian Renewal centre in Northern Ireland, Christians of all denominations try to deepen their faith and their understanding of one another.

area. (The examples given by Taizé should give you a few ideas.)
3. Share your ideas with the rest of the class. Plan to put *one* idea into action.

Assignment

The Corrymeela Summerfest helps to promote peace and reconciliation between all groups of people in society.

In order to truly understand and respect the way of life, beliefs and values of other Christians, we must first understand and respect our own faith's traditions. Answer the following questionnaire to briefly explain what being a Catholic means to you.

As a young Catholic . . .
1. What are my most important beliefs?
2. What are my most important values?
3. What are the important signs and symbols of my faith?
4. How do I take part in the life of my Church community?
5. How do I feel about being a Catholic?

Share your answers with the rest of the class.

If you get a chance, ask some young people of other Christian denominations to answer the same questionnaire to explain what being a Christian means to them. Share your answers with each other.

Reflection: 'By the authority of Our Lord Jesus Christ, I appeal to all of you, my brothers, to agree in what you say, so that there will be no divisions among you. Be completely united, with only one thought and one purpose.' 1 Cor 1:10

Oratory at Columba House, Derry.

Action: Get a tape of the Taizé music and learn some of the chants.

Psalm: I am listening to what the Lord God is saying;
he promises peace to us, his own people,
if we do not go back to our foolish ways.
Surely he is ready to save those who honour him
and his saving presence will remain in our land.

Love and faithfulness will meet;
righteousness and peace will embrace.
(Our) loyalty will reach up from the earth,
and God's righteousness will look down from heaven.
Psalm 85: 8–11

For more information about Taizé, contact:
The Taizé Community
71250 Cluny, France.

DIALOGUE WITH WORLD RELIGIONS

CHAPTER 34
▼

Very Reverend Rabbi Ephraim Mirvis, Chief Rabbi of Ireland

Judaism

In the following interview, Ephraim Mirvis, the Chief Rabbi of Ireland, explains the main beliefs, teachings and way of life of Orthodox Jews today.

Q. What are the main Jewish beliefs?

A. The unity of God is our most important belief. I think it's important to quote the verse from Deuteronomy, Chapter 6:

'Hear, O Israel, the Lord, our God, the Lord is One.'

This is a verse which one is advised to recite on one's deathbed, (God forbid!) and we are also instructed to say it twice a day. In this particular verse, we have an expression of our very deep belief that there is one God and that He is the power which created the universe and who continues to rule the world.

We also believe in the Bible. The Jewish Bible is what Christians call the Old Testament. We believe that the first five books of the Bible, the books of Moses, have particular sanctity or holiness because they came directly from heaven. We call these books the Torah. The rest of the Bible does not have the same sanctity, but it is still very important. Jews follow the teaching of the Bible to the letter.

The Talmud, which was written by wise rabbis, is also very important to Jews. It explains how we should apply the teachings of the Bible to our daily lives.

Q. Is Judaism, then, mainly about following laws?

A. Only to some extent. One sometimes finds that there is an unfair comparison being made between Christianity and Judaism, suggesting that Christianity is a religion of love whereas Judaism is a religion of law and this is very much not the case. The Talmud tells us that the most important commandment of the

Torah is to love your neighbour as yourself. We should love everyone and always have compassion for other people. And indeed the main purpose of being the Chosen People is to set an example of love to others by our whole way of life. I have no doubt that the fact that Jesus concentrated so much on aspects of love and consideration was because of his Jewish background and upbringing.

Q. Are festivals important in Judaism?

A. Yes, they are very important. Our calendar is filled with special dates and occasions. To a large extent these tell the story of the Jewish people, and there are many wonderful happenings to celebrate. At the same time, unfortunately, we have many sad and tragic events which we commemorate. We celebrate Passover, Pentecost, Tabernacles, New Year (the Jewish New Year) and Yom Kippur, as well as many minor festivals like Hanukkah. There are also six public fast days on our calendar, on which we remember tragedies of the past. So we have a good mixture of the happy and the sad.

Special foods are used at Passover.

In this regard, I think its important that people should appreciate the extent of the suffering of the Jewish people over the ages. The holocaust of the Second World War is only one example of numerous occasions during the history of our people when we have suffered terribly because of anti-semitic sentiment. There is no doubt that one of the greatest miracles ever to take place in the history of the world is the survival of the Jewish people. It is of tremendous significance to us that God has kept His people alive, and that in modern times, He has returned His people to the land of Israel.

Q. How do Irish Jews feel about the land of Israel today?

A. Israel is very important to Irish Jews. This was reflected in the fact that, with the establishment of the state of Israel, quite a large number of Irish Jews went to live in that country. I think it's important for people to be reminded that the president of the state of Israel is Chaim Herzog, an Irish Jew, someone who was born in Belfast, raised in Dublin and who is very proud of that fact. At this time Irish Jews fully support Israel, pay visits to Israel, and some of those who leave the country settle in Israel. There is a very close link between Jews in Ireland and Israel. In this regard there is an interesting similarity between the Jewish people and the Irish people. I think Irish people should find it easy to understand the sense of belonging to a

The candles at Hanukkah.

country, to a nation, to a people, even though one lives elsewhere and one has never even visited one's homeland, so to speak. One finds situations occasionally in which Irish-Americans can be even more Irish than those in Dublin and Cork. Yet they are still loyal to the country in which they are living. Similarly, the fact that we owe allegiance to Israel and support Israel does not raise any conflicts with our Irishness. In the same way as there are Irish Catholics and Irish Protestants, there are also Irish Jews. We don't consider ourselves to be Jews living in Ireland: rather, we are Irish Jews and we are proud to be citizens in this country and to be fully involved in every aspect of public life.

Q. How important is it for Jews to attend services in the synagogue?

A. It is preferable to pray in the synagogue with the community, but one may also pray alone. There are three synagogue services on weekdays and four on the Sabbath. Those who find it difficult to attend the synagogue pray at home. Even on the Sabbath there is no obligation to attend service, even though we prefer and expect people to do so.

Blessing the Sabbath candles.

Q. Apart from attending services in the synagogue, how do Jews celebrate the Sabbath?

A. The Sabbath lasts from just before Sunset on Friday evening until there are three stars in the sky on Saturday evening. Our Sabbath is a very enjoyable day of family togetherness, coupled with spiritual joy and upliftment. In remembering that after the 6 days of creation God rested on the Sabbath day, we too rest from creative activity, which includes, amongst other things, not working for a living or turning on electrical equipment. However, do not imagine that we sit in darkness on our Sabbath or that we have cold food and so on. Some people leave their lights on in certain rooms right through the Sabbath, others could use a time switch. And then we place an absestos sheet over a gas hob and that keeps the food on the sheet warm right through the day. There are delicious recipes for food which matures overnight. Therefore we are able to properly observe the Sabbath day while enjoying all pleasures.

The family celebrates the Sabbath Kiddush when the father comes home from the synagogue.

Q. How important is family life in Judaism?

A. Meaningful family life is a well known feature of Jewish existence. We stress the importance of very close family units. We feel that on Friday evenings at the Sabbath table, all members of the family should be present, sometimes even the extended family as well. Members of Jewish families feel very close to one another. Our tradition insists that parents should instruct their children and this they do both formally and informally, and also through example.

Q. Do you try to convert people to Judaism?

A. No. Judaism is not a missionary faith. We do not believe that salvation will come to the world only through every person being a member of the Jewish faith, or accepting God as Jews do. Consequently, we do not consider it of great importance to spread our doctrine and our faith. People may convert to Judaism, but it is difficult to do so. We believe there is more than one way for people to come close to God, so we hope that people who are members of other faiths will try to be faithful to their own traditions. As the Chosen People, we should serve as an example to the other peoples of the world, with the Torah as our guide.

Q. How do you see the relationship between Judaism and Christianity?

A. There are a number of very basic and important differences between the two. For example, Jews do not attach any significance to Jesus, to his life or to what he stood for as perceived by Christians. At the same time we have much in common such as the values of love and justice. Christianity has in its roots the Jewish faith and therefore has taken much from Judaism. We have a lot to build on towards having a meaningful relationship between members of the two faiths.

The synagogue decorated with flowers for the festival of Tabernacles.

Q. Are there any efforts being made at present in Ireland to improve the relationship between Jews and Christians?

A. There is an Irish Council of Christians and Jews. Representatives from all the major Christian denominations and from the Jewish community sit on this Council. It was established in 1980, under the patronage of the Cardinal of Ireland, the Archbishop of Dublin, the heads of all the Churches and the Chief Rabbi of the day. The existence of the Council shows that there is a common desire for Jews and Christians to work together towards greater understanding.

(December 1990)

QUESTIONS

1. What is your reaction to Judaism as it is presented here?
2. Does anything appeal to you about this religion? Explain.
3. Is there anything about Judaism you find difficult to understand? Explain.
4. (a) What do you think are the main similarities between Judaism and Christianity?
   (b) What are the main differences?

Islam

In the following interview, the *Imam Al Hussein* explains the main beliefs, teachings and way of life of Muslims.

Q. What does the word 'Islam' mean?

A. Islam is an Arabic word. It means both peace and submission. The follower of Islam is called a Muslim; this literally means 'the one who submits'. In some texts a Muslim would be referred to as a 'Mohammaden' and this is not correct. Muslims do not worship Mohammad, but they worship God, or they submit to God.

Q. Where do the Islamic teachings come from?

A. There are two main sources of the Islamic teachings. The first one is that the Qu'ran [Koran] is the word of God transmitted to the Prophet Mohammad through the Archangel Gabriel. The revelation continued for twenty-three years, bit by bit, until it was completed. The most important message of the Qu'ran is that there is one God, Allah, the creator of the Universe. Everyone should worship that God alone.

The second important source of Islam is called the Sunnah or the recorded practices and sayings of the prophet Mohammad. The prophet, in his words and in his actions, was a living model of the Qu'ran. He translated the Qu'ran into actions so he is the model for the Muslims.

The Qu'ran and the Sunnah provide the Muslim with guidance in every situation, whatever it is — personal, domestic, economic, social or political.

For example, family law is derived from religion — marriage, divorce, wills — there are teachings for this area both in the Qu'ran and the Sunnah. Then there are certain punishments in

Some members of the Dublin Muslim community outside the Mosque.

the Qu'ran and in the Sunnah for certain moral offences, such as stealing and murder. Also, there are certain teachings on the area of food and drink. For example, Muslims cannot take alcohol or drugs. They cannot eat pork.

Q. What are the main Islamic beliefs?

A. There are five main beliefs.
1. We believe in one God. We must only worship that God.
2. We believe in angels, for example the Archangel Gabriel.
3. We believe in all the books of God, the Scriptures. We believe in the Torah, the Gospel and the Qu'ran.
4. We believe in the messengers sent by God. There are twenty-five of them mentioned in the Qu'ran, including Adam, Abraham, Joseph, Jacob, Moses and Jesus.
5. We believe in life after death. On the last day, we will be raised and brought to life and we will have to account for our efforts in this life. If a man does something evil, he will be punished. Whoever does something good will be rewarded. We believe in paradise and we believe in hell.

Imam Al Hussein preaching in the Dublin Mosque.

Q. What are the moral teachings in Islam?

A. The Islamic teachings relating to morals resemble those of other revealed religions in many respects. There is the prohibition on all bad moral conduct on the one side, such as lying, cheating, being dishonest and so on. On the other hand there is the call to be truthful, honest, fair and so on. However the Islamic teachings go many steps further, embracing the whole of man's life in all its aspects — personal, social, political, and economical. In many ways the Islamic teachings are also far more clear and specific.

Q. How do Muslims practise their religion?

A. Muslims have five basic practices. These are called 'The Five Pillars of Islam'.
1. The first pillar is the Shahadh. This means the declaration of the faith. It comes from the Qu'ran which is in Arabic:

> 'La ilaha illa Allah;
> Muhammad Rasul Allah.'

This means:

> 'I bear witness that there is no God except Allah;
> and that Muhammad is the Messenger of Allah.'

2. The second pillar is the Salat, or prayer. We pray five times a day — at dawn, noon, afternoon, sunset and at night. Muslims should pray at a mosque if possible. Otherwise, they should pray wherever they happen to be at the time.

3. The third pillar is Zakat, or the welfare tax. This is a percentage of our wealth that we should pay to the poor and needy in the community. This is not optional, like charity. Zakat is the minimal obligation which a Muslim should pay every year when his wealth reaches a certain amount.

4. The fourth pillar is fasting during the month of Ramadan. During this month, the Muslim abstains from eating, drinking and sexual intercourse from dawn until sunset.

5. The fifth pillar is the major pilgrimage to Mecca (where the Prophet Muhammad lived). There is a special meaning behind this pilgrimage. It is a withdrawal from this life and a journey towards God. The pilgrim wears symbolic clothes, a seamless two pieces of cloth to cover himself. It is a reminder of the shroud which covers a man when he is dead.

Q. For Muslims working in Ireland, would there be any difficulty in stopping at the different times of the day for prayer, if they are working with other people who are not part of the Muslim community?

A. It is not really a serious problem. The time of prayer extends for two hours and the person can pray at any time during these two hours.

Q. You are the Imam of this community. How is the Imam chosen?

A. The Imam is chosen by the community. Any knowledgeable male member of the community could take the position of Imam.

Q. How are children brought up in a Muslim family?

A. In a Muslim family, the parents would teach the child the basic rules regarding Islam before the children go to school and would also begin teaching the practices, for example, prayer, or learning short pieces from the Qu'ran. They would teach them about God, about good conduct.

Muslim children have special religious education classes at the weekend.

Q. Are the children taught the Arabic language from a very early age?

A. Yes, they learn some short chapters of the Qu'ran as a form of prayer. If possible, they will be taught to read the Qu'ran in Arabic.

Q. If a young Muslim boy or girl is growing up in a Western culture, does this create a problem in any way?

A. It is not as easy as living in a Muslim society. There is not the same example for the young Muslim from the rest of society apart from parents and family, school and local community. However, I don't think living in a Western culture should cause any great conflict for Muslims. Everything depends on the individual. If he has a strong belief in his religion, then there will be no problem.

(November 1990)

The Muslim National School, Dublin.

QUESTIONS

1. What is your reaction to Islam as it is presented here?
2. Does anything appeal to you about this religion? Explain.
3. Is there anything about Islam that you find difficult to understand? Explain.
4. What do you think Islam and Christianity have in common? What strikes you as being most different about Islam?

Buddhism

In the following interview, John, an Irish Buddhist, explains the main beliefs, teachings and way of life of Buddhists.

Q. Where does Buddhism come from?

A. It comes from the teachings of the Buddha, a wise man who lived in Nepal and Northern India in the sixth century B.C.

Q. What are the main teachings of Buddhism?

A. The main teachings of Buddhism are called the Four Noble Truths.

The shrine at the Buddhist Centre, Dublin, which shows the traditional figure of the Buddha.

271

Rimpoche is a Buddhist teacher, originally from Tibet, now living in India. He visited Ireland and many other countries to teach people more about Buddhism.

1. The first Noble Truth is that there is suffering in everyone's life. Even when we are happy, our minds are not at peace, as we wonder if it will last and what suffering we may face in the future.
2. The second Noble Truth is that suffering is caused by ignorance — having a mistaken view of the world — and desire based on this. For example, people put so much energy into their possessions — their cars, their houses — as though they were going to last forever. This leads to suffering because these things don't last. Suffering is also caused by being too self-centred, seeing myself as the most important figure in the universe.
3. The third Noble Truth is that there is a way to overcome suffering and the causes of suffering in our lives.
4. The fourth Noble Truth shows us how to do this and how to become truly wise. The Buddha explained this as an eight-fold path.

Q. What is the eight-fold path?

A. 1. First comes *Right Understanding*. We must begin by understanding that nothing in our lives is permanent — that positive actions bring good results and negative actions bring bad results. We must be aware of the sufferings and difficulties of others.
2. Secondly *Right Motive*. Not being a Buddhist out of a wish for fame, for example, but to develop one's wisdom and compassion.
3. The third step is *Right Speech*, not lying or speaking harmfully.
4. Next, *Right Action*. This means trying to avoid harming others. This includes animals as well as human beings, even the planet itself, not abusing its resources. If we can help others in practical ways — the sick, the old, the hungry and so on — this is excellent, but at least we try to avoid harm. Its also important to try to develop the wish to help others, even if we can't do much at the present time.
5. The fifth one is *Right Livelihood*. This means not earning one's living by a destructive means. For example, a Buddhist wouldn't like to be a butcher, or a soldier or an arms trader. A Buddhist would not be involved in dealing in drugs or substances that would tend to harm people.
6. Next is *Right Effort*. This means devoting at least some of our time and energy to study, meditate and grow in understanding of the teachings of the Buddha.
7. The seventh step is *Right Mindfulness*. This means developing a reflective attitude to life, not being continually distracted. It

Meditation is very important in the life of a Buddhist.

doesn't mean that you need to give up what you enjoy. It means that you spend some time every now and again being quiet, thinking a little bit more deeply about things and carrying this through into your life.

8. The last step is *Right Concentration*. Most Buddhists try to practise meditation every day to help calm their minds and become more receptive to truth. Right Concentration applies to this. With meditation it is considered important to have the advice of experienced and trustworthy teachers.

These 'steps' are, of course, practised together, not one-by-one.

Rimpoche holds a Buddhist book.

Q. Does 'Right Livelihood' mean that a Buddhist couldn't be a farmer with animals, or sell alcohol in a shop?

A. In reality one can never avoid harm altogether. You may be a vegetarian but how many creatures are killed in digging the earth for the food that you eat? Every time you breathe you are killing microscopic beings. It is wrong to think 'because I can't do it perfectly, I'll not bother at all'. This is a form of pride. The point is sincerely to do one's best in avoiding and reducing harm. So if you are a farmer, or someone who grows plants for a living, you do the best you can in accordance with your conscience.

Many lay Buddhists in the West do take an occasional drink socially, but drunkenness and the meditative life don't really go together!

Q. Are there any commandments in Buddhism, for example, anything you are forbidden to do?

A. There are no commandments as such. However, we do have the 'five precepts' which are the basis of Buddhist ethics. Some Buddhists take these formally as vows, but all are expected to observe them as best they can.

The precepts are to avoid harming life, human or animal; not to steal; not to tell lies or deceive people; not to misuse sexuality and not to stupefy or cloud the mind with drink or drugs.

Doing any of these harmful things leads, sooner or later, to suffering both for yourself and for other people, so the 'precepts' are seen as a matter of common sense.

Rimpoche teaches some Irish Buddhists.

Q. Do Buddhists believe in reincarnation?

A. The answer to that is yes and no. We believe that there is a continuity in life. Unless one becomes a Buddha, free from ignorance and beyond suffering, one will continue to be 'reborn' from moment to moment; day to day; year to year, and from life to life.

When a person is reborn in another life, he is not the same 'self' as in the previous life. He is a new 'self' or person, but his new life will depend upon his actions in his previous life or lives. This is sometimes compared to one candle lighting another, lighting another and so on. The flame is the same, and yet it is different.

The most important thing about this is that my future, or my destiny, is in my own hands. My actions in this life will affect my future life. Bad actions will bring suffering. Good actions will bring greater wisdom and understanding.

Q. What would a day be like in the life of a Buddhist?

A. There would be as many days in the life of a Buddhist as there are Buddhists, in the sense that every one of them would be different. For somebody who took the teachings a little bit to heart, they would try to fit in somewhere in the day, some time for meditation practice. That might be ten minutes or half an hour in the morning or in the evening. But apart from that, I don't think there is anything different about the Buddhist's day. There are no special dietary requirements. Many Buddhists happen to be vegetarians, but this is a matter of individual choice. Unless one has taken vows as a monk or nun, there are no special clothes and one doesn't have to attend temples or services. At the simplest level, its sufficient to have an acquaintance with the teachings, and to try and live one's life as well as one can in accordance with that.

(February 1991)

The Buddhists pray and meditate together.

QUESTIONS

1. What is your reaction to Buddhism as it is presented here?
2. Does anything appeal to you about this religion? Explain.
3. Is there anything about Buddhism that you find difficult to understand? Explain.
4. What does Buddhism have in common with Christianity? What is different?

Exercises

1. Briefly outline the main teachings of each of the three religions:
   (a) Judaism
   (b) Islam
   (c) Buddhism.
2. Do you see any similarities between each of these religions? Explain.
3. What are the main differences between:
   (a) Judaism and Islam?
   (b) Judaism and Buddhism?
   (c) Islam and Buddhism?
4. Which of these religions is closest to Christianity? Explain your answer.
5. Which of these religions is most different from Christianity? Explain your answer.

Declaration on the Relation of the Church to non-Christian Religions (Second Vatican Council)

The Church, therefore, urges her sons [and daughters] to enter with prudence and charity into discussions and collaboration with members of other religions. Let Christians, while witnessing to their own faith and way of life, acknowledge, preserve and encourage the spiritual and moral truths found among non-Christians, also their social life and culture.

(Taken from Paragraph 3)

Questions

1. According to the Second Vatican Council, how should Christians relate to people of other religions?
2. What does it mean to enter into discussion with 'prudence' and 'charity'?
3. How could Christians collaborate with people of other religions in the world today?
4. How can Christians 'witness' to their own faith and way of life?

5. What does it mean to:
   (a) acknowledge
   (b) preserve and
   (c) encourage the good things in the religions of other people?
6. As a Christian, what do you think is the most important thing you can learn from:
   (a) the Jewish faith
   (b) the Muslim faith
   (c) the Buddhist tradition?

Discussion: Are all religions the same?

Reflection: 'The Gentiles do not have the law; but whenever they do by instinct what the law commands, they are their own law, even though they do not have the law. Their conduct shows that what the law commands is written in their hearts. Their consciences also show that this is true, since their thoughts sometimes accuse them and sometimes defend them. And so, according to the Good News I preach, this is how it will be on that day when God through Jesus Christ will judge the secret thoughts of all.' Romans 2:14-16

Action: Find out more about the founders or important leaders in the three religions mentioned in this chapter.

Psalm: Praise the Lord, all nations!
Praise him, all peoples!
His love for us is strong
and his faithfulness is eternal.
Psalm 117

THE LITURGICAL YEAR

THE LITURGICAL YEAR

CHAPTER 35

What do the following statements tell you about time?

1. It's six o'clock.
2. The time just flew by.
3. All in good time.
4. Is this the last time?
5. Have a wonderful time.
6. School-time.
7. Time heals all things.
8. Is it time yet?
9. She's doing overtime at work.
10. I had the time of my life.
11. At the end of time.
12. A time of change.
13. A life-time.
14. I've got time to kill.
15. I'm trying to save time.

Time

Time is very important to people in many ways. For example, we organise it into minutes, hours, days, weeks, months and years to bring order into our lives. We plan to do things at a certain hour or on a certain day. Although we live in the 'present' time, we remember and are influenced by the 'past' time, and we look forward to a 'future' time.

However, we are also aware of another kind of 'time' which cannot be measured in minutes, days or years. This 'time' has everything to do with the most important and meaningful experiences in life. A time of joy or sorrow, a time of healing, or a time of change can be very important in our lives. We cannot usually plan these 'times'. We can only hope for them, or learn from them in some way. We are often surprised to find ourselves in the middle of them. Yet these are the 'times' that we remember when we think back on our life story. Long after we have forgotten what day of the week it was, we may still remember the 'time' we started going to school, the time we made a new friend or the time a much loved pet died.

QUESTIONS

1. In what ways is your life 'ruled by the clock'?
2. What time of year do you enjoy most? Why?
3. Give examples of really special 'times' in your past or present life.
   Do you celebrate these times? If so, how?

A birthday party.

The Liturgical Year

We often use 'ordinary' time as a way of celebrating the 'special' times which are most important to us. For example we usually celebrate our birthday every year. Although we cannot remember it, being born was certainly one of the most significant times in our lives. For most people, however, their birthday is more than just a celebration of something that happened many years ago. Their birthday is an important event in the *present*. For young people it is a time when they are the centre of attention from their families and friends. For older people it is less important, but still a day which celebrates that they are special and loved. A birthday is also a time to look to the future — what will happen to me this year, now that I am sixteen; forty; seventy-six?

> The Christian community also uses the hours, days, weeks and years of 'ordinary' time to celebrate the special times and experiences in the life of the community. Just as the ordinary year is divided into seasons, so the Christian community divides the year into religious or Liturgical seasons — the season of Advent, the season of Christmas, the season of Lent, the season of Easter and two other seasons of 'Ordinary Time' in which we celebrate God's love for us. Each of these special seasons in the 'Liturgical Year,' as it is called, celebrates a special time in our lives.

Many of these celebrations are based on and recall the special saving acts which God has done for us in our history, for example, sending Jesus to live among us (Christmas); or Jesus' death and resurrection (Holy Week and Easter). However, these occasions are also celebrations of important events which are happening in our lives at the *present* time. When we celebrate Advent we do not simply remember that the Jews waited for the Messiah to come for hundreds of years — *we* actually wait for Jesus to come into *our* lives during Advent. We know that he has already come to the

world, but we also know that in many ways we have not allowed him into our lives. So during Advent we prepare to accept him and follow him in our lives more fully.

> In another way, each of these celebrations looks forward to the future. During Advent we look forward to Christ's second coming at 'the end of time'. During Easter we look forward to our resurrection from the dead. During Lent, we prepare in a special way for the life in the Kingdom of God.

The Liturgical Year is a celebration of all the most important experiences in the life of the Christian community, past, present and to come. The highpoint of the year is the celebration of Jesus' resurrection on Easter Sunday. Every other celebration throughout the Liturgical Year is linked to this celebration.

The themes, readings and prayers, and even the clothes worn by the priest at Mass on Sunday, and at daily Mass, are all based on the particular season of the Liturgical Year. By taking a full part in the celebration of the Eucharist and paying attention to the readings and the prayers, we have the chance to reflect more deeply on all the different aspects of our faith, past, present and future. This can encourage us to live better Christian lives every day.

Exercises

1. Give examples to show how an important celebration involves:
   (a) remembering the past
   (b) rejoicing in the present
   (c) looking forward to the future.
2. What is your favourite celebration in the Liturgical Year? Why?
3. Examine the following chart which shows some of the major festivals which we celebrate during the seasons of the Liturgical Year.

Season	Festivals
Advent	Immaculate Conception — 8 December
Christmas	Christmas Eve — 24 December Christmas Day — 25 December Mary, Mother of God — 1 January The Epiphany (Visit of the Magi) — 6 January
Ordinary Time	Baptism of the Lord } date varies from year to year.
Lent	St Patrick's Day (Ireland) — 17 March Ash Wednesday Palm Sunday Holy Thursday } dates vary from year to year. Good Friday Holy Saturday
Easter	Easter Sunday Ascension Thursday } dates vary from year to year. Pentecost
Ordinary Time	Trinity Sunday } dates vary from year to year. Corpus Christi Assumption of Our Lady — 15 August All Saints' Day — 1 November All Souls' Day — 2 November

Exercises

1. Make a note of what we remember as a community on each of the main festivals mentioned.
2. Are there any feast days which are not mentioned on this brief outline which are important to you? Briefly describe them if this is the case.
3. Why do you think the Liturgical Year starts in late November/early December instead of January, like the secular calendar?

Reflection: 'Sing to the Lord, all the world! Proclaim every day the good news that he has saved us. Proclaim his glory to the nations, his mighty acts to all peoples.' 1 Chronicles 16:23-24

Action: When you are celebrating a class liturgy, make sure that the theme is in keeping with the season of the Church's year.

Psalm: Sing a new song to the Lord!
Sing to the Lord, all the world!
Sing to the Lord and praise him!
Proclaim every day the good news that he has saved us.
Proclaim his glory to the nations,
his mighty acts to all peoples.

Praise the Lord, all people on earth;
praise his glory and might.
Praise the Lord's glorious name;
bring an offering and come into his Temple.
Bow down before the Holy One when he appears;
tremble before him, all the earth!
Psalm 96: 1–3, 7–9

ADVENT

CHAPTER 36

▼

John the Baptist

Characters: The Angel Gabriel, Zechariah, Elizabeth, Mary, Neighbour, Priest, Levite, Woman, Tax Collector, Soldier, Jesus, Herod, Daughter, Herodias, and five Narrators.

Scene One: The birth of John the Baptist is announced.

Narrator 1: During the time when Herod was King of Judaea, there was a priest named Zechariah, who belonged to the priestly order of Abijah. His wife's name was Elizabeth; she also belonged to a priestly family. They both lived good lives in God's sight and obeyed fully all the Lord's laws and commands. They had no children because Elizabeth could not have any, and she and Zechariah were both very old.

One day Zechariah was doing his work as a priest in the temple, taking his turn in the daily service. According to the custom followed by the priests, he was chosen by lot to burn incense on the altar. So he went into the temple of the Lord, while the crowd of people outside prayed during the hour when the incense was burnt. An angel of the Lord appeared to him, standing on the right of the altar where the incense was burnt. When Zechariah saw him, he was alarmed and felt afraid. But the angel said to him:

Angel Gabriel: Don't be afraid, Zechariah! God has heard your prayer, and your wife Elizabeth will bear you a son. You are to name him John. How glad and happy you will be, and how happy many others will be when he is born! He will be a great man in the Lord's sight. He must not drink any wine or strong drink. From his very birth he will be filled with the Holy Spirit, and

283

	he will bring back many of the people of Israel to the Lord their God. He will go ahead of the Lord, strong and mighty like the prophet Elijah. He will bring fathers and children together again; he will turn disobedient people back to the way of thinking of the righteous; he will get the Lord's people ready for him.
Zechariah:	How shall I know if this is so? I am an old man, and my wife is old also.
Gabriel:	I am Gabriel. I stand in the presence of God, who sent me to speak to you and tell you this good news. But you have not believed my message, which will come true at the right time. Because you have not believed, you will be unable to speak; you will remain silent until the day my promise to you comes true.
Narrator 1:	In the meantime the people were waiting for Zechariah and wondering why he was spending such a long time in the temple. When he came out, he could not speak to them, and so they knew that he had seen a vision in the temple. Unable to say a word, he made signs to them with his hands. When his period of service in the temple was over, Zechariah went back home. Some time later his wife Elizabeth became pregnant and did not leave the house for five months.
Elizabeth:	Now at last the Lord has helped me. He has taken away my public disgrace!

Scene Two: The birth of Jesus is announced.

Narrator 2:	In the sixth month of Elizabeth's pregnancy, God sent the Angel Gabriel to a town in Galilee called Nazareth. He had a message for a girl promised in marriage to a man named Joseph, who was a descendant of King David. The girl's name was Mary.
Gabriel:	Rejoice! The Lord is with you and has greatly blessed you!

Narrator 2: Mary was deeply troubled by the angel's message, and she wondered what his words meant.

Gabriel: Don't be afraid, Mary; God has been gracious to you. You will become pregnant and give birth to a son, and you will name him Jesus. He will be great and will be called the Son of the Most High God. The Lord God will make him a King, as his ancestor David was, and he will be the king of the descendants of Jacob for ever, his kingdom will never end!

Mary: I am a virgin. How, then, can this be?

Gabriel: The Holy Spirit will come on you, and God's power will rest upon you. For this reason the holy child will be called the Son of God. Remember your relative Elizabeth. It is said that she cannot have children, but she herself is now six months pregnant, even though she is very old. For there is nothing that God cannot do.

Mary: I am the Lord's servant. May it happen to me as you have said.

Narrator: And the angel left her.

Scene Three: Mary visits Elizabeth.

Narrator 2: Soon afterwards Mary got ready and hurried off to a town in the hill country of Judaea. She went into Zechariah's house and greeted Elizabeth. When Elizabeth heard Mary's greeting, the baby moved within her. Elizabeth was filled with the Holy Spirit and said in a loud voice:

Elizabeth: You are the most blessed of all women, and blessed is the child you will bear! Why should this great thing happen to me, that my Lord's mother comes to visit me? For as soon as I heard your greeting, the baby within me jumped with gladness. How happy you are to believe that the Lord's message to you will come true!

Narrator: Both Elizabeth and Mary were filled with joy, and praised God together. Mary stayed about three months with Elizabeth and then went back home.

Scene Four: The birth of John the Baptist.

Narrator 3: The time came for Elizabeth to have her baby, and she gave birth to a son. Her neighbours and relatives heard how wonderfully good the Lord had been to her, and they all rejoiced with her.

When the baby was a week old, they came to circumcise him, and they were going to name him Zechariah, after his father.

Elizabeth: No! His name is to be John.

Neighbour: But you have no relatives with that name!

Narrator: Then they made signs to his father, asking him what name he would like the boy to have. Zechariah asked for a writing tablet and wrote 'His name is John.' How surprised they all were! At that moment Zechariah was able to speak again, and he started praising God. The neighbours were all filled with fear, and the news about these things spread through all the hill-country of Judaea. Everyone who heard of it thought about it and asked:

Neighbour: What is this child going to be?

Narrator: For it was plain that the Lord's power was upon him. John's father Zechariah was filled with the Holy Spirit and he spoke God's message in a powerful prophecy, proclaiming that John would be a prophet and prepare the way for the Messiah.

The child grew and developed in body and spirit. When he grew up, he went to live in the desert, to be close to God, until the time came for him to appear publicly to the people of Israel. He wore clothes made of camel's hair, with a leather belt round his waist, and his food was locusts and wild honey.

Scene Five: The preaching of John the Baptist.

Narrator 4: It was the fifteenth year of the rule of the Emperor Tiberius; Pontius Pilate was governor of Judaea, Herod was ruler of Galilee, and his brother Philip was ruler of the territory of Iturea and Trachonitis; Lysanias was ruler of Abilene, and Annas and Caiaphas were high priests. At that time the word of God came to John, son of Zechariah, in the desert. So John went throughout the whole territory of the River Jordan, preaching:

John: Turn away from your sins and be baptised, and God will forgive your sins.

Narrator: Crowds of people came out to John to be baptised by him.

John: You snakes! Who told you that you could escape from the punishment God is about to send? Do those things that will show that you have turned from your sins. And don't start saying among yourselves that Abraham is your ancestor. I tell you that God can take these stones and make descendants for Abraham! The axe is ready to cut down the trees at the roots; every tree that does not bear good fruit will be cut down and thrown in the fire.

Woman: What are we to do, then?

John: Whoever has two shirts must give one to the man who has none, and whoever has food must share it.

Tax Collector: Teacher, what are we to do?

John: Don't collect more than is legal.

Soldier: What about us? What are we to do?

John: Don't take money from anyone by force or accuse anyone falsely. Be content with your pay.

Narrator: The Jewish authorities in Jerusalem sent some priests and levites to John, to ask him:

Priest:	Who are you?
John:	I am not the Messiah.
Levite:	Who are you then? Are you Elijah?
John:	No, I am not.
Levite:	Are you the Prophet?
John:	No.
Priest:	Then tell us who you are. We have to take an answer back to those who sent us. What do you say about yourself?
Narrator:	John answered by quoting the prophet Isaiah:
John:	I am the voice of someone shouting in the desert: Make a straight path for the Lord to travel!
Levite:	If you are not the Messiah nor Elijah nor the Prophet, why do you baptise?
John:	I baptise you with water to show that you have repented, but the one who will come after me will baptise you with the Holy Spirit and fire. He is much greater than I am; and I am not good enough even to carry his sandals.

Scene Six: Jesus is baptised by John.

Narrator 4:	At that time Jesus arrived from Galilee and came to John at the Jordan to be baptised by him. But John tried to make him change his mind.
John:	I ought to be baptised by you, and yet you have come to me!
Jesus:	Let it be so for now. For in this way we shall do all that God requires.
Narrator:	So John agreed. As soon as Jesus was baptised, he came up out of the water. Then heaven was opened to him, and he saw the Spirit of God

coming down like a dove and alighting on him. Then a voice said from heaven, 'This is my own Dear Son, with whom I am pleased.'

Scene Seven: The death of John the Baptist.

Narrator 5: In many different ways John preached the Good News to the people and urged them to change their ways. But John reprimanded Herod, the governor, because he had married Herodias, even though she was the wife of his brother Philip.

Herod himself ordered John's arrest, and he had him chained and put in prison. Herodias held a grudge against John and wanted to kill him, but she could not because of Herod. Herod was afraid of John, because he knew that John was a good and holy man, and so he kept him safe. He liked to listen to him, even though he became greatly disturbed every time he heard him.

Finally, Herodias got her chance. It was on Herod's birthday, when he gave a feast for all the chief government officials, the military commanders and the leading citizens of Galilee. The daughter of Herodias came in and danced, and pleased Herod and his guests. So the king said to the girl:

Herod: What would you like to have? I will give you anything you want. I swear that I will give you anything you ask for, even as much as half my kingdom!

Narrator: So the girl went out and asked her mother:

Daughter: What shall I ask for?

Herodias: The head of John the Baptist.

Narrator: The girl hurried back at once to the king.

Daughter: I want you to give me here and now the head of John the Baptist on a dish!

Narrator: This made the king very sad, but he could not refuse her because of the vows he had made in front of all his guests. So he sent off a guard at once with orders to bring John's head. The guard left, went to the prison and cut John's head off. Then he brought it on a dish and gave it to the girl, who gave it to her mother. When John's disciples heard about this, they came and took away his body and buried it.

(Based on Lk 1:5–80; 3:1–200; Jn 1:19–27; Mt 3:13–17; 6:17–29)

QUESTIONS

1. What do you think about John the Baptist?
2. In what way do you think John 'prepared the way' for Jesus?
3. In what way does his 'infancy narrative' show who John was, and what his mission was?
4. Would you call John a prophet? Explain.

EXERCISES

1. In what ways is John's message relevant or important to us today?
2. In what way does the story of John the Baptist help us to understand the meaning and purpose of Advent?

The Liturgical Year: Celebrating the Mystery of Christ and his Saints (U.S. Catholic Conference of Bishops, 1985)

The first Advent was Christ's birth. The third will be his return in glory and judgment. The second Advent refers to Christ present in us now. Celebrating the past and future Advents . . . we can become open enough to recognise the present Advent that is here on our journey.

Taken from Chapter VI, 'The Proper of Seasons'

Questions

1. How did John the Baptist prepare the people for Christ's first Advent?
2. How can the story of John the Baptist help us to celebrate:
   (a) the first Advent
   (b) the second Advent
   (c) the third Advent?
3. How does the Advent season help us to prepare for Christmas?
4. How does it help us to prepare for Christ's Advent at the end of time?
5. In what ways can Christ come into our lives in the present? How can the season of Advent help us to recognise Christ in our lives?

Reflection: ' A virgin will become pregnant and have a son and he will be called Immanuel' (which means "God is with us").' Matthew 1:23

Action: Prepare a series of posters for use in your school, home or oratory. Each poster should refer to either the first, second or third Advent.

Hymn of Praise: Let us praise the Lord, the God of Israel!
He has come to the help of his people
and has set them free.
He has provided for us a mighty Saviour,
a descendant of his servant David.
He promised through his holy prophets long ago
that he would save us from our enemies,
from the power of all those who hate us.
He said he would show mercy to our ancestors
and remember his sacred covenant.
With a solemn oath to our ancestor Abraham
he promised to rescue us from our enemies
and allow us to serve him without fear,
so that we might be holy and righteous before him
all the days of our life.

'You, my child, will be called a
prophet of the Most High God.
You will go ahead of the Lord
to prepare his road for him,
to tell his people that they will be saved
by having their sins forgiven.
Our God is merciful and tender.
He will cause the bright dawn of
    salvation to rise on us
and to shine from heaven on all
those who live in the dark shadow
    of death,
to guide our steps into the path of
    peace.' (Luke 1:68-79)

CHRISTMAS

CHAPTER 37

That Christmas

Vera often had a dirty face, told lies, and on winter nights when all we kids would be standing looking at the sweets in Miss Casey's shop window, Vera'd put a piece of paper in her mouth and chew it. Then she'd say: 'I'm just finishing off the last of me bar of chocolate.'

As the nights got colder, the shop window where we used to stand got brighter and a big card said . . .
JOIN OUR CHRISTMAS CLUB
PAY WHAT YOU LIKE
HAVE WHAT YOU LIKE

One night as we stood looking at the sweets, she asked: 'What are you getting for Christmas, Dan?' I began to tell her all the things I hoped to get, and she said, 'Well I'm getting three dolls, a bike, ten blocks of chocolate, three big books and a new hat and coat.'

On Christmas Eve my mother went out shopping. My elder brother Pat put a lot of hair oil on his head and sent me out for a new pair of cufflinks and a tiepin. He gave me ninepence and there was a penny change, which he told me to keep. He was going out to a dance and I went out into the street and over to the shop window.

After I'd been there for a few minutes Vera came and began talking. She asked me if I believed in Father Christmas. 'No,' I said, 'not now, I used to.' Then she said: 'What are you getting for Christmas, Dan?' 'I don't know. I might get a gun, a book and some chocolates.' 'Is that all???'

The way she said it made me feel that it was my own fault. I wished we didn't have a Christmas like this, where you had to compare what you got, and where no one was any richer than me, or, I was as rich as everyone else.

In the shop window I could see a big bundle of chocolates and the price was half a crown. Vera had gone, but I still stared at the chocolates. I walked down the street to the main road. 'Oh God,' I prayed, 'let me find half a crown so that I can buy that bundle of chocolate.'

All along the main road I went looking into the gutters to see if my prayer was answered. But I wasn't lucky. It was late when I got home and my mother said to me: 'Try them boots on.' They fitted me well, and as I walked around the room in them, I wondered would they ever grow old and look as my other boots did. Funny, I thought, how you never notice boots growing old. It happens suddenly: like one day you go into a shop and notice that you can see over the counter. *You* grow up without knowing it.

'Those,' said my mother, looking down at the boots on me, 'are your Christmas present.' My eyes saw them now, not as new boots, but as something that had stopped me getting a gun, or chocolate. I felt that they were really a present for my mother, not for me. I didn't want them.

'Well,' she said, 'aren't you going to say thanks?'

'Thanks,' I said, as though it wasn't myself talking, as though I wasn't myself, only some big lump of disappointment. I closed my eyes tight, hoping that the tears wouldn't come out, but they did just the same. And when my mother saw me crying, she took hold of me by the shoulders and pulled me close against her. 'I'm sorry, child, but you had to have the boots first, you know.'

On Christmas morning I didn't want to go out into the street. I watched through the window at all the kids with their toys. Then my mother gave me a shilling and said, 'Go and buy yourself some sweets.'

I didn't go until the streets were empty. Then I rushed over to the shop and bought a big block of chocolate.

Just as I reached my own door, I heard Vera call me.

'What did you get?' she asked.

I told her a lot of lies, then I showed her the block of chocolate. 'Oh, I nearly forgot. I got this chocolate, too.'

She was wearing new boots I noticed, so I said, 'And, I got new boots!'

She looked down at mine, then at her own and said, 'Oh yeah, I got boots — but a lot of other things as well.'

'What kinds of things?'

When she'd finished telling me, I knew she'd been telling lies, for she said, 'I've not even opened all the parcels yet.'

'I don't believe you,' I said.

'You come and look then . . .'

We went to her house, and she said: 'Now look through the window at all those big parcels on the table.'

Sure enough, I could see lots of parcels on the table, and as I looked at them, I said to her, 'Why don't you open them out?'

'Not yet,' she said, 'I've not finished playing with all the other toys I got.'

Looking in at all the parcels made me terribly sad. 'Can I come in and see your other toys?' I asked.

'No,' she said, 'they're girls' toys, not boys'.'

'Please.'

'No.'

'I'll give you a big piece of chocolate!' I said.

She looked at the block of chocolate in my hand, then turned and looked at the parcels on the table. Again, she looked at the chocolate, then at the parcels. Then she looked away from me up the empty street.

'Where's everyone gone?' she asked, and her voice was crying. There was nothing for me to say. I just looked again at all the parcels and wondered why she was so sad.

She looked through the window and said to me, 'I was telling lies.'

'About . . .'

'There's nothing in them parcels. I got nuthin' but these boots.'

I don't think I ever felt so happy as I did at that moment. I broke the chocolate into two equal pieces.

'I only got these boots,' I said, as I handed her the chocolate.

'Did you?' she asked, and before I answered she began to laugh. Then we sat down on her doorstep talking about all the wonderful things we'd do some day.

And when I looked at her boots and at mine, I didn't see them like boots. It was as though my boots were my mother's heart and her boots were her mother's. And I saw that her boots were like mine, and somehow I thought she must feel just like me when I'm lonely, unhappy and afraid.

'You know,' I said, 'I love . . . your boots, Vera.'

'I love your boots, Dan,' she answered.

Soon I had told her that I loved her, and she had said that she loved me. And although years afterwards we forgot about it, I always remember that Christmas.

Well, now she's grown up, and I am, yet whenever we meet, we blush, because we know something about each other: but what it is, I'm not sure either of us understands.

by Dan Treston

(Taken from *Sunday Miscellany 2*, Editor, Ronnie Walshe)

QUESTIONS

1. What is your reaction to this story?
2. Briefly describe: (a) Vera; (b) Dan; (c) Dan's mother. Which of them do you like the best? Why?
3. What did Dan like about Christmas? Was there anything he did not like? Explain your answer.
4. What do you think Dan's mother thought about Christmas?
5. In what ways does Dan change by the end of the story? Explain why each of these changes happens.
6. What do you think is the most important moment in the story? Why?
7. What is the main meaning or message in the story?

Christmas

Presents are a very important part of Christmas, especially for young people. It is exciting to open a parcel and discover what it contains. It also makes us feel good when someone cares enough to give us a present.

Dan and Vera were very unhappy they had no new toys to play with, but they were even more upset because they felt no one really cared about them. Dan felt that if his mother loved him, she would give him a *real* Christmas present, and not a pair of boots. He would not go out with the other children on Christmas morning because he knew he would be the odd one out, the only one without a Christmas present.

When Dan discovered that Vera was in the same situation as he was, he suddenly felt very happy. He realised that he was not the odd one out, that he was no longer alone. Someone else knew what it was like to feel left out, lonely and unhappy.

Vera and Dan were both happy that it was Christmas, even though they did not have everything they wanted. They were happy because they were real friends. They did not have to feel jealous of each other. Neither of them looked down on the other. They did not even have to lie to each other any more. Instead, they understood and accepted each other. Happily, they shared the bar of chocolate and talked about the future.

Life can often be boring, miserable and painful. Our problems do not go away just because it is Christmas time. However, Christmas is a special time for celebrating the fact that joy, love and happiness are also part of human life. The presents, the parties, the decorations, the food and the carols are all ways of saying that it is good to be alive, it is good to share with family and friends, it is good to love and be loved.

Whether people are rich or poor, the best way to have a happy Christmas is to be involved with other people. It was because Vera told the truth to Dan that both of them had a happy Christmas. They both discovered that joy and happiness come from having loving relationships with other people. When people show by their words and actions that they care about other people — family, friends, neighbours and strangers — then they can experience the true happiness of Christmas.

Decorating an old person's house.

Questions

1. What do you like about Christmas? Is there anything you do not like? Explain.
2. Briefly describe an occasion when you felt really happy because you felt loved and wanted. Did this ever happen to you at Christmas? Explain.
3. What do you think people need in order to have a happy Christmas. Why?

The Incarnation

Everything that is loving, joyful and happy in our lives comes from God. When we celebrate all the good things in our lives at Christmas, we praise and thank God for giving them to us. We thank God in a special way for becoming a human being and living among us. This is called the 'Incarnation'. It means that God the Son 'became flesh', or became a human being. St John tells us that:

'God loved the world so much that He gave
His only Son,
so that everyone who believes in him may
not die but have eternal life.' John 3: 16–17

This is great news because it shows us how important we are to God. Not only human beings but the whole of creation is blessed or holy because God became a part of it in Jesus of Nazareth.

At Christmas, many young people give up their time to sing carols and collect money for those in need.

The Incarnation shows that there is no need to despair about the bad things in the world. God loves us and will give us the strength and courage to keep on working for justice and to build up loving relationships with each other. Because God the Son became one of us, God understands us completely and knows our every need. At Christmas, we celebrate the Incarnation and we praise and thank God for loving us so much.

QUESTIONS

1. Mention some of the good and happy things in your life. How does each of these things come from God?
2. What does the birth of Jesus tell us about God? What does it tell us about ourselves?
3. What is your favourite part of the religious ceremonies at Christmas? Why?

Reflection: 'The Word became a human being, and full of grace and truth, lived among us. We saw his glory, the glory which he received as the Father's only Son.' John 1:14

Action: Prepare a thanksgiving Christmas service as a class. Use symbols or signs to show all the good things for which you want to thank God.

Psalm: Sing a new song to the Lord;
he has done wonderful things!
By his own power and holy strength
he has won the victory.
The Lord announced his victory;
he made his saving power known to the nations.
He kept his promise to the people of Israel
with loyalty and constant love for them.
All people everywhere have seen the victory of our God.

Sing for joy to the Lord, all the earth;
praise him with songs and shouts of joy!
Sing praises to the Lord!
Play music on the harps!
Blow trumpets and horns,
and shout for joy to the Lord, our King.
Psalm 98: 1–6

LENT

CHAPTER 38

Here is a list of some of the things in our life which many people enjoy, but which we do not actually *need*.

(a) Television
(b) Chocolate/Sweets
(c) Cakes/Biscuits
(d) Your most important non-essential possession
(e) Pocket money
(f) Video
(g) Magazines/Books (not school books)
(h) Cinema
(i) Your favourite article of clothing
(j) Staying in bed late on Saturday morning.

(You may wish to add some items to the list, as a class, before doing the following exercise.)

1. In the case of each item, write down whether you could:
   (a) do without it very easily;
   (b) do without it with a bit of effort; or
   (c) do without it only with great difficulty.
2. If you had to give up every item on the list except one, which one would you choose to keep? Why?
3. Would you say that this item is essential for your happiness? Explain.

Christians have always gone at times to lonely places to help them remember how much they need God.

Lent

All of us are totally dependent on God in every way. All our happiness, all our joy comes, in the end, from God. Without God there would be no food, no friendship, no success, no happiness. However, sometimes we forget that this is true. Usually we try to remember to thank God for all the gifts we have, but sometimes we value the gifts more than we value the giver.

Lent is a time for getting our priorities right. It is a time to get back to basics, to remind ourselves of our dependence on God. One of the ways in which we can do this is to notice how much we need God's gifts, by giving up some of them for a time. The 'emptiness' that we feel when we no longer enjoy something which makes us happy is a sign of our need for God in our lives. It is a sign of our need for love, for justice, for prayer, for reconciliation.

Our own 'emptiness' should remind us of the 'emptiness' in others — an emptiness which we should try to fill with love, respect, support, help and companionship. In this way Lent reminds us that we are called to see Jesus in every person, and to be him to every person.

Exercises

1. Why do we call Lent a 'penitential' time?
2. How can penance lead to joy?
3. Which do you think is more important — giving something up for Lent, or doing something for Lent? Explain.
4. (a) What do you think are the most important things in your life?
   (b) What can you do in Lent to remind yourself of one of these things?

Reflection: 'My deep desire and hope is that I shall never fail in my duty, but that at all times, and especially just now, I shall be full of courage, so that with my whole being I shall bring honour to Christ, whether I live or die.' Phil. 1:20

Action: Take the opportunity this Lent to try to become free from any 'addiction' you may have. Choose one habit which you would like to break and concentrate on that. If possible, substitute a good habit for the old one, preferably one which will help you to love others.

Irish monks lived a life of prayer and penance on Skellig Michael.

Psalm: Be merciful to me, O God,
because of your constant love.
Because of your great mercy
wipe away my sins!
Wash away all my evil
and make me clean from my sin!

I recognise my faults;
I am always conscious of my sins.
I have sinned against you — only against you —
and done what you consider evil.

Sincerity and truth are what you require;
fill my mind with your wisdom.
Remove my sin and I will be clean;
wash me and I will be whiter than snow.
Let me hear the sounds of joy and gladness;
I will be happy once again.

Create a pure heart in me, O God,
and put a new and loyal spirit in me.
        Psalm 51: 1–4, 6–8, 10

EASTER

CHAPTER 39

A
. . . as he went down in the water for the third time he felt that his lungs would burst. With all his heart and mind and body he longed for one breath of air . . .

B
The proud parents described their 7lb daughter as 'a little miracle' . . .

C
Day after day the people waited for the rain. And day by day their need grew greater . . .

. . . and every green shoot was a promise that filled the people with hope.

QUESTIONS

1. What is the single most important thing to each of the people in these examples?
2. What do each of these people have in common?

Easter

Easter is a celebration of life:
- the life of the Risen Jesus;
- our life as Christians, dead to sin and alive to love;
- our future life forever with God.

The drowning person, the parents of a newborn child, the villagers waiting for the seed to grow are all strongly aware of the preciousness of life, of the importance of life, of how easily life can be lost. At Easter, Christians praise and thank God for this unbelievable gift of life, past, present and future.

> Christians believe that we are now living in the 'last days' or 'end times'. Our life now is an eternal life. It will not end with our physical death. This is the promise of the resurrection which we celebrate at Easter. Therefore our life now is a resurrected life. It is already in some way, part of the Kingdom of God. So Christians are not just people waiting around for 'life after death', as a reward for putting up with misery in 'this' life on earth. The resurrection means that we can (and do) experience real, 'eternal' happiness when we live like Jesus in our daily lives. The Cross reminds us that mixed in with this happiness there will be suffering. It will not be until the last day that our joy will be complete, and every tear will be wiped away.
>
> However, this life is not all sorrow. Denying ourselves, being unselfish, really trying to love others, working for justice against impossible odds — all of these experiences of 'dying' to ourselves will lead to experiences of the resurrection, real happiness in this world and in the world to come.

EXERCISES

1. Give examples to show how people can become aware of the value of life.
2. Give an example of a time when you experienced real happiness, even if only for a short time.
3. Do you believe that denying yourself can lead to happiness? Why/Why not?
4. Why, do you think, is Easter the high point of the Church's year?

Reflection: Jesus said to her, 'I am the resurrection and the life. Whoever believes in me will live, even though he dies, and whoever lives and believes in me will never die. Do you believe this?' John 11:25-26

Action: Celebrate your 'new' life in Christ by having a class party.

Psalm: I praise you, Lord, because you heard me,
because you have given me victory.

> The stone which the builders rejected as worthless
> turned out to be the most important of all.
> This was done by the Lord;
> what a wonderful sight it is!
> This is the day of the Lord's victory;
> let us be happy, let us celebrate.
> *Psalm 118: 21–24*

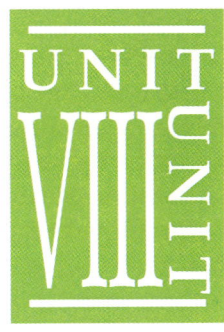

UNIT VIII

WORSHIP AND PRAYER

WORSHIP

CHAPTER 40

The Jews have worshipped God for over 3,000 years.

The ancient Egyptians worshipped the sun-god.

Muslims have prayed to Allah since the year 537.

Hindus have prayed to the gods for over 4,000 years.

UESTIONS

1. What do these photographs tell you about human beings?
2. Do you think that people will still behave and think like this in 2,000 years' time? Explain your answer.

Worship and Prayer

Human beings have always responded with awe, wonder and a kind of fear to the mystery and grandeur of the world in which we live. Right from the beginning, from prehistoric times, there is archaeological evidence to suggest that people believed there was a significance, a deeper meaning, to their lives. Many people showed by the way they buried their dead that they believed in an afterlife. They put food and weapons with the dead person, perhaps thinking these would be needed in the afterlife. They seem to have believed that their lives had a purpose which was more important than just being born, living and dying.

Some groups of people have believed that the world itself, the trees, animals, stones, the sun, moon and stars, have special, meaningful powers and can have an influence on human life. For example, the Egyptians worshipped the sun god, Ra, who they believed gave life to the earth. Other groups gradually began to believe that beyond the physical world there was a spiritual power or powers which had some connection with human life. For example, the native peoples of North America worship the Great Spirit who is present in all of creation.

Worship means acknowledging our dependence on a greater power or powers. It can involve praise, sacrifice, petition, fear or love. Where people believe that this power is harsh and cruel, their worship usually takes the form of trying to prevent the power from harming people and their world. Where people believe this power is loving and caring, their worship often takes the form of adoration and praise, prayers for help, and the desire to be close to the power at all times.

> Jews, Christians and Muslims believe that this power is God who reveals Himself to people, or communicates with them. This revelation shows that there is only one God who loves people and wants to be close to them. The worship which is an essential part of these three religions involves praise and thanksgiving, sorrow for sin against a loving God, and prayer for God's continued help and support. Their worship celebrates the ways in which God has acted in their lives in the past, and continues to be involved in their lives in the present.

There are many different forms of worship — formal, with set words and actions; or informal, using no set form of words or actions. People can worship individually, in a group or in a community. The greatest act of formal, community worship for Christians is the celebration of the Eucharist. All prayer is a form of worship. Indeed, for a Christian, any thought, word, attitude, action, or a person's whole way of life can be an act of worship. When people try to live their lives according to God's plan of love, they are showing their love, respect and need for God, which is the meaning of worship.

EXERCISES

1. Why do you think people feel the need to worship God?
2. Explain how the Eucharist is an act of worship, i.e. in the Eucharist how do we:
   (a) praise God
   (b) thank God
   (c) show that we need God
   (d) celebrate the saving actions of God?
3. Give examples to show how you can worship God in your life.
4. Do you think it would make any difference in people's lives if they did not perform any acts of worship? Explain your answer.

Reflection: ' . . . the time is coming and is already here, when by the power of God's Spirit people will worship the Father as He really is, offering Him the true worship that He wants. God is Spirit, and only by the power of His Spirit can people worship Him as He really is.' John 4:23-24

Action: Is there evidence in your locality of the worship of people in the past? Try to find out the story behind this evidence.

Psalm: The Almighty God, the Lord speaks;
he calls to the whole earth from east to west.
God shines from Zion,
the city perfect in its beauty.

> 'Listen, my people, and I will speak;
> I will testify against you, Israel.
> I am God, your God.
> I do not reprimand you because of your sacrifices
> and the burnt-offerings you always bring me.
> And yet I do not need bulls from your farms,
> or goats from your flocks.
> All the animals in the forest are mine
> and the cattle on thousands of hills.
> All the wild birds are mine
> and all living things in the fields.
>
> Let the giving of thanks be your sacrifice to God,
> and give the Almighty all that you promised.
> Call to me when trouble comes;
> I will save you, and you will praise me.'
> *Psalm 50: 1–2, 7–11, 14–15*

PRAYER

CHAPTER 41

The Little Box
Not so very long ago, most people were not very well off. But what every family did possess was a little box wrapped in a finely-embroidered cloth. Some kept it in a case with rounded glass and gilt surround; others under a glass bell or in a kind of tabernacle or in a special place inside the cabinet. Their little box was very important to people then. Just by looking at it they got the strength to carry on, to keep going when things were very difficult. It seemed to give them strength. Something emanated from it.

From time to time, children would ask what there was inside that little box. Then the people would invariably assume a great air of mystery, because they were not really very sure about it themselves. You didn't ask, you just had to believe . . . It was something very special, for sure, because they had got it from their parents and they in turn from theirs, and it still worked.

The day was bound to come when somebody could not contain his curiosity. He simply had to know, once and for all, what was in that little box. Somewhat timidly he opened it. Then he burst out laughing. It was empty! He would not have believed it!

What a rotten trick! A worthless old box — and quite empty! The news spread like wildfire, everywhere, in whispers at first, but before long with barefaced effrontery, from one family to another.

The old people denied it vehemently. They were positive: there was a precious stone inside; no, said another, some special word of wisdom; gold-dust . . . grain . . . something alive . . . whatever each of them had always imagined.

The children dared their parents to open up the box. And when they let themselves be talked into it, then they were forced to admit: indeed, it was empty . . . worthless! How dreadful! How was it possible? They were terribly upset about it: had they been made fools of, then, all along? Even so, most of them could not bring themselves simply to throw the box away. They stuffed it into a dark corner of the cabinet as a cherished memento. But it didn't work its spells any more.

The younger generation felt pleased with themselves: after all, they had only given the lie to a gross deception! Yet from then on things did not go better with these people. On the contrary, a great emptiness entered their lives. For the first few years they made hasty efforts to fill that void with one thing or another: with knowledge and science, conferences, and parties, wealth and luxury, love and sex, sport and play, recreation and tourism, but ever faster and more frequently the loneliness, the emptiness, crept up on them; and they didn't know what to do about it.

When they were confronted with things which proved rather difficult, they had nothing to latch on to, to pull themselves up by and persevere with. So one after another they snapped and fell away. Even the best of marriages went to pieces, and more and more people found themselves in trouble. They would often feel utterly miserable, old and young, for the older ones no longer had anything they could hand on to the youngsters.

At their wits' end, they turned to a wise man who had managed to preserve his peace of mind. They told him just how empty they felt and how desperate that made them. And what were they to pass on to their children now that they themselves had nothing left any more? For in the old days they had been duped, made to look like fools, with a box that had nothing in it.

The wise man said: 'Didn't you know that the box was empty? It's bound to be empty, anyway, since it is the gift of self, a reminder of him who is the fulfilment of our existence.

In every person he has a space, an empty place created by himself. Your heart will be restless till it rests in him. If your empty place, your life, is filled with him, it will be no empty box that you bequeath to your children.' Then the older people fetched out their little boxes again and with the greatest care presented them to their children.

(Taken from *Living the Faith Together* by Wim Saris)

QUESTIONS

1. What is your reaction to this story?
2. Why was the little box important to people at the beginning of the story?
3. What happened when people discovered that the box was empty?
4. How had the people's attitude to the box changed by the end of the story?

5. What do you think is the most important moment in this story? Explain.
6. What is the most important message or meaning in this story for you?

Prayer

Christians, and the members of many other faiths, believe that without God, a person's life is empty. We believe that neither wealth, possessions, status or power alone can make a person truly happy. Love, peace, justice, reconciliation and hope are just some of the things we need to make us truly happy, and all of these things come from God. For many people the empty box in the story is a symbol of the human person, waiting to be filled with God's love, joy and happiness.

As Christians we use many symbols and images to remind ourselves of our need for God and of God's love and concern for us. The sacraments are full of these signs; our churches and homes display reminders of God, such as the Bible, the crucifix, images of Jesus, Mary and the saints; while the Liturgical Year is a constant reminder of our dependence on God. All of these can help us to grow closer to God, to get to know God better and allow God to make us happy.

> Prayer is one of the most important ways by which we can get to know God. Prayer means placing ourselves in the presence of God, allowing ourselves to become aware that God is present. Prayer reminds us that our lives are empty unless they are filled with God's love and support. Prayer means seeing life as it really is — a gift from God. Without praying — in the Eucharistic celebration; in the other sacraments; with others in the community; in the family; or on our own — we could easily forget the true meaning and purpose of living. We sometimes think of prayer as 'talking to God'. It might be truer to say that prayer is answering God, or responding to God who speaks to us all the time. The more we pray, the more we will 'hear' God speaking to us in our lives.

The following prayer methods are often used in the Christian community.

The First Method of Prayer (St Ignatius of Loyola)

This is a very simple way to pray. Choose a prayer which you know well. Say it slowly to yourself, one phrase at a time. When you have said the first phrase, think about it for a while, turn it over in your mind, see what it means to you. After a little

while, when you feel that you want to move on, say the next phrase to yourself, and think about it in the same way. Continue until you have finished the prayer. This is a simple form of 'meditation', which means pondering deeply about something. It involves more than just 'thinking', because when we meditate we are also *listening* to God's message in our prayer.

The Jesus Prayer (The Orthodox Tradition)

This is another simple form of meditation in which we pray with our whole mind and heart and body. It involves using one phrase or sentence and repeating it several times. One sentence which is often used is 'Lord Jesus Christ, have mercy on me.' Sit down comfortably and relax. When you are breathing quietly and easily, begin to say the sentence slowly to yourself. As you are breathing in, say 'Lord Jesus Christ.' As you breathe out say 'have mercy on me.' Continue in this way, following the rhythm of your breathing — allow the words to follow your breath, rather than breathing 'in time' to the words.

Other sentences can be used besides the one given above, for example 'Be still and know/that I am God'; or 'Glory be to the Father, to the Son,/and to the Holy Spirit.'

A quiet hospital oratory.

The Rosary (St Dominic)

The rosary is a meditation on the important events in the lives of Jesus and Mary. We ponder on these events because they were very important to Jesus and Mary, and also because they are important for us. At the end of the rosary we often pray that we may 'imitate what (the events) contain and obtain what they promise'. So praying the rosary should lead us to be loving as Jesus and Mary were, and it should remind us that one day we shall join Jesus and Mary in eternal happiness.

The rosary consists of fifteen events or 'Mysteries':

The Five Joyful Mysteries
1. The Annunciation
2. The Visitation
3. The Nativity
4. The Presentation of Our Lord at the Temple
5. The Finding of the Lord Jesus in the Temple

The Five Sorrowful Mysteries
1. The Agony in the Garden
2. The Scourging at the Pillar
3. The Crowning with Thorns
4. The Carrying of the Cross
5. The Crucifixion

The Five Glorious Mysteries
1. The Resurrection
2. The Ascension
3. The Descent of the Holy Spirit
4. The Assumption of Our Lady into Heaven
5. The Crowning of Our Lady Queen of Heaven

The rosary begins with the sign of the Cross, the Our Father, three Hail Marys and the Glory be to the Father. Then, as we think about the first mystery, we say one Our Father, ten Hail Marys and a Glory be to the Father. These prayers are intended to help us concentrate on the mystery so that we will not be distracted. They also measure out a certain period of time for us to spend on one mystery before going on to the next. This means that the way in which we pray the Our Father in the rosary is different from the way, we might pray it using St Ignatius' 'First Method of Prayer'.

We usually end the rosary by praying the 'Hail, Holy Queen'.

Exercises

1. In what way does each of the sacraments remind us of our need for God?
2. How does prayer remind us of our need for God?
3. In what ways does God speak to ordinary Christians in their lives?
4. What methods of prayer do you find easiest? Explain your answer.

Project

1. Get into five groups.
2. Let each group prepare a presentation on three of the mysteries of the rosary; one Joyful, one Sorrowful and one Glorious. Use paintings, posters and written work to explain something of the meaning of each mystery. Make sure to include the connection between each mystery and our lives today.
3. Display your project over a period of weeks in the oratory, or some quiet place in your school. Put up one mystery at a time, to help the other students to meditate on it.

Preparing to Pray

Spontaneous prayers are a very important part of our lives — sharing our happiness, sorrow, anxiety and fun with God in our own words whenever it occurs to us. However, if we are to build up our relationship with God and take it seriously, then we have to plan our prayer-life, much as we would plan to meet our friends, or keep in touch with them. Another reason for 'planning to pray' rather than just praying whenever we happen to feel like it, is that it is important to pray even when we don't 'feel like it'. It is often when we feel least inclined to pray that we most need to pray. Set prayers or formal prayers can be a great help when we have no words of our own. At the time of a death in the family, or some personal crisis, or when we feel bored and fed up with life in general, this kind of prayer can help us and strengthen us. The following suggestions may help you to develop the habit of praying.

Reading a well-used family Bible.

1. *Plan to pray at the same time each day.* This does not mean that you could not also pray at other times, but it is good to have at least one fixed time, in the morning or in the evening.
2. *Find a place to pray which you can use every day.* If possible, lock the door so that you will not be interrupted.
3. *Decide on a posture for prayer which will help you to be attentive.* Standing, sitting or kneeling can all be good. Lying in bed, however, can sometimes make you fall asleep!
4. *Use some action to prepare to pray, to quieten your busy mind.* For example it is good to begin with the sign of the cross, followed by some short relaxation exercises, or a reading from a Christian book.
5. *Plan to pray for five to fifteen minutes.* It is not necessary to spend hours in prayer. It is better to spend five minutes praying every day than to pray for an hour once in a blue moon.
6. *Use different methods of prayer and different kinds of prayer.* This will help you to grow in prayer. You could include prayers of petition, praise, thanksgiving, sorrow for sin, prayers for yourself and prayers for other people.

(Based on Chapter 15 of *Haircuts and Holiness* by Louis Cassels, 1972)

Discussion: Are these suggestions for prayer useful in any way?

Reflection: 'But when you pray, go to your room, close the door, and pray to your Father, who is unseen. And your Father, who sees what you do in private, will reward you.' (Matthew 6:6)

Action: Try to put some of the suggestions for prayer into practice on a regular basis in your life.

Psalm: Lord, I have given up my pride
and turned away from my arrogance.
I am not concerned with great matters
or with subjects too difficult for me.
Instead I am content and at peace.
As a child lies quietly in its mother's arms,
so my heart is quiet within me.
Israel, trust in the Lord,
now and forever!
Psalm 131

Some Prayers

Our Father
Our Father, who art in Heaven, hallowed be thy name; thy kingdom come, thy will be done on earth as it is in heaven. Give us this day our daily bread; and forgive us our trespasses, as we forgive those who trespass against us; and lead us not into temptation, but deliver us from evil. Amen

Hail Mary
Hail Mary full of grace, the Lord is with thee; blessed art thou among women, and blessed is the fruit of thy womb, Jesus. Holy Mary, Mother of God, pray for us sinners, now and at the hour of our death. Amen.

Glory Be To The Father
Glory be to the Father, and to the Son, and to the Holy Spirit; as it was in the beginning, is now and ever shall be, world without end. Amen.

Hail Holy Queen
Hail, holy Queen, Mother of mercy; hail, our life, our sweetness and our hope. To thee do we cry, poor banished children of Eve. To thee do we send up our sighs, mourning and weeping in this valley of tears. Turn then, most gracious advocate, thine eyes of mercy towards us, and after this our exile, show unto us the blessed fruit of thy womb, Jesus. O clement, O loving, O Sweet Virgin Mary.

    Pray for us, O holy Mother of God.

    That we may be made worthy of the promises of Christ.

PILGRIMAGE

CHAPTER 42
▼

1. Many Irish parishes and dioceses have an annual pilgrimage to Knock in honour of Our Lady.

2. Lough Derg may be Ireland's oldest place of pilgrimage, where people go to do penance for three days.

3. Pilgrims travel to Assisi in Italy to feel something of the spirit of St Francis.

4. Lourdes is not only famous for healing, but also for the welcome given to each sick or disabled person.

Every year, thousands of pilgrims travel to these and other places, made holy by the presence of Mary or one of the great saints.

QUESTIONS

Bathing in the river Ganges.

1. Do you know the story of any of the places of pilgrimage? Briefly explain the ones you know about.
2. What other places of pilgrimage do you know besides those shown above?
3. Have you ever been on a pilgrimage? Do you know anyone who has been a pilgrim? Explain.
4. What do people do on a pilgrimage?
5. Why do you think people go on pilgrimage?

Pilgrimage

Going on pilgrimage to a holy place is a part of all the major religions of the world. Hindus visit the river Ganges, their sacred river, to bathe in it and drink the waters. In this way they believe their sins are forgiven, they are purified and strengthened. In the Christian tradition, pilgrimage has been important from the earliest times. The place of pilgrimage was first and foremost the Holy Land, made holy because Jesus lived, worked, died and rose from the dead there. By visiting Bethlehem, Jerusalem and Nazareth, people have shown in a physical way that they are Jesus' followers, and that he is important to them.

Other places of pilgrimage evolved over the centuries, including Rome, the shrine of St James of Compostella in Spain, Canterbury in England, Bruges in Belgium, Tours in France and so on. In Ireland, Lough Derg and Croagh Patrick became popular. Today Lourdes, Knock, Fatima, and Czestochoura (in Poland) are important centres of pilgrimage. What these islands, mountains, shrines, cities, tombs and other holy places have in common is that God communicated with people in a special way at those places. This 'communication' or 'revelation' can take place through the life of a saint, or a community, or through a vision of Our Lady. All places of pilgrimage are therefore great centres of prayer because people feel particularly close to God there. Many are also centres of healing, penance, reconciliation and peace. They are a sign of joy and hope to the whole Christian community.

Bethlehem at sunrise.

A pilgrimage is an act of worship. It involves taking time out from our ordinary, everyday lives and consecrating a special time to God, who is always at the centre of our lives. The true pilgrim is not just a tourist who happens to have faith; the pilgrim is someone who wants to 'touch' God, to come close to God. The pilgrim's journey to a holy place is a sign of trust and faith in God. The journey home is a sign that the pilgrim brings back a renewed enthusiasm for living the Christian life.

Jerusalem, Good Friday. The Cross is being carried down from the first station in the Via Dolorosa, the journey Jesus made to Calvary.

EXERCISES

1. How do you think a pilgrimage could help someone feel closer to God?
2. What place of pilgrimage would you most like to visit? Why?

PROJECT

1. Get into groups of three or four.
2. Each group should research and present a project on one of the great centres of pilgrimage. Remember to include some of the history of the shrine, and the way in which the manner of pilgrimage has changed over the years, e.g. the means of travel, the accommodation available etc.
3. If possible, interview someone who has done this pilgrimage and include their impressions in your project.
4. Make a note of the message which your particular place of pilgrimage has for people today.

The Pope in Ireland, Addresses and Homilies (Pope John Paul II, 1979)

I know very well that every people, every country, indeed every diocese has its holy places in which the heart of the whole people of God beats, one could say, in more lively fashion; places of special encounter between Him and human beings; places in which Christ dwells in a special way in our midst . . .

Do we not confess with all our brothers, even those with whom we are not yet linked in full unity, that we are a pilgrim people? As once this people travelled on its pilgrimage under the guidance of Moses, so we, the People of God of the New Covenant, are travelling on our pilgrim way under the guidance of Christ.

Pilgrims on Croagh Patrick.

QUESTIONS

1. Are there any 'holy places' near your home? Explain.
2. In what way is a place of pilgrimage a place of special encounter, or a special meeting between God and people?
3. In what way is the life of a Christian like a pilgrimage? In what way is the life of the whole Christian community like a pilgrimage?

Reflection: 'Every year the parents of Jesus went to Jerusalem for the Passover festival. When Jesus was twelve years old, they went to the festival as usual. When the festival was over, they started back home, but the boy Jesus stayed in Jerusalem. His parents did not know this; they thought that he was with the group, so they travelled a whole day and then started looking for him among their relatives and friends. They did not find him, so they went back to Jerusalem looking for him. On the third day they found him in the Temple, sitting with the Jewish teachers, listening to them and asking questions. All who heard him were amazed at his intelligent answers. His parents were astonished when they saw him, and his mother said to him, "My son, why have you done this to us? Your father and I have been terribly worried trying to find you."

He answered them, "Why did you have to look for me? Didn't you know that I had to be in my Father's house?" But they did not understand his answer.

So Jesus went back with them to Nazareth, where he was obedient to them. His mother treasured all these things in her heart. Jesus grew both in body and in wisdom, gaining favour with God and men.' Luke 2:41-49

Action: If you can, go on a pilgrimage with a group of pilgrims, maybe from your school or parish. Try to make the pilgrimage a real journey towards God in your life by taking part in the actions and prayers.

Psalm: I was glad when they said to me,
'Let us go to the Lord's house.'
And now we are here,
standing inside the gates of Jerusalem!

Jerusalem is a city restored
in beautiful order and harmony.
This is where the tribes come,
the tribes of Israel,
to give thanks to the Lord
according to his command.
Here the kings of Israel
sat to judge their people.

Pray for the peace of Jerusalem:
'May those who love you prosper.
May there be peace inside your walls
and safety in your palaces.'
For the sake of my relatives and friends
I say to Jerusalem, 'Peace be with you!'
For the sake of the house of the Lord, our God,
I pray for your prosperity.
Psalm 122

PHOTO CREDITS

Photo Research: Anne-Marie Ehrlich

For permission to reproduce photographs, grateful acknowledgment is made to the following:

Science Photo Library: pages 3, 88 (top), 97 (bottom), 98, 100 (bottom);
John Walmsley/Impact Photos: page 4;
Robert Allen: pages 5, 35 (bottom), 114 (bottom), 145, 179, 180, 228 (top), 231, 232 (middle), 247 (bottom), 264, 278, 311 (bottom), 312;
Sally and Richard Greenhill: pages 13 (top), 19, 66 (top and middle), 76, 82 (top and middle), 96, 107, 111, 113 (both), 120, 125 (bottom), 189, 221 (bottom), 223, 226, 227, 255 (bottom), 302 (top), 305 (top right), 314;
Barnaby's Picture Library: pages 13 (bottom), 42, 62, 187 (centre and right), 225 (both), 257, 298, 302 (bottom), 318 (top);
Concern: page 20 (both);
Frank Spooner Pictures: pages 14, 18, 36, 88 (bottom), 97 (top), 110, 135, 297 (top);
Popperfoto: page 27;
Gamma/Frank Spooner: pages 33, 37 (both), 66 (bottom), 67 (top), 87, 89 (all three), 144, 197 (bottom), 202, 297 (bottom), 305 (top left and bottom right), 307, 317 (bottom left);
Network Photographers: pages 34, 35 (top), 43, 63;
Camera Press: pages 44, 95 (bottom), 100 (top), 211, 249 (bottom), 313;
B. and C. Alexander: pages 45 and 109;
Stephen O'Reilly: pages 45 (middle and bottom), 46 (both), 48 (both), 49, 185, 215 (bottom), 221 (top), 232 (bottom), 234, 235, 256, 311 (top), 317 (top left), 319 (bottom right);
Hutchison Library: pages 67 (middle and bottom), 82 (bottom), 108, 125 (top), 186 (top), 302 (middle);
E.T. Archive: pages 88 (middle), 244 (middle), 247 (middle);
Biofotos/Heather Angel: pages 95 (top), 197 (top), 300, 306 (both);
CMAC/Robert Allen: page 114 (top);
Chris Fairclough Colour Library: pages 136, 232 (top), 255 (top);
Juliette Soester: pages 171 (top and middle), 172, 174, 266 (both), 267;
Zefa Picture Library: pages 171 (bottom), 173 (both), 228 (bottom), 229, 265 (both), 266 (both);
Trocaire: page 186 (bottom);
Harry Smith Horticultural Photographic Collection: page 187 (left);
Sonia Halliday Photographs: pages 195, 239 (top left), 318 (bottom), 319 (top);
Rex Features/SIPA: pages 214, 250 (both), 251 (both), 259, 260, 261, 317 (bottom right);
Scala: pages 215 (top), 239 (bottom), 241, 244 (top), 245 (centre), 247 (top);
Jean-Loup Charmet: pages 239 (top right), 246, 248, 249 (top);
Bridgeman Art Library: pages 243, 244 (bottom);
National Portrait Gallery, London: page 245 (right);
KNA-Bild, Frankfurt: page 249 (middle);
Christian Renewal Centre, Rostrevor: page 262;
Corrymeela Community Ballycastle: page 263 (top);
Columba House, Derry: page 263 (bottom);
Islamic Foundation of Ireland: pages 268, 269, 270, 271 (top);
Samyé Trust/Robert Allen: pages 271 (bottom), 272 (both), 273 (both), 274;
Bord Fáilte: pages 301, 317 (top right);
C.M. Dixon: page 305 (bottom left).